剑桥 文学名家研习系列（英国卷）之一

The Cambridge Introduction to
Shakespeare
威廉·莎士比亚

U0745356

Emma Smith ◎ 著

何其莘 ◎ 导读

上海外语教育出版社
外教社 SHANGHAI FOREIGN LANGUAGE EDUCATION PRESS

CAMBRIDGE
UNIVERSITY PRESS

图书在版编目（CIP）数据

威廉·莎士比亚 / 史密斯（Smith, E.）著；何其莘导读.
—上海：上海外语教育出版社，2008
（剑桥文学名家研习系列. 英国卷）
ISBN 978-7-5446-0748-3

Ⅰ. 威… Ⅱ. ①史… ②何… Ⅲ. 莎士比亚, W.（1564~1616）—人物研究
Ⅳ. K835.615.6

中国版本图书馆CIP数据核字（2008）第046158号

图字：09-2008-084号

Shakespeare, 1st (ISBN 978-0-521-67188-0) by Emma Smith first published by
Cambridge University Press 2007.

出版发行：**上 海 外 语 教 育 出 版 社**
（上海外国语大学内）　邮编：200083
电　　话：021-65425300（总机）
电子邮箱：bookinfo@sflep.com.cn
网　　址：http://www.sflep.com.cn　http://www.sflep.com
责任编辑：张传根

印　　刷：上海叶大印务发展有限公司
经　　销：新华书店上海发行所
开　　本：787×965　1/16　印张11.5　字数216千字
版　　次：2008年8月第1版　2008年8月第1次印刷
印　　数：3 100 册

书　　号：ISBN 978-7-5446-0748-3 / I · 0037
定　　价：32.00 元

本版图书如有印装质量问题，可向本社调换

总 序

　　为了帮助广大读者特别是英语专业学生学习英国文学，上海外语教育出版社从国外引进了这套"剑桥文学名家研习系列"丛书。正如封底文字所说，本系列丛书旨在向学生介绍英美经典作家，而普通读者如果想进一步了解自己所喜爱的作家作品，也会发现这套丛书富有吸引力。

　　英国文学是英国人民在漫长的历史发展进程中创造的英国文化与文明的精华，是世界文学宝库中一颗璀璨的明珠。文学是语言的艺术，英国文学是英语语言艺术的结晶。英语表意功能强，文体风格变化多，或高雅，或通俗，或含蓄，或明快，或婉约，或粗犷，其丰富的表现力和独特的魅力在英国作家作品里得到了最为淋漓尽致的发挥。要真正掌握英语，必须阅读和了解优秀的英国文学作品，英国文学因此成为高校英语专业课程设置不可或缺的组成部分。

　　英国文学源远流长，经历了长期、复杂的发展演变过程。在这个过程中，文学本体以外各种现实的、历史的、政治的、文化的力量对文学发生着影响，文学也遵循自身规律，历经了盎格鲁—撒克逊、文艺复兴、新古典主义、浪漫主义、现实主义、现代主义、后现代等不同历史阶段。"剑桥文学名家研习系列"丛书（英国卷）是开放式的，首批推出莎士比亚、奥斯丁、康拉德、叶芝、T·S·艾略特、乔伊斯、伍尔夫、贝克特等8位名家，他们均为英国文学史上的里程碑式人物，对推动英国文学的发展作出了重要贡献。8位名家的创作领域涵盖了小说、诗歌和戏剧，而叶芝、T·S·艾略特和贝克特分别为1923、1948、1969年度诺贝尔文学奖得主，这也从一个侧面说明了本系列丛书入选名家的经典性。

　　大学本科课程要符合基础性、研究性和前沿性的要求。本科教育的重要任务是让学生掌握专业的基础理论、基本知识和基本技能；同时培养学生的研究能力，使之有较强的"问题意识"，能够发现问题、思考问题、解决问题，学会使用研究方法，进行学术探讨；另外，要让学生知悉学科发展的最新动态，对专业领域内的前沿课题有所了解。"剑桥文学名家研习系列"丛书（英国卷）的设计思想和内容与大学本科教育的要求基本上是吻合的。每册书均由学有所成的专家一人撰写，一气呵成，而不是多人合写的论文集。作者均为专业领域里有着较深造诣的学者，对材料驾轻就熟，可以针对本科生的水平，深入浅出，娓娓道来。每册书的基本内容为作家的简要生平（Life）、主要作品（Works）、历史语境（Context）和作品接受情况（Reception），不仅比较全面地提供相关作家的基本信息，体现基础性特点，而且以作者深厚的学术研究为依托，从独特的视角解读剖析文本，系统梳理各种评论观点，介绍最新研究进展，引导学生开展学术研究。因此，本系列丛书也可用作英语语言文学专业文学方向研究生的参考书。书末附有进一步学习所需的阅读书目，推荐了有代表性的重要文献，对学生撰写课程论文或毕业论文很有帮助。

应当指出，阅读英国文学指南类书籍并不能替代阅读英国文学作品本身。优秀的文学作品具有道德（ethical）和审美（aesthetic）指向，正如巴金所说，它们教育人，要人变得更好，同时给人美的享受。我们每一个人都有阅读文学作品的体验：有时，一本小说、一首诗或一出戏会让我们感动，让我们激奋，让我们思绪万千，难以释手。我们之所以能有情感的涌动和心灵的感悟，是因为我们对真善美有追求。部分英语专业学生因为中西文化差异和英语语言水平的障碍，无法从阅读英国文学原著中获得愉悦。我们应努力改变这种局面，让学生对英国文学有发自内心的热忱和需求，在阅读过程中找到对文学的美好感觉，而对英国文学名家的研习可以帮助我们进入文学世界。

近年来国内已出版了几套英国文学指南或导读类书籍，但"剑桥文学名家研习系列"丛书（英国卷）于2006年才问世，是迄今为止最新的一套，材料新，观点新，兼顾普及性和专业性。我相信"剑桥文学名家研习系列"丛书（英国卷）会成为我们学习英国文学的良师益友。

王守仁

南京大学

导 读

◎ 何其莘

　　莎士比亚是中国读者和观众都非常熟悉的名字。虽然，这位世界著名戏剧大师的名字早在19世纪中国出版的书刊上出现，但是，他的作品直到20世纪初才被介绍给中国的读者。1903年，英国作家查理·兰姆和他姐姐玛丽·兰姆改写的《莎士比亚戏剧故事集》首次译成中文，其中10个故事的文言译文被编成一个集子，题名为《澥外奇谭》。集子的"叙例"中写道：

> 　　是书为英国索士比亚（Shakespeare，千五百六十四年生，千六百一十六年卒）所著。氏乃绝世名优，长于诗词。其所编戏本小说，风靡一时，推为英国空前大家。译者遍法、德、俄、意，几乎无人不读。而吾国近今学界，言诗词小说者，亦辄啧啧称索氏。然其书向未得读，仆窃恨之，因亟译述是编，冀为小说界，增一异彩。

　　次年，商务印书馆又出版了林纾和魏易用文言文翻译的同一本故事集的全译本，定名为《英国诗人吟边燕语》。林纾称其为"神怪"小说，并为每个故事取了传奇式的名字。我国20世纪三四十年代上演的莎士比亚作品，大多以此书为蓝本。

　　莎士比亚的剧作直到1919年的"五四"运动之后才被完整地用白话文的形式介绍进中国。1921年，《哈姆雷特》由田汉完整地译成中文，作为中华书局的《莎翁杰作集》的第一种出版。至今，莎士比亚的全部剧作都被译成了中文，每个剧目都有多个中译本。

　　在中国第一个被搬上舞台的莎剧是《威尼斯商人》。1902年上海圣约翰大学外语系的毕业班用英语演出了《威尼斯商人》。1913年，上海的一个专业剧团和一所女子学校分别演了剧中的片断。直到1930年，上海业余话剧团推出的《威尼斯商人》才是莎剧第一次被完整地搬上了中国舞台。20世纪80年代之后，中国的舞台上经常可以看到莎士比亚的剧目。1980至1982年间，北京青年艺术剧院推出的话剧《威尼斯商人》就连演了200多场。

虽然，中国报刊上最早出现有关莎剧的文章是1918年，但是，真正意义上的莎士比亚戏剧评论是在1949年解放之后。50年代的中国莎评受到当时苏联文学评论界的影响，追随"社会主义现实主义"批评流派，基本上是一种偏重政治思想和意识形态的解读方式。这种情况一直延续到了70年代末，和当时中国的政治气氛，文学评论界的运作方式基本一致。

20世纪70年代末以来，中国的莎学发展很快。1984年，中国莎士比亚研究会正式宣告成立，并在北京和上海组织了1986年和1994年两届莎士比亚戏剧节。许多大学的英文系和中文系都把莎士比亚戏剧列为专业必修或专业选修课。莎士比亚成为越来越多的中国读者喜爱的外国作家。曹禺先生在1983年为即将成立的中国莎士比亚研究会会刊《莎士比亚研究》所写的"发刊词"中的一段话极好地描述了莎士比亚在中国读者心目中的地位：

> 有史以来，屹立在高峰之上，多少文学巨人们教给人认识自己，开阔人的眼界，丰富人的贫乏生活，使人得到智慧、得到幸福、得到享受，引导人懂得"人"的价值、尊严和力量。莎士比亚就是这样一位使人类永久又惊又喜的巨人。

基本上与中国经济上的改革开放同步，中国莎学比较明显的变化出现在20世纪80年代，特别是80年代末。随着改革开放，也伴随着中国学者去国外学习，中国的文学评论界和戏剧界有机会接触到了几百年来世界莎学的研究成果，眼界开阔了，学术视野拓宽了。90年代以来，中国学者在他们出版的专著、发表的论文中，就莎士比亚戏剧的艺术性等问题与世界莎学界在学术层面上平等对话，开始展示了中国学术界对世界文坛可能作出的贡献。

埃玛·史密斯撰写的《威廉·莎士比亚》，是上海外语教育出版社最新引进的"剑桥文学名家研习系列"中的一种。2000年前后,外教社曾引进"剑桥文学指南"丛书,其中有一本《莎士比亚》。那是由英国著名莎学家、国际莎士比亚学会主席斯坦利·韦尔斯主编的一本论文集,撰稿人为伯明翰大学、哈佛大学、耶鲁大学、波恩大学、巴黎大学等多国专家学者,比较集中体现了20世纪七八十年代西方莎学的最新进展。

埃玛·史密斯博士是牛津大学英国文学高级讲师,她的主要研究方向是文艺复兴时期戏剧,代表作包含了《Blackwell文学评论导读:莎士比亚悲剧》(2003)、《Blackwell文学评论导读:莎士比亚历史剧》(2003)、《Blackwell文学评论导读:莎士比亚喜剧》(2003)、《莎士比亚演出史:亨利五世》(2002)。

与传统的文学名家导读相比,埃玛·史密斯的《威廉·莎士比亚》确有独特的视角。史密斯博士没有沿用传统导读的模式——从作家生平到作家的创作生涯,再通过剖析几部代表作总结出作家的艺术特点,最后以作家在文学史上的地位作为全书的结束语,而是直接抓住戏剧艺术的主要特点——剧中人物、莎剧的演出、莎剧的文本、剧中语言、戏剧结构、莎剧故事的来源、剧作与时代的关系——直接插入,通过分析莎士比亚的多部剧作,在回顾总结历代学者评论家研究成果的基础上,阐述了她个人对莎剧的看法。因此,埃玛·史密斯的《威廉·莎士比亚》是一部个性化很强的导读。在每一章的结尾处,作者还加上了一份参考书目——不是单纯地列上书名,而是加上了对每本书的详细点评,这对读者进一步探讨这个问题会有很大的帮助。

第一章讨论的是莎士比亚戏剧中的人物。在戏剧评论中,剧中的主题、结构和人物塑造是最受关注的三个方面。从分析《罗密欧与朱丽叶》中的女主人公朱丽叶入手,史密斯博士回顾了几百年来在人物分析方面所经历过的一个演变过程,也指出了在传统分析中所存在的一种倾向,即自觉不自觉地把自己与剧中人物在感情、心理上等同起来,其结果是采用了一种现实主义的手法来剖析莎剧中的角色。当然,这种情况更多的是出现在读者的身上,因为充裕的时间使得读者有机会去挖掘剧中所谓"深层次"的内容。而作者的建议是,在阅读时不要为剧中人物添加"心理因素"，因为这些内容在原剧中并不存在。然而，在把莎剧搬上舞台或银幕时，导演和演员则无法回避这样一个问题，因为他们首先要自己去理解剧本，然后再把他们对原作的理解在舞台上表现出来。一个有趣的例子是《温莎的风流娘儿们》中的福斯塔夫：他与历史剧中单纯的丑角不同，成了一个颇有个性的追逐女人的喜剧人物。

第二章是莎剧的演出，切入点是喜剧《一报还一报》。《一报还一报》一直是一出很有争议的剧目，特别是全剧的结尾：安哲鲁在做尽了坏事之后竟然能得到赦免，仅以与他根本不爱的玛利安娜成婚作为对他的惩罚，而文森修公爵向伊莎贝拉求婚更被看作是非常荒唐的一步棋。在莎士比亚的剧本中，伊莎贝拉并没有对公爵的求婚做出反应，而这种开放式的结尾在演出时则是无法回避的，不同的导演就可能演绎出多种处理方式。作者还讨论了另一出喜剧《驯悍记》，因为这出喜剧的结尾也是开放式的，存在着多种可能性。但是，每一位导演只能选其中的一种，导演的选择往往取决于各种文化背景下的人对于婚姻和男女地位的看法，而导演对结尾的处理方式则决定了他对全剧的理解和释义。在这章中，作者还对比了《麦克白》的两个电影版本和《哈姆雷特》中"To be, or not to be"这段独白在三个电影版本中的处理方式。

莎剧的文本是第三章讨论的主题。文本研究是文学评论的一个重要分支。当代作家的作品一般不存在文本问题，对于19世纪末、20世纪初出版的小说，文本研究主要是对比作家手稿与正式出版的小说、小说不同版本、杂志连载的文本与作为小说出版时文本之间的差别。但是，对于16、17世纪作家作品的文本研究就要困难得多，复杂得多。莎士比亚没有为我们留下自己的手稿，他的笔迹只出现在几份文件的签字当中。另外，保存下来的手稿《托马斯·莫尔爵士》中5种不同的笔迹中可能有一种出自莎士比亚之手。我们现在知道，在莎士比亚的有生之年，他从未把自己的剧本卖给出版商。因此，16、17世纪印刷出版的莎剧4开本和对开本都是出版商通过非正常渠道获得的，可靠性方面都有问题，有些版本之间的差别还相当大。因此，当代莎剧的编者就面临着一个极大的考验：16、17世纪印刷出版的莎剧4开本和对开本之间存在的差异中，究竟哪些是剧作家的原意？

第四章的主题是莎剧的语言。莎士比亚戏剧的语言属于早期现代英语，在英语发展史上这是一个重要的转变时期，英语既受到古希腊古罗马语言和文化的影响，也与欧洲其他国家的语言和文化相互渗透、相互借鉴、相互影响。当然，这种变化中的语言为莎士比亚和他的同代剧作家创造了一个极好的发展空间，但是，对于后来的读者和观众来说，这样的戏剧语言就有很大的难度。作者列举了悲剧《麦克白》中的一个例子：主人公麦克白对女巫三个预言的解读与最后结果之间的差异恰恰说明莎剧语言的多元性，对于21世纪的读者来说这是一个极大的挑战。

第五章讨论的是莎士比亚剧作的结构。在探讨悲剧结构时，我们常常引用德国剧作家格斯塔夫·弗雷泰格的"金字塔"理论，即一个悲剧常常由5个部分组成：展示部分—上升事件—高潮—下降事件—结局（大灾难）。作者分析了《罗密欧与朱丽叶》第三幕第一场的决斗和《哈姆雷特》的第三幕第二场"戏中戏"，认为几乎每个莎剧的中心位置都有一个事件，而这个事件对于全剧剧情的发展有着举足轻重的作用。不仅莎士比亚的悲剧是这样，他笔下的喜剧和历史剧也是这样。众所周知，莎士比亚不是亚里士多德的忠实追随者，他的悲剧和喜剧常常也不符合亚里士多德为悲剧和喜剧所下的定义，因为我们在剧中可以看到悲剧成分和喜剧成分相互交叉。所以，在探讨每一个莎剧的结构时，使我们感兴趣的不是它究竟属于哪一个剧种，而是剧作家是如何处理他手中的素材的。

第六章的主题是莎剧故事的素材。在这章中，作者对比了莎士比亚的《安东尼和克莉奥佩特拉》与1579年出版的史书上对这段历史事件的记载，以及《罗密欧与朱丽叶》与布鲁克同名长诗，指出这就是莎士比亚和他的同代剧作家常用的创作手法，即以一个老故事为基础，在故事情节上做些改动，然后用一种新的方式来重述这个故事。作者似乎很不同意学术界对莎士比亚戏剧故事来源的讨论，因为在她看来，所有的学者都在重复相同的结论：从不那么完美的素材中，诞生出了天才之作。作者认为，这种程式化的讨论没有任何实际意义，而我们在对莎剧故事来源的研讨中，更应该关注莎士比亚是如何具体地处理每一个剧的素材，以及他剧作的最后效果。在作者看来，莎士比亚对于故事来源的处理有许多得意之作，但也有一些并不那么成功的例子。

第七章讨论的是莎士比亚剧作与时代的关系。和他的同代剧作家本·琼森不同，莎士比亚极少评论他自己的剧作。但是，考虑到16、17世纪的英国，一个剧本的演出周期往往只有几个星期，可以肯定莎士比亚的剧作更为当时的观众所理解、所欣赏，与他生活的那个时代的联系更加紧密。但是，莎剧毕竟不是文献，而只是艺术作品，我们很难判断他的剧作是否反映了他那个时代的现实生活，或在多大程度上反映了他的那个时代。但是，从这些剧中我们还是可以体验到生活在那个时代的人们的思维模式、喜怒哀乐。

史密斯博士对莎士比亚戏剧艺术的讨论并没有遵循传统的模式，但是，她是在归纳总结前人研究成果的基础上，通过实例的分析，充分地阐述了个人的观点。对于她的结论恐怕后人还会提出不同的见解，但是，她的这本入门对于21世纪的读者来说确有很多启示。

Contents

Figures and tables

Figures

Tables

Preface

This book is intended as an introduction in two senses. Firstly it is an introduction in a sense available to Shakespeare's contemporaries: that of a first guide to a topic. Readers in sixteenth-century London could purchase 'introductions' to fields from astrology to Welsh, and from swimming to dying well. Like these, I have tried not to assume existing expertise or familiarity: I have wanted the book to be self-standing, acting as an encouragement and guide to further reading and investigation via 'Where next?' sections after each chapter. Each chapter covers a range of examples with a focus on those plays most frequently studied. The emphasis of this volume, unlike the many other great introductory guides that are currently available, is that it engages less with facts than with critical approaches to Shakespeare's plays – with the question of what we 'do' when we read or study Shakespeare. And I have also thought of it as an introduction in a more recent sense: 'the action of introducing or making known personally' (*Oxford English Dictionary*). Meet Shakespeare ('s plays): I think you'll find you have some things in common. I hope you hit it off.

Lots of students – particularly at Hertford College, Oxford, at the Department for Continuing Education in the University of Oxford, and at the Bread Loaf School of English – will find this material familiar, either because they've heard me rehearse parts of it in different forms or on different occasions, or because they recognise their own ideas here too. I'm grateful for the serial privilege of those conversations. Emily Bartels has cast a generous eagle eye over it all; Charlotte Brewer has, among other things, saved me from my most egregious forms of mateyness. And since this is a book which comes out of, and I hope may give something back to, teaching, it's made me think with affection about what I owe to those who have taught me: Rita Chamberlain, John Gregory, Katherine Duncan-Jones, and, differently but especially, Viv Smith.

All suggested websites were accessed in April 2006. Except where I've indicated otherwise, the edition of the plays I have used is the New Cambridge: for *Love's Labour's Lost*, *Two Noble Kinsmen* and *The Winter's Tale* where there is no New Cambridge edition yet, I've used *The Complete Works* ed. Stanley Wells and Gary Taylor (2nd edn, Oxford, 2005).

Chapter 1

Character

Juliet's balcony, Verona

In the Italian town of Verona, the tourist authorities have taken Shakespeare's *Romeo and Juliet*, and in particular the character of Juliet, to their hearts. Despite the historical tenuousness of the association of Juliet with Verona, a suitable medieval townhouse has been designated Juliet's house, and a balcony was added in the 1930s to make the setting photogenically consonant with the play's most iconic moment, when Juliet calls down from her balcony to her new lover. Streams of visitors add lovestruck graffiti to the walls, gain luck from stroking the right breast of a modern bronze statue of Juliet, and apparently address numerous letters requesting help in matters of the heart (rather oddly, since Juliet's wasn't an entirely successful love affair to aspire to) to 'Juliet, Verona', which are duly answered by a multilingual team of agony aunt volunteers known as the 'Juliet club'.

While the curious afterlife of Juliet in Verona is an extreme case, it nicely illustrates two aspects of our abiding interest in, and attitude to, Shakespeare's characterisation. Firstly, projecting a real person from the words of

1

Shakespeare's plays involves an extreme effort of will. We desperately want to believe that Juliet is a real person – a desire bound up here with narratives of travel, of holiday snapshots as consumption, of a sentimental version of romantic love, of the modern vestiges of pilgrimage – and thus the tourist offices provide what we want, complete with medieval-effect balcony and a substitute Juliet in the form of a statue. We might compare this effort to the effort we habitually make in reading or watching plays, by which we supply missing details or smooth over inconsistencies in the name of realism or of helpfully suspending our disbelief in order to help the play along. And secondly, this desire and our exertions to satisfy it postdate the plays, by a long way. Inventing Juliet in this form – as a real person in a real house in a real city, rather than a collection of words written on a page – is a twentieth-century tail on a sixteenth-century play. It's the interpretative equivalent of that Mussolini-era balcony tacked onto the medieval house.

We could therefore argue that Shakespearean characters are *writing* first, *people* second – just as the meanings of the very word 'character' have shifted from its earliest meaning as 'impression' or 'graphic sign or symbol' to the now dominant meaning, first registered after Shakespeare's death, of distinctive individual personality. When they were first printed, Shakespeare's plays had no character lists or *dramatis personae* as we are now used to in modern editions. There was therefore no obvious sense in which the persons of the play pre-existed the words they speak in it. We can see dramatic characters in this way as a product of the language which, strangely, they seem themselves also to produce. Rather than articulating their own words, they are articulated by them. One of the beguilingly circular argumentative movements of character study has been to derive from the characters' speeches an idea of their personality which is then used to interpret and underwrite those same speeches.

Character study – how characters are depicted in the drama, why they behave as they do, and the modes of reading or viewing which encourage empathic identification with them – has been a dominant mode of Shakespearean criticism since its earliest days. In fact, the first appreciations of Shakespeare tended to praise his characterisation above all other aspects of his work, particularly as an antidote to the datedness of his language or to the perceived irregularity of his plotting by classical standards. In recent academic writing, however, the whole notion of 'character' has been placed under question. Critics have argued that personality as a distinctive inner quality would have been less recognisable to Shakespeare's first audiences than it has become for us, and that therefore character study is based on an anachronistic premise. We tend to think that how people perceive themselves and others has been a historical constant across all time; historicist criticism has challenged this assumption and drawn usefully on changing ideas of privacy and the personal, as well as on dramatic technique, in the early modern period. (See 'Where next' for further reading on this topic.) But readers, viewers and performers of Shakespeare have been resistant to this apparent undermining of one of their primary sources of pleasure in the plays. So this opening chapter traces the critical debates about character, aiming to develop and interrogate, rather than entirely to reject, what often seems most appealing about those apparently lifelike personalities such as Hamlet or Falstaff or Beatrice in Shakespeare's plays.

Shakespeare's realism?

Alexander Pope's assertion that 'every single character in Shakespeare is as much an individual, as those in life itself' expresses the claims for psychological verisimilitude often made for Shakespeare's powers of characterisation. When we say that we relate to, or recognise, aspects of Shakespeare's characters, we are willingly entering into a relationship with them in which we endow them with human form, and compare their actions with our own and those of people around us. Thus the characterisation of Beatrice and Benedick – the unwilling lovers of *Much Ado About Nothing* who spend much of the play denying what is plain to all their friends, that they are a passionately compatible and unorthodox romantic couple – is bolstered by our recognition of these kinds of behaviour in the real world; perhaps we think we have all known people whose protestations that they cannot stand each other are a thin cover for deep feelings hidden through habit or fear of hurt, and those people combine in our mind with Shakespeare's characters to give an illusion of verisimilitude. Often Shakespeare presents us with individuals undergoing particular life events which are likely to chime in with readers' own experience: the death of a parent in *Hamlet*, for example; the adolescent search for an adult identity in unfamiliar surroundings in *A Midsummer Night's Dream*; the suffocating burden of parental expectations in *1 Henry IV*; the heady experience of first love in *Romeo and Juliet*; the clash between private conscience and public duty in *Julius Caesar*. In measuring the plays against our own experiences – and, in some cases, vice versa – we do some of the work to animate Shakespeare's words into the shapes of sentient, moral agents like ourselves. Using the language of emotional empathy – identification, sympathy, recognition – literary criticism has often seemed to teach that fully to engage with the plays we have to reach out a hand to their characters.

There are lots of ways in which Shakespeare's works encourage this kind of psychic rapport. We might, for example, adduce those wonderful moments when a single remark gestures towards a whole back-story for a character – as when the foolish gull Sir Andrew Aguecheek in *Twelfth Night* sighs 'I was adored once' (2.3.153), or when Lady Macbeth says that she would have killed King Duncan herself, 'had he not resembled / My father as he slept' (2.2.12–3). Such information does not really help the plot along; rather, it serves to create the illusion of a broader psychological history of which the current play can only be a segment. There's more to me than I get the chance to say here, these lines seem to signal; they're like a marker flag saying 'look at me again'. Shakespeare gestures to a world surrounding, but not articulated in, the play, rather as he does in his habitual device of opening his plays in the middle of a conversation we are to suppose was going on before we came in on it: with 'Nay, but this dotage of our general's / O'erflows the measure' (1.1.1–2), Philo begins *Antony and Cleopatra* with a response to an unheard and unrecorded remark by his Roman interlocutor Demetrius (the term for this is *in medias res*, literally, 'into the middle of things').

If gesturing to a more complete back history is one of Shakespeare's approaches to realistic character presentation, another is to endow characters with recognisable emotions. Thus when Capulet and his cousin discuss the passing of time in *Romeo and Juliet*, they suddenly emerge as recognisable older people at a family reunion: 'His son is thirty.' 'Will you tell me that? / His son was but a ward two years ago' (1.5.38–9). Of course this has a thematic relevance to a play about speed, and particularly the speed with which young people grow into adulthood, often unnoticed by their elders, but significantly it is a brief moment in which the play sees that process not from the point of view of the children but sympathetically from that of the parents. This part of the scene isn't directed at anyone who's been treated as the child they no longer are by relations at a family party; instead, it's for the people who, seeing strapping young adults in place of the chubby infants preserved in their memory, have to realise that they too have aged.

Shakespeare's 'unreal' characters

These examples, and numerous more like them, could be cited in support of Pope's assessment of Shakespeare's verisimilitude. But there are ways in which seeing Shakespeare's characters as people blinds us to other possibilities and limits our understanding of the way the plays work. It is important to register, for example, that elsewhere characters in Shakespeare do not approach this recognisability: they do not gesture towards a knowable past. Sometimes these are 'minor' characters; sometimes it's necessary to the plot that they lack the apparent verisimilitude lavished on some of their peers. Take Mariana, for

example, in *Measure for Measure*. This play works by juxtaposing two interrupted marital unions. The first is that of Claudio and the pregnant Juliet, who
maintain that they are married 'save that we do the denunciation lack / Of
outward order' (1.2.9–10) – meaning, apparently, that they have undergone a
kind of private, rather than church, wedding – and are to be punished by the
new governor of Vienna, Angelo, for unlawful fornication. The other, parallel
couple are Angelo himself and Mariana the 'affianced' bride he abandoned
when her dowry was lost at sea. *Measure for Measure*'s presiding organiser, the
Duke of Vienna who is disguised as a friar, plots to deliver both couples, and
devises a so-called 'bed trick' by which Angelo can be brought to have sex
with Mariana, thinking it is with Isabella the sister of Claudio, and thus by
consummating his relationship with Mariana he be brought to recognise his
marital obligations. With me so far? The point is that Mariana completes a
situation of parallels which is crucial to the design of a play titled after a parallel, 'measure for measure' (editions of the play often have a cover illustration
of a set of scales), in which the notion of equivalence – ethical, legal, moral,
dramatic – is insistently interrogated.

Because this is her role – structural, rather than personal – Mariana is hardly
characterised at all. She isn't even mentioned until Act 3 of the play and first
appears in Act 4. She substitutes for Isabella in Angelo's bed – an action seem-
ingly requiring the complete abdication of individual personality – and goes
on to play out the role the puppet-master Duke has scripted for her as the
means by which Angelo's hypocrisy and harshness will be punished. It is thus
inappropriate to ask of her, as we might of a 'real' person: why does she want
to marry the awful Angelo after the way he's treated her? why does she go
along with the Duke-Friar's seedy plan? why is she still mooning around her
'moated grange' thinking about her worthless fiancé? The answer to these
questions is not primarily psychological but dramatic: because the play
requires it.

There are lots of other examples of characters whose purpose in their play is
functional, structural or thematic, rather than to be uniquely themselves: we
might think of Hotspur as the foil to Prince Henry – the king expresses the
wish that the two boys had been swapped in the cradle, just in case we don't
understand that they are meant to be conceptualised as two sides of the coin –
in *1 Henry IV*, or Sebastian, the twin of Viola in *Twelfth Night*. Rather akin to
Mariana, Sebastian's own role is also a sort of pre-sexual 'bed-trick': having
fallen for Viola who has been dressed as a male page Cesario, Olivia vows to
marry him. No one in the playworld knows of Sebastian's existence, so his arrival
at Olivia's coincides with her rush to the altar and, bewilderedly, he substitutes
for his sister and marries a woman he has only just met. As a figure whose

purpose in the play is to substitute for someone he looks just like – his own twin – it is appropriate that Sebastian has relatively little personality of his own. He's a plot device, although we could argue that a couple of scenes with his devoted companion and rescuer Antonio are unnecessary by this estimation, and serve to establish Sebastian as a character who can himself inspire affection, rather than just mop it up by appearing in the right place at the right time.

Reading Shakespeare's characters on the page

So looking at Shakespeare's characters as if they were, and with the expectation that they can be explained as, real people, may be more appropriate to some characters than others. It may also confine us unhelpfully or lead to questions the text is not supported to answer. A good example might be the issue satirised in the title of L. C. Knights' article 'How many children had Lady Macbeth?' (1933). The title refers to the scholarly controversy prompted by the fact that while Macbeth and his wife apparently have no offspring, there *are* references to a child, particularly in Lady Macbeth's startling image designed to strengthen her husband's resolve to kill King Duncan:

> I have given suck, and know
> How tender 'tis to love the babe that milks me:
> I would, while it was smiling in my face,
> Have plucked my nipple from his boneless gums
> And dashed the brains out, had I so sworn
> As you have done to this.   (1.7.54–9)

So Lady Macbeth has 'given suck' and yet Macbeth sees he has achieved a 'barren sceptre' since he has no heir. One of the most influential character critics of Shakespeare, A. C. Bradley, devoted a section at the end of his *Shakespearean Tragedy* (first published in 1904) to this problem, along with other questions including 'Does Lady Macbeth really faint?' and 'When was the murder of Duncan first plotted?' The form of the questions suggests that there are absolute and knowable answers if only we can interrogate the play skilfully enough to make it confess them. The play is withholding information which we need to uncover. (The terminology is appropriate: the connotations of the interrogation cell are disturbingly present in this interpretative model.) This again puts the onus on us as readers, performers, or viewers to do that work the play does not do for us – mentally to supply the unwritten scenes in which the answers to our questions are provided – but it may be that it is the questions themselves which are unnecessary.

Because Knights' approach, in contrast with that of Bradley, is to see *Macbeth* not as a drama of real, autonomous protagonists but rather as a linguistically and thematically integrated poetic whole, he sees this image as part of a cluster of references to unnaturalness with which the play is structured. Unnaturalness is the keynote of the play's sustained inscription of how bad it is to murder a lawful king, the crime that haunts Macbeth's illegitimate rule in Scotland, and thus it is not associated with, or derived from, particular individuals in the play. It is the play's own timbre, a tone suffusing all of its language. There-fore Lady Macbeth's image is not about a 'real' child: it demands attention not alongside the family situation of the Macbeths but alongside imagery voiced by other characters, such as that of the Old Man (the absence of any sem-blance of individual characterisation in his name is indicative in this context): 'On Tuesday last, / A falcon tow'ring in her pride of place / Was by a mous-ing owl hawked at and killed' (2.4.11–13). For Knights, therefore, the search for the 'truth' of this image, the attempt to reconcile the Macbeths' childless-ness with this perverted image of maternity, is an unnecessary one resulting from a misrecognition of a poetic pattern as lines requiring psychological and realistic explanation (we return to this kind of interpretation in chapter 4, 'Language').

Embodying Shakespeare's characters on stage

It's a significant part of Knights' argument that he calls the drama of *Macbeth* a 'poem'. If we step back from character as a way of interpreting Shakespeare, we are left with a sequence of lines, images, words susceptible to the same kinds of analytical interpretation we might want to perform on the poetry of, say, Wordsworth or Dickinson. For those whose concern is with the play as theatre, however, dismissing the denigrated question about Lady Macbeth's children is not really sustainable. Poems don't tend to come over very well on stage; people do. In order to understand the character, in order to make sense of his or her lines and give them authority in the theatre, the performer often has to imagine motivations and events not explicitly present in the text. In her account of her preparation and performance of the role of Lady Macbeth opposite Antony Sher, directed by Gregory Doran for the Royal Shakespeare Company in Stratford-upon-Avon in 1999, Harriet Walter discusses this missing child, appearing in the text only as a kind of metaphor, in surprisingly material terms: 'it could have been a boy who died. This seemed to us the most likely and contained the richest theatrical juice . . . to create the highest stakes possible for the couple in this short but pivotal scene [1.7], we decided that the couple had not spoken of the child since its death and that, for whatever reason, they could not have any more.'

This tells us as much about dominant modes of classical acting in the UK, perhaps, as it does about Shakespeare. The idea of the Macbeths as bereaved parents, however, does chime interestingly with the specificity of Macbeth's most brutal order, for the massacre of Macduff's family – 'give to th' edge o' th' sword / His wife, his babes, and all unfortunate souls / That trace him in his line' (4.1.150–2) – and with the repeated imagery of children throughout the play. The attempt to find a psychological rationale for characters' behaviour, often through constructing a back-story or history for them which is barely legible in the play itself, is a standard technique when actors work to bring Shakespeare to life on the stage. It develops Bradley's style of questioning into something less absolute and more provisional: as chapter 2 on 'Performance' discusses in more detail, we can answer 'Does Lady Macbeth really faint?' in relation to particular productions, even while we can't do it in relation to the text of the play itself.

Doubling on the early modern stage

Harriet Walter's account of her interpretation of Lady Macbeth reveals how modern theatrical practices shape our encounter with Shakespeare's characters on stage. There are a number of rather different protocols operative in the Elizabethan theatre, however, which have an intriguingly different impact on notions of character. Two particular features of early modern theatre practice seem relevant here: the habitual practice of doubling, and the fact that Shakespeare wrote for particular actors.

As a commercial playwright with a clear sense of the medium for which he wrote, Shakespeare constructed his plays with an abiding consciousness of business discipline. Plays needed to be performable by a company of approximately fourteen actors who between them would take up to forty roles. To give some specific examples, *Antony and Cleopatra* lists thirty-seven named speaking parts and in addition calls for supernumeraries such as servants, soldiers and messengers; *1 Henry VI* has thirty-five named speaking parts; *Cymbeline* has thirty-three named speaking parts; *The Merchant of Venice* has nineteen; even *The Tempest*, set on what is misleadingly labelled an 'uninhabited island', has eighteen. This disparity between the number of actors and the number of roles was bridged by the customary practice of doubling, in which actors took on more than one role in each play.

Doubling may have been initially a logistical convenience, enabling plays with ambitiously large casts to be staged within reasonable financial constraints, perhaps with extras drafted in for supernumerary parts. Some of the stage directions in the early texts seem deliberately permissive in this regard, and give us a glimpse into the contingent practices of the early modern theatre: *Titus Andronicus*, for example, has a stage direction in Act 1 which lists the entrance of all the play's principals and then adds 'and others as many as can be'. But rather than considering doubling merely as a practical necessity, there are some suggestive ways in which to see it as integral to the structure of the plays and as offering significant inflection of our understanding of dramatic character.

As soon as we have one actor playing more than one role, something of the autonomy of individual, unique character is broached. A relationship – visually, at least, but perhaps also thematically or even psychically – between the characters played by the same actor is implied. Sometimes this is a feature of apparently minor characters. Thus in *Henry V*, the play depicting the scapegrace Prince Henry's reformation on his accession to the throne, we begin to see that Henry repeatedly encounters groups of three potential antagonists: the three traitors who have allied with the enemy France; the three disreputable foot-soldiers who are remnants of his riotous youth with Falstaff; the three named English soldiers he meets while in disguise the night before the decisive battle of Agincourt. Doubling may well mean that these trios were all played by the same group of actors – perhaps they also played the French noblemen – and that thus they offer a cumulative, almost choric, locus of resistance to Henry's idealisation. Taken in isolation the roles are minor; cohering around the reiterated physical presence of the same actors, they look more significant: to be sure, Henry keeps besting these trios, dispatching the conspirators with considerable theatrical élan, marginalising the soldiers' concerns, knocking the proud French into a cocked hat, but what is significant is that the play keeps reviving them to provide another, differently costumed but structurally similar challenge.

A more famous example is that of Cordelia and the Fool in *King Lear*. The two characters never appear on stage in the same scene (an obvious prerequisite for doubling), and the idea that the same actor played both parts may help us with the unremarked disappearance of the Fool in Act 3. Perhaps this conundrum needs to be resolved practically, rather than thematically: he has to disappear not because Lear has now become his own Fool, or because his role as Lear's conscience is completed as Lear enters his final madness, or because he has been captured by the forces of Gonerill and Regan, or some other such realist or psychological explanation, but rather because he has to change into Cordelia's costume for her return to the play in Act 4. Lear's apparent association of the two characters when he notes on the death of Cordelia that 'my poor fool is hanged' (5.3.279) adds to the parallels between them. We don't need to complicate this connection by literalising it and hypothesising that Cordelia has actually disguised herself as the Fool in order to remain close to her father, as has sometimes been suggested in modern productions. Instead, we can use the interconnectedness of the two truth-telling roles to explore structures of correspondence in the plot, as Cordelia's scenes with Lear are visually and emotionally echoed and pre-empted by those of the same actor in his role as the Fool.

In this case doubling works to refract a single role across two 'characters'. This isn't to deny Shakespeare's interest in psychology, but rather to disrupt a one-to-one association between dramatic character and individual personality. And there are any number of roles in Shakespeare which, once we recognise that they would have to be doubled, activate a kind of ripple-effect across the surface of their play. Take the ghost of Old Hamlet, for example, who appears in only four scenes of the play, and is therefore apt to be recast elsewhere. It is interesting to consider the different effects of doubling the ghost with the character of Fortinbras who strides onto the stage to assume the throne at the end of the play, or with the Gravedigger, who, as he prepares Ophelia's burial place, may also share with the ghost the trapdoor region below the stage, or with Laertes, or with Claudius, or with the Player King. Or we might consider the parallel human and fairy worlds of *A Midsummer Night's Dream*, a play which moves from the Athenian court of Theseus and Hippolyta to the magical woodland world presided over by the warring Oberon and Titania. The human and fairy sovereigns never appear on stage together, and thus it's quite likely they would have been played by the same actors – Peter Brook's famous production in Stratford for the Royal Shakespeare Company in 1970 is a prominent modern example of this practice. Similarly, it's likely that the play's 'rude mechanicals' (working men of Athens) and the fairies would have been doubled, which may challenge our assumption that these two categories would be physically dissimilar. Doubling gives us a way of conceptualising the relationship between the real and dream worlds, as if Oberon and Titania represent the dream versions of Theseus and Hippolyta engaged in the risky personal and sexual freedoms the wood seems to symbolise in the play. The 'dream' of the title thus becomes a more obviously Freudian one, in which repressed or sublimated sexuality expresses itself in dangerously surreal ways.

Writing for particular actors

If Shakespeare wrote for doubled casting, he also wrote with particular actors in mind. Chapter 3, 'Texts', discusses in detail the early printed versions of Shakespeare's plays and what insight they can give us into their performance and construction. Here, I want merely to touch on an example from *Much Ado About Nothing* which places against the expectations of character plausibility the exigencies of performance. Unlike many of his contemporary playwrights, Shakespeare's association with a particular acting company – the Lord Chamberlain's Men, later becoming the King's Men – meant that he wrote plays for specific actors rather than scripts for sale to the highest bidder. Thus Richard Burbage played the dominant tragic roles, and was so associated with them that an elegy on his death suggested the parts had died with him: 'No more young Hamlet, old Hieronimo [the tragic protagonist of Thomas Kyd's popular revenge tragedy *The Spanish Tragedy*], / Kind Lear, the grieved Moor [Othello], and more beside / That lived in him, have now for ever died.' Playing the dangerously, psychotically attractive Richard III, Burbage was, according to a contemporary joke recorded by the diarist John Manningham, encouraged to visit a female playgoer who had fallen for him in his stage persona: I'll quote the story, since it's one of the only contemporary allusions to a flesh-and-blood Shakespeare.

> Upon a time when Burbage played Richard the Third, there was a citizen grew so far in liking with him, that before she went from the play she appointed him to come that night unto her by the name of Richard the Third. Shakespeare, overhearing their conclusion, went before, was entertained, and at his game 'ere Burbage came. Then message being brought that Richard the Third. was at the door, Shakespeare caused return to be made that William the Conqueror was before Richard the Third.

Shakespeare's comic roles up to 1599 were written for Will Kemp, a clown with a talent for improvisation. The early texts of *Much Ado* register his intimate relation to the character of the comic constable Dogberry, such that in a number of instances the speech prefix for Dogberry is, in fact, 'Kemp'. The sense that Kemp is playing himself, or at least that he is playing his stock role, is therefore preserved in the very fabric of the play as it's come down to us. Kemp's departure from the Lord Chamberlain's Men after some kind of disagreement in 1599 may explain why another of his famous comic creations, Falstaff, did not reappear in *Henry V* (1599) as had been promised in the Epilogue to *2 Henry IV*. Having been so profoundly associated with one actor – just like Burbage's starring tragic roles – Falstaff could not be rewritten to be performed by someone else. Rather, therefore, than being a role serially inhabitable by different actors, a character who can be mobilised in different bodies, Falstaff becomes a version, an avatar, of Kemp.

Falstaff: character as individual or type?

Falstaff's own extraordinary popularity at the end of the sixteenth century may give us some insight into what the Elizabethans enjoyed about dramatic character. This irrepressible fat knight, with his preference for drinking sack and for lying down pretending to be dead on the battlefield, first appeared in *1 Henry IV*, where he is the tavern companion of the young heir to the throne, Prince Henry. His popularity seems to have spawned a second episode, *2 Henry IV*, and he also appears uprooted from the Eastcheap underworld of the history plays in a comedy, *The Merry Wives of Windsor*. He is a character who is literally larger than life, and larger than the plays in which he refuses to be confined. As Shakespeare's own invention – with no real equivalent in his historical source material – Falstaff has been investigated as a kind of vestigial Vice figure – who in medieval drama tried to lure audience and characters into wickedness – as a version of the *miles gloriosus* type of braggart solider, as the Lord of Misrule in early modern festivities, or as a personification of England and an image of greenworld fertility. None of these attempts to account for Falstaff suggest that he is an individual of consummate humanity: rather they offer different ways in which he is a literary or cultural type, as do those readings of *1 Henry IV* which see him as a substitute father-figure or foil to the young prince. Paradoxically, therefore, Falstaff's vitality seems to be exactly because he is not a believable human being, but because he is both more and less than that. He is both stereotype – a locus of a range of influences and archetypes – and individual – a character with a proper name which has become adjectival as a byword for fat, raffish joviality.

Naming and individuality

One of the ways in which character is fixed for us is via that use of a proper name. The experience of a proper name is very different when reading a play – and sometimes, as we'll see, editorial interventions sharpen this difference – from seeing it performed. For example, the second scene of *Twelfth Night* introduces us to a young woman who has been shipwrecked on the shores of Illyria. She is making plans for what to do next now that her brother is apparently drowned, and hears from her companion the sea captain something about two notable local residents, the grieving Lady Olivia and Count Orsino. If we read this scene rather than seeing it performed, we are immediately introduced in the stage directions and prefixes to the woman as 'Viola'. What's more, she remains 'Viola' in the apparatus of the text even as she dresses as a man and takes on the identity of the page Cesario. This is more than just a convenience for readers: giving Viola a consistent name that she does not share with any other character in Shakespeare is like giving her a consistent, unique and knowable personality to which we as readers have privileged access and one which is unaffected by such provisional matters as a change of clothing. Viewing the play is quite a different experience, however. Since Viola's name is never mentioned in the spoken text of the play until, in the very last scene, she is reunited with her lost brother Sebastian – the only figure in the playworld who *can* name her – she is literally unknown and as mysterious to us as she is to the Illyrians she moves among. When she enacts the role of Cesario, we have no firm sense of the known and consistent femaleness which underlies her disguise; at the first performances when, as usual, female parts would be played by males, this must have been even more unsettling than it is when staged now.

Here, the apparatus of the printed play seems to consolidate individual character identity in the case of Viola. But there are examples of early printed texts denying specific individual identity to particular characters. In *Hamlet*, for instance, Hamlet's uncle Claudius is never called by his personal name by anyone in the play. Speech prefixes and stage directions are univocal in apparently endorsing his claim to the throne, calling him 'King': one stage direction alone gives him the additional name 'Claudius'. Modern editors have almost uniformly preferred to humanise him under the forename 'Claudius' than to leave him named for his hierarchical role as in the early texts. What difference does this make to our expectations of his character? Editors do something comparable with the character we tend to know as Edmund, the Duke of Gloucester's malevolent illegitimate son in *King Lear*, who plots against his legitimate brother Edgar. Edmund is called, without ceremony, 'Bastard', in the early texts of the play, as if his personal identity is less significant than the stereotype of the illegitimate malcontent. Perhaps we raise expectations of realistic psychology by naming him 'Edmund' rather than the descriptive label 'Bastard', and then our character criticism struggles to meet expectations which we have in fact superimposed on the play. (There's more on the way editing pre-interprets plays for us in chapter 3, 'Texts'.) Further, we describe the play as *King Lear*, so that it corresponds to that individualist tragic aesthetic already discussed.

Looking at the earliest printed version of the play published in 1608, we can see that it bears the fuller title of 'True Chronicle History of the Life and Death of King Lear and his Three Daughters': the mention of the king and his three daughters not only means that Lear has to share top-billing, but also allies the play to the genre of fairy story. Once we see the resemblances between *King Lear*'s story of two wicked sisters and a young faithful one, and a familiar folk-tale such as 'Cinderella', we might feel that expecting its protagonists to draw out great psychological reserves is irrelevant to the form of the narrative, and that, for example, any attempt to distinguish deeply between the personalities of Gonerill and Regan is a futile one. (There's more on the sources for *King Lear* in chapter 6.)

One of the difficulties of these suggestions for modern readers and spectators of Shakespeare is that they cut across our categories of aesthetic appreciation. To call characterisation 'two-dimensional' seems a term of abuse, an attribution of dramatic failure, rather than a recognition that some characters are necessarily and enjoyably stock types or plot devices rather than rounded individuals. Sometimes they even know they are: have a look at Keanu Reeves playing Don John, another plotting 'bastard', in Kenneth Branagh's film version of *Much Ado About Nothing* (1993) for an example of this. When reviewers criticised Reeves for wooden acting, they seemed to ignore the fact that this is a wooden role: part of the way the play insulates us against the potentially destructive energy of Don John's menace, and thus preserves itself as a comedy, is to make this self-confessed 'plain-dealing villain' (1.3.24) so deliciously transparent. One popular early seventeenth-century genre, rather analogous to modern sketch show comedy, was that of 'characters': pen-portraits of recognisable 'types' such as 'a Jesuit', 'a French cook', 'an ordinary Widow', or even, strikingly, 'an excellent Actor'. The idea of the stereotype was not clearly associated with aesthetic failure as we might now think – this is related to the discussion of originality in chapter 6 on 'Sources'– and it is a measure of our own critical preoccupations that those plays where empathetic identification with a central character seems most difficult – *Timon of Athens*, for example, or *Coriolanus* – have tended to be sidelined in criticism and in the theatre.

Characters as individuals or as inter-relationships

If we look down a title list of Shakespeare's plays, one ready distinction between the ways tragedies and comedies are entitled presents itself. Tragedies are eponymous, that is, they are named for a single – or occasionally, a double – protagonist: *Romeo and Juliet, Julius Caesar, Othello*. Comedies, by contrast, tend to the proverbial, or to evoke a mood rather than reference a person: *As You Like It, Much Ado About Nothing, The Winter's Tale*. This apparently banal difference can tell us something about the different importance of character in the two genres. In tragedies, the central protagonist tends to move towards increasing isolation through the course of the play. Thus Macbeth, initially one of King Duncan's favoured thanes, surrounded by allies and compatriots and hand-in-glove with a wife he calls 'my dearest partner of greatness' (1.5.9–10), recognises in the dying moments of his play that 'that which should accompany old age, / As honour, love, obedience, troops of friends, / I must not look to have' (5.3.25–8): the word 'troops' implicitly substitutes for the forfeited loving companions the hostile forces, captained by Duncan's son Malcolm, advancing on Dunsinane castle as he speaks. Macbeth speaks these lines alone on stage – in a soliloquy – and soliloquy, the habit of articulating thoughts to the audience and achieving most authentic self knowledge and realisation when alone, is a trait of tragedy rather than comedy and one which, like the title, represents the protagonist's own isolation. By contrast, soliloquies tend not to be used much in comedy. Instead the protagonists reveal themselves and achieve their identities through dialogue and interaction. Comedies tend to be social rather than individualistic in emphasis, and their characteristic movement towards marriage suggests both that people need to be accompanied rather than isolated in order for the social world to perpetuate itself, and that to achieve these matches they need to talk to each other rather than, as in soliloquy, to us. (Chapter 5, on 'Structure', discusses generic distinctions, and blurring, in more detail.)

This may suggest that characters in tragedy are autonomous, whereas those in comedy are interreliant. But there are many aspects of Shakespeare's characterisation which challenge this. If we take *Hamlet*, for example, the play on which most theories of Shakespearean characterisation have been premised, we can see different modes of characterisation in simultaneous operation. Hamlet, for example, may think himself uniquely individual. Certainly, the family and friends with whom he is initially surrounded are insistently rejected in favour of solitude: as he contemptuously tells his old college friends Rosencrantz and Guildenstern, 'you would play upon me [. . .] you would pluck out the heart of my mystery [. . .] you cannot play upon me' (3.2.330–1), and they, like Ophelia and Laertes, are marginalised by Hamlet's resolutely centrifugal individualism. Even Horatio, greeted as 'my good friend' in 1.2.162 and thus, as well as a potential ally in the court, a threat to the tragic isolation to which Hamlet is fated and perhaps aspires – cannot reach him.

But at the same time, the play is carefully structured to echo Hamlet's situation as a son avenging a father, and in this structure it contests this view of Hamlet's uniqueness. Perhaps we could say it contests Hamlet's own solipsism.

Laertes and Fortinbras are both sons of dead fathers, both seeking to revenge slights or losses suffered by the earlier generation. Like Hamlet, Fortinbras is saddled with the name of his illustrious father, and seeks to recapture the territory lost to Denmark in a previous battle. Like Hamlet, Laertes suffers the violent death of his father and seeks to redress this injury. It seems unlikely that we will interpret this concatenation of avenging sons realistically; rather, the two secondary protagonists act as foils or contrasts or amplifications of Hamlet himself. Thus we might say that the dominance of Hamlet in *Hamlet* is aided by the fact that Laertes and Fortinbras also represent aspects of Hamlet's own dilemma, alternative responses to the experience of early manhood and the loss of a parent. Celestino Coronada's radical 1976 film of the play, which casts twins Antony and David Meyer as two sides of Hamlet's personality and also as Laertes, suggests this very economically: in the final fatal duel between Hamlet and Laertes, we see simultaneously that the mortal struggle is and always has been within Hamlet himself. We might develop this insight to suggest that other characters, too, might be read as aspects of Hamlet's own refracted personality. So Ophelia's madness and her apparent suicide become a representation or a rehearsal of Hamlet's own; the ghost's shared name – in none of Shakespeare's sources for *Hamlet* do dead father and grieving son share a name – offers us a way in which the melancholic Hamlet is already restively dead at the start of the play; even the Players already know a play remarkably close to Hamlet's own story, as if they, too, are in his head.

We might want to think of this as another kind of doubling, psychic rather than actual, in which this time it is the characters, rather than the actors, who are doubled up. This sense that maybe a number of the characters represent attributes of Hamlet, or echoes of him – or, put another way, that they occupy overlapping psychic space – links Shakespeare's plays suggestively with the legacy of medieval theatre. Plays such as *Mankind* (*c.* 1470) or *Everyman* (*c.* 1520) presented characters whose very names clearly indicated that they were not complete and autonomous human beings. When, for example, 'Everyman' is abandoned by his fair-weather friends 'Fellowship', 'Kindred', and 'Goods', and only 'Knowledge' will accompany him on his final journey to death, we know that these figures are personifications or externalised symbols of an inner struggle rather than 'real' characters: the technical term for this is *psychomachia*, literally, 'conflict of the soul'. Conventionally it has been argued that Shakespeare, with his fellow dramatists of the 1580s and 1590s, breaks free from this representational schema. But it might be useful to see certain Shakespearean characters in a similar relationship, as representing complementary traits, or as rendering an internal conflict legible by splitting it between different protagonists.

Let's look at Othello and Iago, for instance. Iago, the ensign who plots to destroy his general for reasons the play, unlike Shakespeare's sources, does not make clear, has long been an enigma for character critics. Famously, S. T. Coleridge writing in the nineteenth century, discussed their efforts as 'the motive-hunting of a motiveless malignity', and the sense that Iago's wickedness is essentially without motive has itself been used to psychologise him as a psychopath. Even, that is to say, an observation which might seem to mark a failure of psychological plausibility in the representation of Iago – we don't understand why he does what he does – is recast in realist terms. There is, however, an alternative way to conceptualise him: less as a self-contained person and more as a sort of inner voice, or a mechanism, an engine of the plot. In prompting Othello to question his wife's fidelity, Iago functions as the nagging doubt that is part of Othello's own precarious identity as a black man in a white world. Just as later, Shakespeare will rewrite this story of an irrationally jealous husband who needs no external Iago to trigger his rage (in the character of Leontes in *The Winter's Tale*), perhaps here he is showing us a version of psychomachia, as Othello's trust in Desdemona is battling with his doubts as externalised and represented in Iago. Iago's strange early line 'were I the Moor, I would not be Iago' (1.1.58) registers the uncanny interplay between them. Seeing Othello and Iago as part of a psychomachic presentation of dramatic individuals, rather than as separately realised human beings, enables us to see the way the play uses the technique of externalisation to anatomise an inner emotional struggle.

Character: interior or exterior?

The relationship between Othello and Iago might help us to read the interaction between characters as an externalised representation of an interior psychic dynamic. This question of whether character is an essence, an inner quality, or whether it is a performed or externalised property, is key to recent scholarly debates. In *Hamlet* Shakespeare seems to offer us both a way of perceiving character as the project of the interior, and as something registered externally. At his first appearance, Hamlet stands out from the court by wearing black. By setting 1.2. amid the confettied celebrations of the wedding of Gertrude and Claudius, Kenneth Branagh's film (1996) makes this particularly evident, as Hamlet's costume signals a reproachful contrast to all the visual festivity. He is making a point. Everyone else may have forgotten his father's death, but not Hamlet. In case that point isn't clear to everyone, Hamlet makes it explicit. He admonishes the superficialities of Claudius' debased court – as he sees it – by arguing that while his conventional mourning clothes of 'inky cloak' and 'customary suits of solemn black' (1.2.77–8) could be usurped by someone who is only playing at grief, in his case they are the correlative of an inner and ultimately inexpressible state. His articulated 'I have that within which passes show' (1.2.85) demonstrates, however, the frustrations of identity in theatrical form: what is within must be externalised in order to be legible; what is externalised necessarily loses something of the authenticity accorded to the inner. Hamlet simultaneously casts suspicion on the validity of exterior appearance while he draws out a continuum between it and the mysterious human interior.

This conflict, between character as expressed internally and externally, is further developed moments later in Hamlet's first soliloquy. Soliloquies have tended to be seen as moments of supreme self-revelation, when the self turns outward in the dubious privacy of the empty stage. As such they are associated with psychological truth, even as they are clearly profoundly unrealistic: soliloquy does not have an equivalent in the 'real' world. Film versions of the tragedies – for example Laurence Olivier's *Hamlet* of 1948 – have often favoured the cinematic technique of voice-over as a way of translating soliloquies for the screen: here, another non-realist convention – the actor's voice heard over an extreme closeup of his face or head, suggesting access to an inner dialogue – substitutes for that of soliloquy itself. But in the context of the theatre there is no possibility of being alone: even these private moments are observed by, and perhaps therefore articulated for, an audience – something Hamlet, with his particular consciousness of theatrical forms, might be expected to recognise. Everyone else may have left the stage, but the theatre is full, expectant, and Hamlet, in revealing the torment he can only allude to bitingly in public, does not disappoint:

> O that this too too solid flesh would melt,
> Thaw and resolve itself into a dew,
> Or that the Everlasting had not fixed
> His canon 'gainst self-slaughter. O God, God,
> How weary, stale, flat and unprofitable
> Seem to me all the uses of this world!
> Fie on't, ah, fie, 'tis an unweeded garden
> That grows to seed, things rank and gross in nature
> Possess it merely.   (1.2.129–37)

Here in his first soliloquy his rhetoric is finely balanced between revelation and concealment. The opening 'O' establishes the exclamatory mode of the speech, and its use of rhetorical questions as it continues ('Must I remember?') and of repetition ('month', 'father') indicates that it is poetically highly wrought. But it also bends with the progress of his thoughts: amid more developed and flowing thoughts we can see the broken and abrupt sentences. One of the preparatory exercises undertaken by classically trained Shakespeare actors includes reading a speech and moving on each punctuation mark to give a sense of the emotional timbre of the speech: more movement tends to mean more emotional strain or mental agitation, and the middle lines of this speech would be a good example to pace out.

As the play continues, soliloquies come to define Hamlet and his unique relationship with the audience. They mark privileged moments when we are alone together: the first soliloquy breaks off at the entrance of Horatio, Rosencrantz and Guildenstern and Hamlet's realisation 'break my heart, for I must hold my tongue' (1.2.159). We can also, however, see that this moment of self-articulation is marked with its own loss: even as he privately speaks himself as an autonomous agent, Hamlet defines himself in relation to others. Most obvious in this idea of identity produced through dialogue is the presence of the audience. Identity isn't self-contained: it needs to be witnessed. It's like that old philosophical chestnut which asks 'if a tree falls in the forest and there is no one to hear it fall, has it actually fallen?': the eighteenth-century philosopher George Berkeley argued that it hadn't, and that might work as an analogy with Hamlet. If we do not hear him, does he exist? Can the self exist without an audience to witness it?

Perhaps, then, instead of phrasing our critical questions in the form of 'what is this character like?' or 'why does he or she do what he or she does?', we should step back and attend to the constructedness, the fictiveness, of the texts we are reading. Asking 'why is this character in the play?' or 'what would happen without him or her?' may be a better route to appreciating Shakespeare's art of characterisation.

Character: where next?

- Some of the challenges to traditional notions of character can be found in Alan Sinfield's *Faultlines* (Harvester Wheatsheaf, 1992) and in Catherine Belsey's *The Subject of Tragedy: Identity and Difference in Renaissance Drama* (Routledge, 1991). Katherine Maus' *Inwardness and Theater in the English Renaissance* (University of Chicago Press, 1995) offers a historicised rebuttal of Sinfield et al; Harold Bloom's *Shakespeare: the Invention of the Human* (Fourth Estate, 1999) is a more combative, common-sensical defence of character study. I cover some of the debates in more detail in the chapter on

'Character' in *Blackwell Guides to Criticism: Shakespeare's Tragedies* (Blackwell, 2004), and that volume also excerpts from pre-twentieth-century commentators on Shakespeare, including Alexander Pope.

- Other 'functional' or structural characters to be investigated might include Feste in *Twelfth Night* or Jacques in *As You Like It*; the function of the tableau of 'a son that hath killed his father' and 'a Father that hath killed his son' in 2.5 of *3 Henry VI*; choric roles such as that of Enobarbus in *Antony and Cleopatra* or the women in *Richard III*; characters whose names suggest they are functions or personifications, such as Parolles (words) in *All's Well That Ends Well* or Seyton (probably pronounced Satan) in *Macbeth* or Eros (God of love) in *Antony and Cleopatra*.

- L. C. Knights' article is reprinted in his *Explorations* (1946); Harriet Walter's account of her interpretation of Lady Macbeth is published in Faber's Actors on Shakespeare series (2002) – there are other volumes by Vanessa Redgrave on Cleopatra, Simon Callow on Falstaff, Emma Fielding on Viola, James Earl Jones on Othello and Saskia Reeves on Beatrice. Cambridge University Press's Players of Shakespeare series also collects actors' accounts of particular roles; Jonathan Holmes' book *Merely Players? Actors' Accounts of Performing Shakespeare* (Routledge, 2004), analyses this genre and what it can offer Shakespeare studies. On children and the Macbeths, Janet Adelman's *Suffocating Mothers: Fantasies of Maternal Origin in Shakespeare's Plays, 'Hamlet' to 'The Tempest'* (Routledge, 1992), is a clever and subtle argument.

- Thinking more about doubling and its impact on characterisation could take in *The Winter's Tale*: how might the Bohemia scenes in Act 4 reprise and transform the court of Leontes through doubling? How about the good and bad Dukes in *As You Like It*? Or the twins in *The Comedy of Errors*? Or Caliban and Ferdinand in *The Tempest*? Or the armies of York and Lancaster in the *Henry VI* plays, or of Rome and Egypt in *Antony and Cleopatra*? In the television production of *Twelfth Night* directed by John Dexter (1969), Joan Plowright played both Viola and Sebastian; in Celestino Coronada's 1976 film of *Hamlet* Helen Mirren played Gertrude and Ophelia; at Stratford in 1969 Judi Dench played Hermione and Perdita in *The Winter's Tale*: to what purpose? Relatedly, John Barton's decision to have actors Ian Richardson and Richard Pascoe alternate as Richard and Bullingbrook in his 1973 Stratford production of *Richard II* (pictures and discussion in the 'Histories' exhibition online at http://www.rsc.org.uk/picturesandexhibitions/jsp/index.jsp) used the interplay between actor and character rather differently. Trevor R. Griffiths' *Shakespeare in Production: A Midsummer Night's Dream* (Cambridge University Press, 1996), discusses a number of productions which

double Theseus/Oberon and Hippolyta/Titania (and sometimes Philis-
trate/Puck).

- The anecdote about Shakespeare and Burbage's sexual rivalry comes from
John Manningham's diary, written in the first years of the seventeenth century. This introduction doesn't have much to say about Shakespeare's biography (see chapter 3, 'Texts', for a brief comment on its often specious
attractions!), but if you are interested in following this up, Katherine
Duncan-Jones' *Ungentle Shakespeare: Scenes from his Life* (Arden Shakespeare, 2001) and Stephen Greenblatt's *Will in the World: How Shakespeare
became Shakespeare* (Jonathan Cape, 2004) are recommended.
- The fact that women's roles were taken by male actors has been considered
in a range of criticism. Stephen Orgel's *Impersonations: The Performance
of Gender in Shakespeare's England* (Cambridge University Press, 1996),
and Jean Howard's article 'Crossdressing, the Theatre and Gender Struggle
in Early Modern England' in *Shakespeare Quarterly* 39 (1988) are recommended. There have been some attempts to reproduce this performance
style at the 'rebuilt' Globe on London's Bankside (http://www.shakespeares-
globe.org), and more engagingly, in Cheek by Jowl's all-male production
of *As You Like It* and productions of *The Winter's Tale* and *A Midsummer Night's Dream*, among others, by Edward Hall's company Propeller
(http://www.propeller.org.uk).
- On editing and the construction of certain sorts of expectations about character, see Random Cloud's stimulating essay on '"The Very Names of the
Persons": Editing and the Invention of Dramatick Character' in David Scott
Kastan and Peter Stallybrass (eds.), *Staging the Renaissance: Reinterpretations of Elizabethan and Jacobean Drama* (Routledge, 1991): Cloud takes up
the different speech prefixes for the same character – Mother, Countess, Old
Countess, Lady, and Old Lady – in the Folio (see chapter 3 for more on this)
All's Well That Ends Well, arguing provocatively that 'not only is it not philo-
sophically necessary to ascribe a primary or transcendent unity to the notion
of individual, isolated character that so obsesses modern history, but also
the text and Shakespeare's nomenclutter [Cloud's playful neologism] resists
such appropriation'. Margreta de Grazia and Peter Stallybrass's 'The Materiality of the Shakespearean Text' in *Shakespeare Quarterly* 44 (1993) picks up
some similar issues. An online version of Thomas Overbury's *Characters*, a
selection of portraits, is at http://www.eudaemonist.com/biblion/overbury.
- The issue of tragic soliloquies and the kind of access they give us to characters
might be discussed in relation to Richard II's speech 'I have been studying
how I may compare / This prison where I live unto the world' (5.5.1–2):
Richard's first and only soliloquy in the play is also the prelude to his death, as

if the assertion and annihilation of self are intimately linked. The same might be said of Coriolanus, a tragic protagonist with fewer than forty lines of soliloquy all in the last third of the play – among the smallest number in any Shakespeare play – where the absence of articulated introspection is clearly defined: Coriolanus' character, like his very name, is public rather than private. On the other hand, Claudius' soliloquy in 3.3 of *Hamlet* may offer a different perspective on the play's events: could the king be an occluded tragic hero in the manner of fellow regicide Macbeth? Other characters for whom soliloquy seems to cut across other axes of sympathy include *Measure for Measure*'s Angelo or Aaron in *Titus Andronicus*. And what does Iago's habit of soliloquising – particularly when contrasted with Othello's relative distance – do for his relation to the audience?

• Thinking about how actors develop ideas of character through their physical embodiment of Shakespeare's language is a useful counter to more desk-bound approaches. The classic text, full of exercises and tips, is Cicely Berry's *The Actor and his Text* (Virgin, 1993): other possibilities are John Barton, *Playing Shakespeare* (Methuen, 1987) or Patsy Rodenburg's *Speaking Shakespeare* (Methuen, 2005).

　　　人物分析是莎士比亚戏剧研究的一个重要方面。在近400年的文学评论中，读者和观众对莎剧中形形色色戏剧人物的反应，经历了一个不断发展和演变的过程。读者对于剧中人物往往采用一种现实主义的态度，而观众则更容易在感情和心理上认同剧中的人物。其实，莎剧中的有些角色在剧中仅起到了功能性或结构性的作用，有些则是满足了剧中主题的需要。熟悉文艺复兴时期剧团运作模式的读者不难猜到，有个别角色是剧作家为持有剧团股份的主要演员量身定做的。作者建议在今后阅读莎剧时不要为剧中的人物增添心理因素。你认为这个建议有道理吗？我们可能做到吗？为什么？

Chapter 2

Performance

Measure for Measure: staging silence

At the end of *Measure for Measure* we have one of Shakespeare's most enigmatic silences. During the play, Isabella, a novice nun, has been attempting to secure her brother Claudio's release from jail on charges of fornication. She has been accompanied by the Duke of Vienna, who has been disguised as a friar, apparently in order to test the virtue of his deputy Angelo. The friar-Duke manipulates all the characters so that the final act sees them acknowledge their failings and gain a troubling sort of punishment/restitution in a series of marriages. It's a dark comedy in which the nagging doubts we may often experience at the multiple marriages typical of the genre are blown into a profoundly unsettling conclusion.

At least, they may be. The ending of *Measure for Measure* gives us the option. The Duke's final piece of tidying up is to propose marriage to Isabella. There has been no previous textual evidence to suggest that they might be a romantic couple, other than the specious coincidence of their matching friar-and-nun outfits, which, even by Shakespearean standards, is not much of a basis for marriage:

> Dear Isabel.
> I have a motion much imports your good,
> Whereto, if you'll a willing ear incline,
> What's mine is yours, and what is yours is mine.
>
> (5.1.526–9)

Two lines later, the play is over. Isabella does not respond, either in words or with an action indicated by the stage directions. Does she accept the Duke, or not?

Now as readers of the play we can recognise that she could do either – and that in the text of the play on the page she does neither. Perhaps the value of the moment, for readers, is that it could be interpreted either way. We often validate Shakespeare with reference to the simultaneous interpretative possibilities in his texts, and thus Isabella's silence or aporia is precisely neither acceptance nor rejection but the chance to do either. Performance is, I think, slightly different. Few directors will leave this moment without any kind of interpretative gloss. If the Duke turns to Isabella as he speaks, does she turn away? Does he hold out his hand? Does she take it? Is her wordlessness glossed by an unmistakeable action – perhaps throwing herself into his arms with a passionate embrace? Turning on her heel and going back to the nunnery? Or does the play end with indecision – will she or won't she?

We could interpret Isabella's silence as consent, or as disbelief, or as rejection, or as part of her decline which sees a feisty and argumentative woman turn into a quiet and apparently exhausted one. All of these have sanction in performance. Paola Dionisetti, who played Isabella at the Royal Shakespeare Company in a production directed by Barry Kyle in 1978, tried to make sense of the relationship between her character and that of the friar by making him into a paternalistic figure of total and unquestioned authority. When Act 5 revealed him as the Duke making her beg for Angelo's life before revealing that Claudio, her brother, is not in fact dead, she felt utterly betrayed. In the end, she did not take the Duke's outstretched hand, but the veil of her nun's habit had fallen to the floor, and she could not, or would not, pick it up. The production suggested that she could not go back to how she was, and that there was little ultimate choice about marrying the Duke – but this was not a happy romantic ending, rather an indication of how few choices there are for women in this play which repeatedly sees them all – the prostitutes and bawds of Vienna, Mariana, the jilted fiancée of Angelo, and Isabella herself – as sexual objects. During Dionisetti's performance of Isabella, the pale-coloured habit she was wearing at the outset became increasingly muddied to symbolise the impossibility of absolutes in a grubby and human world.

Five years later in 1983 the RSC put the play on again, this time directed by Adrian Noble, with Juliet Stevenson as Isabella. She interpreted the Duke's proposal as the final reinstatement of masculine power – the return of the status quo along with the return of the Duke. 'Men are organising things', Stevenson reflects in a book collection of women talking about Shakespearean roles called *Clamorous Voices*, 'So what should Isabella say or do? I used to take a long, long, pause, in which I looked at everyone. Then I took the Duke's hand.' Again, Isabella's silence is interpreted as reluctant consent: her options, always seen in terms of constraint and compulsion have become so circumscribed that she can only agree. The foregone all-female space of the convent, where she initially begs for harsher restrictions, has been replaced by the male world of the Duke's judicial and marital authority.

At the end of the Cheek by Jowl touring production of the play directed by Declan Donnellan in 1994, Isabella responded to the Duke's proposal by slapping his face, then kissing him, and then breaking away sharply and standing in tears. A few moments earlier, Claudio, whose silence in this last scene is another silence or aporia in the play-text, had pointedly rejected her by turning away from her as he embraced Juliet. Earlier than that, another silence, that of Juliet, was explained by having her gagged and held back by a prison warder, although she tried to break free to accuse Angelo. The Duke spoke his final speech nervously as the stage darkened and Isabella wept helplessly. One reviewer of Andrew Hilton's production of 2001 at the Tobacco Factory in Bristol described its ending: 'In the closing sequence, as Lucy Black's taut, concentrated Isabella is claimed by the Duke in marriage as by right, she looks at him not with docile pleasure but bleakly, as if suddenly realising she's been betrayed; you can almost see the colour draining from her face' (Susannah Clapp, *Observer*, 4 March 2001). The Complicité production (dir. Simon McBurney, 2004) ended with the Duke's louche gesture towards a large double bed upstage in the final moments: the sexual threat to Isabella's self-appointed virginity which the play initially locates in the hypocritical Angelo is thus terrifyingly transferred to the Duke in this final tableau (perhaps we could see them as Jekyll and Hyde type doubles, as discussed in chapter 1, 'Character').

By contrast, Trevor Nunn directing the play in 1991 for the RSC, set it in the turn-of-the-century Vienna of Freud – bringing out the play's obsession with sex, repression, coercion and punishment. Perhaps surprisingly, then, Nunn's production had an unashamedly happy ending, with Claudio and Angelo shaking hands, Isabella accepting the Duke without hesitation, and all dancing off stage – creating an almost entirely different play by leaving the audience with a different image. A similar ending, with much smiling, embracing, and comic happiness, can be viewed on the widely available BBC film version, directed by Desmond Davis (1979).

Because Isabella's silence, and the interpretation directors place upon it, is the final image of the play, it has a significant effect on the whole tenor of *Measure for Measure*. It thus shapes wider critical debates about the play, particularly on the question of its genre. There's more discussion of the category of 'problem play' often attached to *Measure for Measure* in chapter 5, but we can see that these different stage interpretations work differently with the notion of what is problematic – i.e. uncomic, uncomfortable, unresolved – about the play. Trevor Nunn's happy ending erases the category of the problem play: this is *Measure for Measure* firmly back among the comedies; Declan Donnellan's Isabella's ambivalent response to the Duke's proposal works to accentuate, rather than dissolve, those generic discomforts.

'Going back to the text': the challenge of performance

How might we assess the interest, the usefulness, the validity of these varying stage interpretations of *Measure for Measure*? We would probably do it with reference back to the text, and to the interestingly moralised vocabulary used of staging or other adaptation: its 'fidelity' or 'faithfulness' to the text. But the *Measure for Measure* example shows us the limits of this kind of interpretative authorisation. Since what the directors are dramatising is a textual *silence* we cannot really go back to the text to delimit the meanings of that silence. Approaching Shakespeare's plays through performance, therefore, can significantly reformulate our notion of the 'text' to which we refer and defer. It's a sacred disciplinary cow of English studies that we support our interpretations with reference to the text: close reading has survived all manner of theoretical developments to remain the corner stone of almost all methodologies in the study of literature. We are told to back up arguments with reference to the text, to reread or go back to the primary text, as if this is where the answers to our questions will always be found. But that these texts are plays – or, rather, that the text of a play isn't necessarily the same as its *script*, and we might want to see the text of a play as its performance on the stage – challenge this foundational assumption. Reading drama, reading Shakespeare, is different from reading other types of writing, since drama's first life is arguably not on the page (there's more on this in the next chapter, 'Texts').

When we ask a question of a play – is Hamlet really mad or feigning madness? does Gertrude know anything about the murder of her first husband? is the ghost really there? is Fortinbras going to be a good ruler? to take examples from *Hamlet* – it is therefore totally inadequate to counsel a return to the text to find a definitive answer. The text, or as the next chapter discusses in more detail, texts, of *Hamlet* doesn't *answer* these questions; rather it *produces* them. That's what's interesting about the play. But if we return to the text not on the page but on the stage, we can begin to offer provisional answers: for example, how do different productions deal with the central line, Gertrude's answer to Hamlet's accusation at 3.4.28–30, 'Almost as bad, good mother, / As kill a king and marry with his brother' when she asks 'as kill a king?' (Or, as the first text of the play prints it, 'How! kill a king!': the way editors choose to punctuate the line, as the next chapter on 'Texts' explores, may prescribe certain meanings and suppress other possibilities.) The line can be delivered with the sudden terrible realisation of what has gone before, with the brazen implication 'prove it', or with genuine bewilderment, or any number of emotions.

The important point here is that a singular and authoritative answer does not – cannot – reside in the text on the page, but that any one of a range of answers can be mobilised in performance. The consequence is that the *text does not itself have stable or singular meaning*: that concept is shifted over to the theatre or the production. There are certain questions we can never conclusively answer by poring over the words: we can only offer multiple and provisional answers by taking up performance information. To put it another way, we need to amplify our notion of a play-text to encompass not simply the words on the page, but the range of their possible materialisation on different stages, real and imaginary.

Performance interpretations: *The Taming of the Shrew*

Let's try to develop this point – the shift of interpretive authority away from the page to the stage – in relation to *The Taming of the Shrew*. Providing enough of a synopsis of this early comedy to introduce the discussion immediately brings out the central difficulty with which performance criticism is engaged: even the apparently neutral procedure of summarising the action depends on a pre-interpretation. So we could give an account of *The Taming of the Shrew* like this: Kate, a shrewish and out-of-control woman at odds with her family and with society at large, meets her match in the humorous and quirky Petruchio. They are married; Kate leaves behind her inconsiderate ways and becomes a loving wife. Or we could summarise it like this: Katherina, a feisty and independent woman who does not seek a husband, is married off by her father to a bounty-hunter Petruchio, who treats her cruelly and breaks her spirit. Or like this: two oddballs meet: neither is looking for an orthodox relationship.

Their passionate and tempestuous relationship turns out to be stronger than the conventional romantic courtships of those around them. Or like this: married to Petruchio, Katherina maintains her independence while mouthing the platitudes of wifely obedience that her husband demands in front of their friends. The most basic thing we might do with a Shakespeare play, therefore, tell someone what it is about, is already fraught with interpretative difficulties. However hard we look, the play on the page will not, I think, resolve these alternatives. But in performance, different directors have given us answers to these questions.

As with *Measure for Measure*, let's focus here on the play's conclusion, on Katherina's last big speech – in fact, her longest speech in the whole play. Petruchio has made a bet with his incredulous male friends that Katherina will come at his command. Her arrival, right on cue, is made the more extraordinary by the contrast with the response of her previously docile sister, Bianca, the honey-pot around whom several suitors have been buzzing. Bianca is also newly married, but she sends a message to *her* husband saying that if he has something to say to her he can come and tell her himself. Not only does Katherina come when she is summoned, she delivers herself of a lengthy speech on the obligations of wives to husbands (and, to a lesser extent, *vice versa*):

> A woman moved is like a fountain troubled,
> Muddy, ill-seeming, thick, bereft of beauty,
> And while it is so, none so dry or thirsty
> Will deign to sip, or touch one drop of it.
> Thy husband is thy lord, thy life, thy keeper,
> Thy head, thy sovereign, one that cares for thee [. . .]
> Such duty as the subject owes the prince
> Even such a woman oweth to her husband.
> And when she is froward, peevish, sullen, sour,
> And not obedient to his honest will
> What is she but a foul contending rebel
> And graceless traitor to her loving lord?
> I am ashamed that women are so simple
> To offer war where they should kneel for peace,
> Or seek for rule, supremacy and sway,
> When they are bound to serve, love and obey. [. . .]
> Then vail your stomachs, for it is no boot,
> And place your hands below your husband's foot.
> In token of which duty, if he please,
> My hand is ready, may it do him ease.

(5.2.142–79)

There are only ten lines of the play left after Katherina has delivered this spousal bombshell – so it's crucial to the mood of the ending and to those varying synopses of the movement of the whole play above. So how have different productions delivered this speech?

A review of Michael Bogdanov's 1978 production at Stratford had Katherina 'spit out her lines with such indomitable scorn that Petruchio flinches and turns away'. A Canadian production from 1988 had the speech as a kind of 'verbal sexual foreplay' – a promise of submission which was the willed masochism of sexual experimentation rather than domestic drudgery, followed by Petruchio's sexualised invitation 'Come on and kiss me, Kate' (5.2.180). Some productions have suggested that Katherina knows there is money at stake – and have had her enter the stage with Grumio whispering to her to fill her in on the situation so that together she and her husband win the substantial bet he has placed on her obedience. Franco Zeffirelli's 1967 film version with Elizabeth Taylor and Richard Burton (the well-publicised offscreen tumults of this on-off couple add much to the film's characterisation of Katherina and Petruchio's passionate encounters) suggests that Katherina's speech is part of an agreed *modus operandi*. These are among a range of readings which have attempted to reclaim the play for modern audiences for whom the spectacle of female submission is unpalatable. But there are other readings too. The ever-provocative New York director Charles Marowitz had his Katherina come in in a pale, surgical-type shift as from a psychiatric ward, mumbling her speech as if sedated or lobotomised. A Turkish production had Katherina sink to the ground at the end of the speech – she had cut her wrist and bled to death during it.

Even if you don't have the chance to see or read about different productions, it is still necessary to ask of the text the same questions as would a director and actors. This process is crucial to our recognition of the play's own provisionality. There are no stage directions in the early texts of *The Taming of the Shrew* to indicate the blocking (the choreography of the actors on the stage): how might the speech have different implications if Katherina were kneeling and Petruchio standing, or vice versa, or if they shake hands in a pact between equals, or if Katherina's remarks are directed to the characters other than her husband, or to the audience? When she says her 'hand is ready' to be placed under her husband's foot, does she demonstrate through gesture this self-abnegation, or does it remain a rhetorical possibility? And what is everyone else on stage doing during the forty-five lines of her speech? Are they uncomfortable, convinced, shifty? Are the women behaving differently from the men? All of these questions for performance interpret, and draw on existing interpretations of, the play and shape our understanding of its thematic and emotional dynamic. We cannot revert to the play-text to prove one of these alternatives 'correct' or 'true' and thereby discount the others; instead, choices in production bring out the range of elements in a stage play in addition to, and in excess of, the words on the page.

Topical performance: the plays in different theatrical contexts

These varying interpretations of the relationship between Petruchio and Katherina are partly matters of academic or scholarly analysis, but they also abut wider cultural notions about what is considered appropriate in relations between men and women outside the theatre. Since Shakespeare has such a privileged status in English-speaking cultures, particularly in the education system and in the subsidised Royal Shakespeare Company in the UK, there are considerable expectations that his works should conform to current ideas of social propriety. If Shakespeare were merely a writer of the sixteenth and seventeenth centuries, we might expect his attitude to, say, the role of women within marriage, to be different from our own. But because, culturally, we have invested in the idea that Shakespeare is timeless (chapter 7, 'History' has more on this), we have tended to want to see in Shakespeare the anticipation of our own attitudes: productions of *The Taming of the Shrew* become, in this critical context, a mirror of wider attitudes towards women's roles in society. Or, to take another example, *Othello*, a play in which a marriage between a black man and a white woman ends in wife-murder, used to be seen as a warning against such 'unnatural' interracial liaisons; it has been reinvented as a play generally seen to be disinterestedly *about*, rather than partisanly enacting, the terrible and corrosive effects of racism. We don't want Shakespeare to look like an unreconstructed sexist or racist, after all: that would really screw up our continued investment in the literary canon.

The ways in which we shape the plays so that they catch up with us are fascinating, and this can often be seen most clearly in thinking about performances in historical context. If we take the case of *Henry V*, for example, we have a play that seemed to be about a heroic English king spurring his compatriots through a rhetoric of motivation into winning a miraculous, God-given victory against the French. Not surprisingly, its stage history has been almost entirely associated with times of war or national crisis. In order to construct a Henry with whom audiences could identify, the text of the play in performance has, until recently, been very heavily cut, so that those elements that might compromise the idealised portrait of Henry were stripped away. Thus the episcopal conspiracy with which Shakespeare begins the play, in which the bishops identify war with France as a tactic to divert the monarch from legislation potentially damaging to the church, is omitted. A heroic stage Henry doesn't threaten the virgins of Harfleur with rape, nor to spit the town's children on pikes (3.4.20–30); he tends not to be implicated in the death of the popular rogue Falstaff, and the decision to execute another of his former comrades, Bardolph, is also cut. Heroic versions of his character usually avoid the clear textual evidence that he orders the execution of the French prisoners before the outrage on the English camp. We can see a version of this kind of idealised Henry, and the cuts that are deemed necessary to protect his reputation, in Laurence Olivier's famous epic film of 1944, itself closely identified with contemporary warfare in its explicit dedication 'to the Commandos and Airborne Troops of Great Britain, the spirit of whose ancestors it has been humbly attempted to recapture in some ensuing scenes'.

Inevitably, perhaps, as attitudes to warfare and to an unexamined glorification of military heroics shifted, so too did *Henry V*. Those elements of the play – the savagery of Henry's threats to Harfleur, the execution of the French prisoners, the abandonment of Falstaff and Bardolph – which had previously been omitted became among the most significant scenes in a new breed of anti-war productions, stimulated by that most unheroic of conflicts, the Vietnam war. Michael Kahn's disturbing and radical production of *Henry V* at Stratford, Connecticut, in 1969 against rising anti-war protests figured the whole play as a sinister game, with Henry as its tyrannical captain. Terry Hands in a stark 1970s production at the RSC presented the savage slaughter of Agincourt as the violent underside of chivalric pageantry: literally, as a richly decorated caparison was lowered to cover the stage in muddy folds for the battle scenes. In 1984 Adrian Noble's Agincourt saw troops sheltering from unremitting rain under dirty tarpaulins as Bardolph was executed in front of them, recalling the trenches of the First World War. Kenneth Branagh as Henry was capable of personal violence one reviewer dubbed 'psychotic'. Some of this demythologising – and the weather – finds its way into Branagh's own film version of the play (1989) which makes a great point of contrast with Olivier's (see 'Where next' for some suggestions on this).

Perhaps the ultimate rereading of the play, and one available on video, was Michael Bogdanov's controversial touring production as part of the English Shakespeare Company's 'Wars of the Roses' during the 1980s. One seasoned reviewer described it as the only production he'd ever seen 'where you wanted the French to win'. Bogdanov's uncompromising interpretation made for some striking moments: after the Eastcheap crowd set out for France in Act 2, the poignancy of their farewells was immediately undercut by their chant, football-supporter style, of 'here we go', as Union flags, bunting, and a banner proclaiming 'Fuck the Frogs' were unfurled from the balcony. The Chorus walked across the stage to the patriotic music of 'Jerusalem', holding a placard spelling 'Gotcha', the infamous headline from *The Sun* on the sinking of the Argentinian warship the *General Belgrano* during the Falklands War. Henry's campaign in France was thus implicated in the unedifying contemporary discourses of Falklands militarism, tabloid jingoism, soccer-hooligan racism, and 'Last Night of the Proms' flag-waving. Turning *Henry V* into a satire on war and its apologists may seem extreme, but it's striking that Bodganov's production preserved a much fuller Shakespearean text (see chapter 5 on 'Structure' for further discussion of the ways the play both enacts and undercuts its idealisation of the central character) than heroic versions such as Olivier's.

Citing performances

Thinking about these different performance possibilities is not a decorative or arty adjunct to standard reading practices. Rather it is crucial to mobilising the range of meanings afforded by Shakespeare's texts. Stage directions – these are discussed in more detail in the next chapter on 'Texts' – are often scanty in early texts, and, even where they are present, they never indicate the way in which a particular line should be delivered. Thinking about performance is not, that is to say, trying to recover the illusory 'original' performance, although 'Where next' suggests some avenues to pursue this fascinating question. Rather, it is a task of imagining multiple possibilities. So reading consciously with a sense of which characters are on stage and how their placement might affect the dynamic between them, imagining what they might look like or the context in which they might be presented, and how the parts might be cast can suggest all kinds of hypothetical performances or performance options which do not need a theatre and a company of actors to be realised. 'Fantasy casting' – who, from the history of film, television and theatre, you would cast in a particular role – can reveal a good deal about different perceptions of the same character. It's been suggested (by Camille Paglia in *Sexual Personae*, a provocative and wideranging book not only on Shakespeare), that Tina Turner would make a good Cleopatra; we might think about the different readings of Hamlet's character suggested by casting the political dissident Innokenti Smoktunovsky (Grigori Kozintsev, 1964), the action hero Mel Gibson (Franco Zeffirelli, 1990), or the melancholy slacker Ethan Hawke (Michael Almereyda, 2000); preferring Christopher Lee over Ian McKellen, following the *Lord of the Rings* films, would make a particular statement about the powers of the magician Prospero in *The Tempest*. Does it make a difference whether Bertram and/or Helena in *All's*

Well That End's Well is conventionally good-looking, or if Beatrice is taller than Benedick in *Much Ado About Nothing*, or if King Lear looks frail? It's worth remembering, too, that characters who do not speak but are on stage have very little presence on the page, but can be enormously significant in performance. Just as Isabella's silence discussed above becomes a space for a range of meanings in production, so, for example, when Prospero forgives his brother Antonio at the end of *The Tempest*, the latter's failure to reply might suggest abject repentance, defiance or bewilderment.

Performances, then, either hypothetical or real, are not merely a matter of the delivery of particular lines. Blocking, casting, costuming, set, lighting, pace, cuts to the script, interpolated characters or stage business, music – all these performance elements shape the director's interpretation of the play, and all can be cited as evidence in an interpretative argument.

Using film

Perhaps the easiest way to access the meanings mobilised through Shakespearean performance is through film. Film has a democratic advantage over theatre: it can be shared by a much wider public, and through video and DVD technology it can be reviewed repeatedly to pinpoint its varying meanings. Rather than reading about performance, therefore, film allows us to experience it directly. It is, however, often in discussions of film that the issues of 'fidelity' to the text emerge most pressingly. A review in the *Washington Post* of Baz Luhrmann's updated *Romeo + Juliet* (1996) speaks for a significant strand in the reception of this film adaptation: 'traditionalists are sure to despise the psychedelic tunes and the flashy sets of this audacious adaptation'. For some critics, film's transformation of Shakespeare will always be debasing or 'dumbing down'.

It is clear that cinema has its own commercial and aesthetic priorities: all films, for example, will cut Shakespeare's dialogue, retaining on average 20–30 per cent of the original lines. It also has its own syntax and generic codes, and thus Shakespeare films have as many formal connections to adjacent films as they do to the plays: the sequence in Joseph Mankiewicz's *Julius Caesar* (1953) as Mark Antony's forces ambush those of Brutus in a canyon is straight out of contemporary Westerns; the visual and thematic characterisation of Lady Macbeth in Orson Welles' *Macbeth* (1948) owes much to the *femme fatale* of film noirs such as Billy Wilder's *Double Indemnity* (1944) or Tay Garnett's *The Postman Always Rings Twice* (1946); Adrian Noble quotes archly from *The Wizard of Oz* and other non-realist cinematic texts in his film of *A Midsummer*

Night's Dream (1995); Kenneth Branagh's *Love's Labour's Lost* (2000) takes the form of a 1930s Hollywood musical. It is by inhabiting the cultural referents of cinema rather than the academic referents of the written play that Shakespeare on film has succeeded aesthetically, particularly in the last decades of the twentieth century. Thus the most obviously 'faithful' adaptation – those of the BBC Shakespeare series, for example – may fail cinematically precisely because it is too reverent of the play, too unwilling to make the changes necessary to make a successful film; by contrast, the Japanese director Akira Kurosawa's film version of *Macbeth* as *Throne of Blood* (1957) is widely judged to be the 'best' Shakespeare film, despite (because of?) having none of Shakespeare's lines and transforming many aspects of plot, character and setting. Judging a film adaptation by its closeness to Shakespeare's play is to ignore the representational differences between the media of theatre and cinema and the historical differences between then and now.

Jack Jorgens has usefully distinguished three modes of Shakespearean film, the 'theatrical', which has the 'look and feel of a performance worked out for a static theatrical space and a live audience' (for example filmed stage plays such as John Gielgud directing Richard Burton as *Hamlet* in 1964, or the BBC Shakespeare series); the 'realist', in which the plays are presented in visual settings, with an emphasis on 'showing' rather than telling (the Shakespeare films of Branagh or Zeffirelli come into this category, and are often praised for bringing a comprehensible Shakespeare to wider audiences); and the 'filmic', described as 'the mode of the film poet, whose works bear the same relation to the surfaces of reality that poems do to ordinary conversation' (Orson Welles and Akira Kurosawa are the directors most often put into this category: we might add a film like Julie Taymor's *Titus*, 1999, which translates a sometimes bewilderingly surreal play into a sometimes bewilderingly surreal film). Even if Jorgens' taxonomy is over-rigid and perhaps over-evaluative, it does offer a framework through which we can view Shakespeare films not only in relation to the play-texts but in relation to modes of visual representation. We need to be able to assess what a Shakespeare film is trying to do before we can judge its success.

Even in Jorgens' 'theatrical' and 'realist' modes, differences between film and theatre make themselves felt in the directorial decisions made in a number of films. Sometimes, for example, narrative film needs to explain things that are left implicit or are unimportant in Shakespeare's plays. It's not necessary, for example, to ask why Viola, on being shipwrecked in Illyria at the opening of *Twelfth Night*, chooses to dress as a man and enter the service of the local count Orsino: as we saw in the previous chapter on 'Character', the answer to the question might be 'because the play demands it'. This kind of causation by plot rather than by character is unwelcome in realist cinema, and thus

Trevor Nunn's film of the play (1996) reverses Shakespeare's 1.1 (Orsino's love-sickness) and 1.2 (Viola's arrival), introduces a preface of the twins presenting gender impersonation as entertainment on the ship, an amniotic underwater sequence as they are separated by the waves, and then interpolates a sonorous speech explaining that the shipwreck victims have arrived on a hostile shore, in which darkly uniformed horsemen and forbidding cliffs emphasise the danger and prompt Viola's subterfuge. Or, to take another example, Michael Radford's *The Merchant of Venice* (2004) begins with an extensive sequence in the Venetian ghetto, placing the story within the context of systematic prejudice against the Jewish community.

While causation or narrative may need to be differently configured to meet the demands of film, the biggest change is the translation into the primarily visual medium of the cinema from the primarily verbal medium of the Shakespearean theatre, in which everything – castles, night-time, forests, cities – was conjured through words rather than materially. Russian director Grigori Kozintsev, writing of his film of *King Lear* (1969) registers the challenge: 'the problem is not one of finding means to speak the verse in front of the camera, in realistic circumstances ranging from long-shot to close-up. [This would be Jorgens' 'realist' mode.] The aural has to be made visual. The poetic texture has itself to be transformed into a visual poetry, into the dynamic organisation of film imagery'. There are a number of ways we can see this kind of cinematic transformation. For example, in Oliver Parker's film of *Othello* (1995) we register the paranoid sequences in which Desdemona and Cassio are seen in bed together as projections of Othello's diseased sexual jealousy to which the play gives verbal rather than visual expression. Less literally, the use of chiaroscuro lighting in Orson Welles' film of the same play (1952) is a visual correlative to the pervasive imagery of black and white in the play, just as the dizzying pan in the opening sequence registers the captive Iago's point of view in a manner analogous to the play's insidious creation of a kind of sympathy with its villain. Kurosawa's *Throne of Blood* uses the visual imagery of the dense forest as an equivalent for the central character's inner confinement; similarly, the shadows in Laurence Olivier's *Richard III* (1955) symbolise in visual terms Richard's dark dominance, or Mankiewicz's preference for close-ups and intimate shots establishes the human scale of his *Julius Caesar*.

Using film comparatively: *Macbeth*

One advantage of studying Shakespeare's major tragedies through films is that there are often multiple versions to compare. Here I want to suggest how a comparison of the openings of two different film versions of *Macbeth* can open up interesting interpretative questions about the play. The versions, both readily available on DVD or video, are directed by Orson Welles (1948), and Roman Polanski (1971).

Because the opening of a film works to establish its visual, emotional and thematic palette – and because it is the only part of a film which, in viewing, is independent of any previous sequence – it can be useful to compare these explicitly, and it can sharpen our sense of how Shakespeare chooses to structure the opening of his plays to look at alternative modes of beginning. The opening of Shakespeare's play is, memorably, a short, atmospheric scene with the witches agreeing to meet Macbeth 'upon the heath', and intoning as they depart: 'Fair is foul, and foul is fair, / Hover through the fog and filthy air.' (1.1.12–13). The next scene introduces the King of Scotland who is being briefed about the bravery of Macbeth and Banquo in the battle against the Norwegians. Duncan hears that the Thane of Cawdor has defected to the enemy, but is now captured. He orders that Cawdor be executed and his title given to Macbeth. 1.3 reintroduces the witches, this time discussing their malicious powers, and predicting the arrival of Macbeth. Macbeth and Banquo enter – significantly, Macbeth is echoing the witches in his first line 'So foul and fair a day I have not seen' (1.3.36). The witches greet him with three titles: Thane of Glamis (Macbeth's title inherited from his father), Thane of Cawdor, and future King. They also predict for Banquo that 'Thou shalt get [beget] kings, though thou be none' (1.3.65). They disappear, refusing to give further information. Two messengers from the king arrive to bestow the king's gift of the thanedom of Cawdor; Macbeth recognises that one of the witches' prophecies has come true and immediately meditates on the third, telling himself 'If chance will have me king, why chance may crown me / Without my stir' (1.3.142–3). In the next scene Macbeth's internal musings grow stronger as Duncan nominates his own son his heir; in 1.5 Lady Macbeth makes her first appearance, reading a letter from her husband.

Chapter 5 on 'Structure' discusses some examples of the ways in which the internal architecture of Shakespeare's plotting works to create meaning, pace and tension. Here we can see that the juxtaposition of the witches' scenes with those of Scottish politics raises the vital question of their agency. In the first scene they arrange that they will meet Macbeth: does this mean that they can foresee the future (they know that they will meet him) or that they can shape it (they can make him come and meet them)? In their second scene they tell Macbeth something we already know – the technique of dramatic irony: that he will become Thane of Cawdor. Here it is clearer to us that they know something that has already been ordered, rather than that they make it happen by proclaiming it, but the effect on Macbeth is quite different: he hears an unexpected prophecy –

'the Thane of Cawdor lives / A prosperous gentleman' (1.3.70–1) – which is almost immediately fulfilled, raising the expectation that their further prophecy will also come true. And if we look at the way in which Shakespeare builds up the effect at the opening of the play, we might further notice that Lady Macbeth's entry into the power dynamic is delayed, and that her first lines are written for her by her husband as she reads aloud his letter; he has already considered the means by which he might become king, and interestingly, albeit figuratively, one of his first words about the subject is 'murder' (1.3.138). Those readings of the play which suggest that Macbeth would never have murdered Duncan without Lady Macbeth's promptings might look again at this sequencing.

What, then, do the two film versions of the play do with this opening sequence? Neither keeps it entirely intact, nor should we expect them to. The job of the director is to interpret and shape the text into a film, to translate across media, rather than to try to recreate the stage play.

Welles begins with a shadowy image of three shapeless witches bent over a cauldron placed on a crag in a swirling, surreal landscape. They speak – with rather dodgy Scots accents, it must be said – the famous lines from 4.1, 'Double, double toil and trouble' (4.1.10), and list some of the monstrous ingredients of the potion over an extreme close-up of the bubbling contents of the cauldron. Lines from 1.1. are patched into the scene, and as they speak 'there to meet with Macbeth' (1.1.8), the witches' hands complete their moulding of a clay figurine of Macbeth from the contents of the cauldron. A climactic piece of music introduces the credit sequence; the theme music has some suggestions of a military pipe band. The next image is of Macbeth and Banquo galloping through the same misty landscape, cutting to the witches' 'By the pricking of my thumbs, / Something wicked this way comes' (4.1.44–5). Shakespeare's 1.2, the discussion of the battle, is thus entirely cut. The witches deliver their prophecies and then are driven away by the arrival of the messengers, who bring news of Macbeth's elevation to the thanedom of Cawdor. The badge of office is taken from the neck of their wretched prisoner and passed to Macbeth, whose asides are delivered as voice-overs against a close-up of his troubled face. The witches watch the party gallop away to the king. The scene changes: by firelight, Macbeth dictates the letter to his wife, and he and Banquo discuss the witches' prophecies. Macbeth's dictation dissolves into her reading the letter, lying on a bed with heaving bosom and looking out into the dark night as she urges the spirits to 'unsex me here' (1.5.39).

As with any other text, there are a number of ways to interpret Welles' direction here. One result of his cutting and rearranging seems to be that the witches have more power. They make an image of Macbeth from their cauldron as if he is their creature – thus amplifying the suggestion in Shakespeare's 1.1.

that they control him even before he appears on stage. The clay model of Macbeth is used later in the film, including a striking cut away from Macbeth to the figurine at the moment of his decapitation by Macduff, substituting the slicing of the neck of the image for that of Macbeth himself. By omitting the scene which explains the rational, political reason for Macbeth's promotion – he has been a brave and loyal warrior whereas the Thane of Cawdor has been a traitor – news of his elevation comes as a surprise in Welles' film. The audience does not have prior knowledge as it does in Shakespeare's play, and thus we share with Macbeth a sense of the witches' power: they predict something and immediately it happens. How does this affect our relation to Macbeth? It's akin to the issue of Banquo's ghost at the banquet in 3.4: should the Banquo actor enter, and thus the audience sees what Macbeth sees and is allied with his tortured imagination, or should we be distanced from him by watching him respond to an apparently empty chair?

If we compare this version of the opening scenes with that of Polanski we can see some interesting differences of emphasis and visual effect. Polanski, too, places the first witch scene as a kind of prologue, separated from the rest of the film by the opening credit sequence. A pink dawn lightens on a damp beach: the tide is out, and on the sand a group of three women dig silently in the wet sand, performing a ritual burial of a noose and a dissevered arm holding a dagger. They speak the lines of 1.1. The atmosphere is heavy and mysterious, but there is none of Welles' mist or shadows. As the credits run we hear the noise of battle: horseback charges, the clash of swords, men shouting. The scene opens to the aftermath of the battle on the same stretch of beach, as soldiers move among the dead. One casualty stirs, only to be brutally clubbed into the sand. The king arrives on horseback with a fanfare to hear the news of the battle, laughing appreciatively at the description of Macbeth 'unseam[ing] him from the nave to th'chaps' (1.2.22). Cawdor is brought in, bleeding, tied to a litter: the king uses his sword point to take the chain of office from him and hands it to his messengers for delivery to Macbeth. A moody close-up of Macbeth, in front of the gallows being prepared for the prisoner, does not give us quite the triumphant military hero previously discussed. He and Banquo are sheltering from the rain when they hear the witches singing and seek them out: the witches do not seem particularly interested in their presence and deliver their prophecies in an unemotional way. There is a sense of time passing between this encounter and the meeting with the king's messengers: Macbeth and Banquo ride away talking, Macbeth is seen musing in his tent.

The keynote of Polanski's film – sometimes attributed to the violence in the life of the director whose wife Sharon Tate was murdered by the Manson gang in 1969 – is violence and blood. A. C. Bradley wrote that *Macbeth* 'leaves a decided impression of colour . . . that colour is the colour of blood', and in these opening scenes the images are steeped in reds, from the dawn sky to the phial of blood sprinkled on the witches' burial, from the wounded face of the captain to the sickening circle of blood which flowers on the back of the soldier clubbed to death on the beach, from the bright blood on Cawdor's naked shoulders to the king's pennants decorated in heraldic red. In this Polanski might be thought to translate the predominant mood of *Macbeth*'s linguistic texture in Jorgens' 'filmic' mode – this is a play in which the word 'blood' and its cognates echo over forty times – into the visual language of film. And what is interesting about the film is that this violence is associated with the playworld even *before* Macbeth's act of regicide. Sometimes a sentimental view of the play prevails in which the murder of Duncan is the aberrant act which sets a Scottish Eden at odds; Polanski's film shows a world which is built on the valorisation of male violence, on which Duncan's power, as well as Macbeth's in turn, relies. In this, it seems that the witches have rather less influence, even as they are presented less explicitly supernaturally than in Welles' version. By comparing the two versions different possibilities are articulated: often it is the version furthest from our initial imagining of the scene which has most to tell us about the play's interpretive range.

Hamlet: 'To be or not to be'

Even moments in the plays which seem so familiar as to be beyond different interpretations can be revitalised through comparative study of performance. *Hamlet*, the most filmed of Shakespeare's plays, gives us a range of cinematic interpretations to compare. Here I want to look at films by Laurence Olivier (1948), Kenneth Branagh (1996), and Michael Almereyda (2000), to see what performance might be able to add to one of the most discussed speeches in Shakespeare's works, the soliloquy which begins 'To be or not to be' in 3.1.

Olivier's settings throughout his black and white film are the claustrophobic interiors of Elsinore castle. He introduces the speech with a dramatic and hectic ascending shot up a long spiral staircase to the castle's battlements: Hamlet leaves a distraught Ophelia crying at the foot of the stairs and the camera looks down at the top of his head as he looks down to the sea crashing way below him. The setting literalises the 'sea of troubles' metaphor (3.1.59) and also gives us a visual correlative for the waves of emotion in Hamlet's troubled mind. The camera whirls as if inside his mind, blurring the external and internal images as he speaks, deliberately and carefully. For much of the speech the camera settles on a middle-shot showing him sitting on a rocky outcrop framed against the sky; he drops his (rather small) dagger impotently into the sea; he leaves by walking away dejectedly down some misty steps and into a dissolve to the next scene.

Branagh's film is shot in the lavish surroundings of a British stately home, Blenheim Palace, and this scene takes place in the large, echoing hall of mirrors. Branagh frames the soliloquy with Claudius and Polonius hiding themselves behind a two-way mirrored door on Hamlet's arrival: the prince walks into an apparently empty room, tiled in tessellated black and white and lined with mirrors. He delivers the speech looking at himself in the mirror, advancing with a dagger on himself, and the camera pans as he steps slowly forward, enhancing the increasing claustrophobia of the encounter. Branagh's delivery is urgent, a hoarse whisper; he threatens his own reflection with the dagger; the camera jumps to Claudius flinching, unseen, behind that reflection, neatly visualising the way in which Hamlet seems to turn against himself the violence the Ghost commands him to expend on his uncle. Gradually the camera pans to focus on the reflection, rather than on Hamlet himself. The speech is broken by the entrance of Ophelia: Hamlet is gentle, and takes her regretfully in his arms.

Almereyda's version of *Hamlet* is set in modern day New York. Hamlet begins his soliloquy as a voice-over as he mooches disconsolately through the empty Blockbuster video rental store, surrounded by action narratives. He begins to speak aloud, looking at the video screens showing explosions and flames. His tone is depressed and wearied.

We can ask a number of questions of Hamlet's speech by looking at these alternative interpretations. What is its mood? How does the speech relate to what goes before and after it? How might its visual context affect the interpretation of the words? How does it add to Hamlet's characterisation? Olivier seems to interpret it as a private, isolated discussion of suicide, in which the crashing sea below both symbolises and literalises the pull of what Hamlet has previously called 'self-slaughter' (1.2.132). Branagh imagines a divided Hamlet, talking with himself and threatening himself, but with his uncle and Polonius as onlookers (have a look at the film and see whether you think Hamlet suspects their presence). For Almereyda, Hamlet's mood is one of urban alienation: he is in a public space, a rental store, but alone with his thoughts, and these thoughts work to juxtapose the exciting and teleological plots of contemporary cinema with the attenuated and detached process of his own narrative. We can see that these different visualisations offer us the cinematic equivalent of critical readings of the character, play, and moment, and that to compare them is to participate in crucial debates about *Hamlet* and its meanings.

Adaptations: Shakespearean enough?

For some viewers, setting *Hamlet* in late twentieth-century corporate America was to go 'too far'. This metaphor of distance – how far *is* too far? – is worth considering further, and to do so, we could add a fourth category to Jorgens' taxonomy of Shakespeare films: adaptation. This category I take to include films based on Shakespearean plots, modernised versions which rewrite Shakespeare's language and/or settings, or which place a performance of a Shakespeare play at the heart of their plot.

This might seem an unnecessary category to include. But because such free-form adaptations happily shoot to pieces any residual critical investment in the notion of 'fidelity' to the Shakespearean text, they can actually free up and radicalise our understanding of their host plays. What can we learn say, about *The Taming of the Shrew* from *Ten Things I Hate About You* (dir. Gil Junger, 1999), a teen movie in which Kat Stratford, a rebarbatively clever young woman even her school counsellor calls a 'heinous bitch', has no interest in boys and wants only to graduate from Padua High School and leave her overprotective father for Sarah Lawrence College? Her attractive younger sister Bianca is forbidden to date until Kat is fixed up; Bianca's would-be boyfriend Cameron arranges for the mysterious oddball Patrick Verona to date Kat, and the couple eventually fall for each other.

Well, we can see immediately from the names – 'Stratford', 'Padua', 'Verona' – that there are a number of barely coded allusions to Shakespeare, even though nothing in the film's publicity highlighted its connection to the play. More importantly, perhaps, we can develop the discussion of the gender politics of Katherina's last speech in *The Taming of the Shrew*, discussed above, as it is redacted for a modern largely young female audience. The equivalent to that final speech in *Ten Things* is Kat's assignment to rework Sonnet 141 – a clever miniature version of the film's own relation to its source text – for her English class. Her (woeful) poem – 'Ten Things I Hate About You' – registers in the film as a public declaration of her changed emotions towards Patrick: ending 'I hate it that you're not around, and the fact that you didn't call. But mostly I hate the way I don't hate you. Not even close, not even a little bit, not even at all.' Perhaps this can help with the ambivalences around the emotional timbre of Katherina's speech; perhaps, too, the fact that Kat ends with love *and* her academic ambitions intact – she can have it all – is the modern cinematic correlative of those critical manoeuvres trying hard to see Shakespeare's Katherina not as subjugated and broken but as whole and fulfilled. The adaptation – a success on its own terms as a teen movie – self-consciously engages with the critical issues in Shakespeare's play and, like all performances, enacts its own interpretative priorities on Shakespeare's text.

Performance: where next?

- The interviews with Paula Dionisetti and Juliet Stevenson are collected in *Clamorous Voices: Shakespeare's Women Today* edited by Carol Rutter (The Women's Press, 1988); a number of women actors discuss their roles including Lady Macbeth, Isabella, Katherina, and Helena from *All's Well That Ends Well*. The Players of Shakespeare series currently in six volumes from Cambridge University Press has readable, informative essays by Royal Shakespeare Company actors describing particular roles and productions. Reviews of recent productions can most easily be found by searching online versions of newspapers: in the UK the *Guardian* (http://www.guardian.co.uk), *The Independent* (http://www.independent.co.uk) and *The Daily Telegraph* (http://www.telegraph.co.uk) do not currently charge for access to their internet archives. The leading Shakespeare journals *Shakespeare Survey* (Cambridge University Press) and *Shakespeare Quarterly* (Folger Shakespeare Library) both include measured and lucid reviews of major UK and US productions. The Royal Shakespeare Company has online exhibitions of production stills and review snippets from its archives, available at http://www.rsc.org.uk/picturesandexhibitions/jsp/index.jsp
- The idea that 'the text itself does not have intrinsic meaning: that concept is shifted over to the theatre' might be tested or explored in relation to other interpretative cruxes (points of interpretative difficulty or debate) in Shakespeare's works. For example, consider the presentation of Cleopatra's character in *Antony and Cleopatra*, or Brutus' decision to kill Caesar in *Julius Caesar*, or the extent to which Shylock is motivated by sectarian hatred in *The Merchant of Venice*, or the sincerity of Bullingbrook's regret at the murder of Richard II.
- My account of productions of *The Taming of the Shrew* derives heavily from *Shakespeare in Production: The Taming of the Shrew* edited by Elizabeth Schafer (Cambridge University Press, 2002). Other volumes in the same series offer longitudinal stage histories of *Othello* (ed. Julie Hankey, 2nd edn 2005), *Henry V* (ed. Emma Smith, 2002 – I've used this for the section in this chapter on the play), *A Midsummer Night's Dream* (ed. Trevor Griffiths, 1996), *Much Ado About Nothing* (ed. John Cox, 1997), *Antony and Cleopatra* (ed. Richard Madelaine, 1998), *Hamlet* (ed. Robert Hapgood,

1999), *The Tempest* (ed. Christine Dymkowski, 2000), *As You Like It* (ed. Cynthia Marshall, 2004), *Romeo and Juliet* (ed. James Loehlin, 2002), *The Merchant of Venice* (ed. Charles Edelman, 2002), *Macbeth* (ed. John Wilders, 2004), and *Troilus and Cressida* (ed. Frances Shirley, 2005). Manchester University Press's Shakespeare in Performance series is also recommended.

The representation of Katherina can be linked with approaches from adjacent chapters. (Laurie E. Maguire discusses what's at stake in calling her Kate – as Petruchio does – Katherine – as she does – or Katherina – as the stage directions (often) do and as Ann Thompson chooses for her New Cambridge edition in her essay in *Gloriana's Face: Women, Public and Private, in the English Renaissance*, eds. S. P. Cerasano and Marion Wynne-Davies (Harvester Wheatsheaf, 1992).)

There's a quarto text of a play printed without authorial attribution in 1594 called *The Taming of A Shrew* – scholars are divided about whether it represents a version of Shakespeare's play as it's printed in the Folio, or is a source for it – which makes for an interesting comparison with the play. The earlier play ends with the completion of the Sly framing device we get in the Induction to Shakespeare's play, and thus closes with the hungover and bewildered Sly:

> Slie: Sim, gis some more wine, whats all the
> Plaiers gon: am not I a Lord?
> Tapster: A Lord with a murrin: come art thou drunken still?
> Slie: Whose this? Tapster, oh Lord sirra, I have had
> The bravest dreame to night, that ever thou
> Hardest in all thy life.
> Tapster: I marry but you had best get you home,
> For your wife will course you for dreming here to night.
> Slie: Will she? I know now how to tame a shrew,
> I dreamt upon it all this night till now,
> And thou hast wakt me out of the best dreame
> That ever I had in my life, but Ile to my
> Wife presently and tame her too
> And if she anger me.
> Tapster: Nay tarry Slie for Ile go home with thee,
> And heare the rest that thou has dreamt to night.
>
> (*The Taming of A Shrew*, 1594)

That Sly proposes to use the wife-taming instructions of the play in his own home may corroborate the reading that Katherina is brought to heel by her husband; or the fact that he's a drunk and the whole plot is distanced as a play-within-a-play may ironise that final speech discussed above. Either way, it's worth comparing, as is *A Shrew*'s equivalent of Katherine's final speech. Leah Marcus' chapter in her *Unediting the Renaissance: Shakespeare, Marlowe, Milton* (Routledge, 1996) discusses the relation between the two, as does Ann Thompson in an appendix to her New Cambridge edition of *The Taming of the Shrew*. John Fletcher's play *The Woman's Prize, or the Tamer Tam'd* (*c.* 1611) gives us another approach to the question of whether Katherine is, or isn't, tamed: his sequel to Shakespeare's play opens as the widowed Petruchio is about to remarry, and this time get his comeuppance from a militant wife who announces from her barricaded bedroom window:

> Ile make ye know and feare a wife Petruchio,
> There my cause lies.
> You have been famous for a woman tamer,
> And beare the fear'd-name of a brave wife-breaker:
> A woman now shall take those honours off,
> And tame you;
> Nay, never look so bigge, she shall, belleve me,
> And I am she.

There's an online text of Fletcher's play at http://www.uq.edu.au/emsah/drama/fletcher/ff/prize/prizeindex.html

- Other points of comparison between Branagh's and Olivier's films of *Henry V* might be (a) the depiction of the chorus, particularly the prologue and epilogue (b) the comedy Olivier makes at the expense of Ely and Canterbury in 1.1, compared with their serious and conspiratorial whispering in Branagh (c) their flashbacks to the life of Falstaff (d) the speech before Harfleur, which Olivier cuts so Henry enters the unresisting cardboard battlements in bright armour with a band of cheerful soldiers, sharply contrasting with Branagh's psychotic yelling from the darkness at a beleaguered city surrounded by desperately battle-weary men (e) the battle of Agincourt itself, which Branagh films as an elegiac and slow-motion sequence, expressing a terrible beauty amid the slaughter, and which Olivier films in technicolour sunshine and without a drop of blood being visibly shed. I discuss these films and the other landmark productions in the play's stage history in my *Shakespeare in Production: King Henry V* (Cambridge University Press, 2002); there's an excellent book by James Loehlin on the play in Manchester University Press's Shakespeare in Performance series (1996).
- Thinking about early modern performance, and the ways in which it might have impacted on the plays, Tiffany Stern's *Making Shakespeare: From Stage to Page* (Routledge, 2004) has great suggestive ideas about – for example – the ghost in *Hamlet* emerging from the stage trapdoor and thus being spatially

identified as a denizen of hell. The 'rebuilt' Globe theatre on London's Bankside has been pioneering 'authentic' performance styles: Pauline Kiernan's book *Staging Shakespeare at the New Globe* (Macmillan, 1999) gives a readable and scholarly account of the findings from their initial productions, and the Globe's own website is at http://www.shakespeares-globe.org.

- On the topic of Shakespeare and film, see Russell Jackson (ed.), *The Cambridge Companion to Shakespeare on Film* (Cambridge University Press, 2000); Deborah Cartmell, *Interpreting Shakespeare on Screen* (Macmillan, 2000) and Richard Burt and Lynda E. Boose, *Shakespeare the Movie II: Popularising the Plays on Film, TV, Video, and DVD* (Routledge, 2003). The taxonomy of different approaches to filmed Shakespeare is from Jack Jorgens, *Shakespeare on Film* (Indiana University Press, 1977); Kozintsev's filming diary of *King Lear* is published in English as *King Lear: The Space of Tragedy* (Heinemann, 1977).

- Both Welles' and Polanski's films of *Macbeth* return to the witches at the end: Welles, by importing the line 'Peace, the charm's wound up' (1.3.37) suggests that the evil movement of the play is completed; Polanski shows a malcontent Donalbain about to encounter the witches just as Macbeth and Banquo did at the start of the film, thus suggesting that the violent cycle might be just about to begin again. Comparing these endings with that of the play itself is illuminating: what's happened to the witches in Shakespeare's play? Are they still at large, or does their disappearance allow us to connect them more directly with Macbeth's own psyche – perhaps as the external projections of his ambition (see chapter 1, 'Character', for more suggestions on this approach). Bradley's observation on *Macbeth* is from his *Shakespearean Tragedy* (1904; much reprinted).

- Other filmic adaptations which are in interesting relation to their Shakespearean sources include *O* – a high school version of *Othello* (dir. Tim Blake Nelson, 2001) or the Western *Jubal* (dir. Delmer Daves, 1956), *Joe Macbeth* (dir. Ken Hughes, 1955) and *Men of Respect* (dir. William Reilly, 1991) as gangster versions of *Macbeth*, the science fiction *Forbidden Planet* (dir. Fred McLeod Wilcox, 1956), Paul Mazursky's 1982 *Tempest* or Peter Greenaway's *Prospero's Books* (1991) as versions of *The Tempest* stressing its psycho-sexual, familial and aesthetic dynamic respectively, or Akira Kurosawa's corporate *Hamlet* as *The Bad Sleep Well* (1960) or Ernst Lubitsch's satiric *To Be or Not To Be* (1942) or even Arnold Schwarzenegger's unexpected cameo as Olivier in *Hamlet* in John McTiernan's *Last Action Hero* (1993). Tony Howard's article in Jackson (ed.), *The Cambridge Companion to Shakespeare on Film*, gives an overview of these and other 'cinematic offshoots'.

从《一报还一报》的开放式结尾谈起，作者强调了每位导演所面临的一个挑战：要对莎剧中每一处模棱两可的台词或舞台提示有自己的解读方式。作者在分析《训悍记》时指出，对剧本结尾——凯瑟琳被训服——的理解，决定了对全剧的解读，而每位导演只能任选其中的一种解读方式。你同意这种说法吗？

Chapter 3

Texts

Shakespeare's hand

The Book of Sir Thomas More, a play about a riot in London and dating from the early 1590s, was probably never performed and exists only in a hectic and partial manuscript including the handwriting of at least five individuals. It has, however, become significant to Shakespeareans because of the widely held belief that one of the writers who contributed to the manuscript may have been Shakespeare. If this is indeed so, the manuscript provides the only example of his literary work that we have in his own writing. No other contemporary hand-written script of a Shakespeare play exists, and the only samples of his handwriting that we do have are signatures to business and legal documents. If the handwriting scholars call 'Hand D' in the manuscript of *Thomas More* is indeed Shakespeare's, then those leaves of paper offer us something like a holy relic: even the common synecdoche 'hand' for 'handwriting' works to suggest that we are getting something of the physical man himself.

The truth is that the evidence that Shakespeare wrote this part of *Thomas More* is actually rather slight, although many collected editions, including those under the Oxford, Norton and Riverside imprints, now include the speeches as part of the canon. But our *desire* for the manuscript to give us access to

Shakespeare's creative processes as he wields his quill is something that under-scores all our work on the attributed plays of Shakespeare – it's the same impulse which drives the perennial interest in Shakespeare's biography. 'Hand D' offers us a fantasy of proximity to Shakespeare, rather as Juliet's statue in Verona offers us a fantasy of proximity to one of his characters (see chapter 1), or source study a fantasy of Shakespeare in the act of composition (see chapter 6). What's more, the passages attributed to Shakespeare in *Thomas More* are admirably poetic and liberal: they offer us a Shakespeare we can be proud of. The play's eponymous hero addresses the rioting crowd who are directing their rage against immigrants, and encourages them to think themselves in the place of their adversaries in a feat of imaginative empathy worthy, we might want to think, of Shakespeare's habitual understanding of different points of view in his other plays. The yearning expressed in the discussion of *Thomas More* for phys-ical evidence of what Shakespeare wrote, for the lost manuscripts underlying the printed texts on which we rely, gives textual studies a sort of elegiac quality – a sense that through new and different editions we are trying to reconstruct something tangible which is forever lost.

So what did Shakespeare write?

Asking what Shakespeare actually wrote may seem an extraordinary question. After all, we have the plays available to us in any number of printed and online forms. But crucially, all of these have been mediated by different agents other than their author. Because we do not have a manuscript version of any play, we cannot see how much of the printed play we do have was added to or altered by actors, theatre managers, printers, publishers, censors, or others, by design or by accident. There is no 'original' to refer back to: all the texts we have are secondary, or, rather, they take on the status of dubious originals. In what follows I will use the phrasing 'early texts' to refer to those printed versions of Shakespeare's plays published up to 1623, as being the nearest thing we have to an 'original'. But in some cases – *King Lear* and *Hamlet* are important examples discussed in more detail below – we have two different versions of a single play – sometimes with major differences, sometimes with minor verbal divergences – and no way of verifying how those differences relate to what Shakespeare wrote when. This chapter is going to discuss the ways in which this uncertainty can be exhilarating rather than demoralising, and to suggest that looking at the earliest texts of Shakespeare's plays can give us insight into his working methods, into the industries of the theatre and of printing, and into the texture of the drama itself.

We will see that recovering what Shakespeare wrote is an impossibility – a kind of holy grail of textual scholarship. But in the process of examining the means by which Shakespeare's plays have been transmitted to us, both by their earliest redactors and by the recent editors of the texts on your bookshelf, other, more stimulating questions emerge to substitute for the question of what Shakespeare wrote. Rather than striving after this impossibility, modern textual scholarship is inclined to embrace the energy of a more dynamic model of authorship than the singular creative genius writing the good bits of *Thomas More*: an intrinsically collaborative model in which the theatre and the printing house have their own creative input into the plays.

Stage to page

Often academic books and university or college courses considering the plays in performance use the happy phrase 'page to stage': the order of priorities here is decidedly not that of the context in which Shakespeare wrote. In the Elizabethan period performance, using a manuscript text was the first, primary life of a play, and publication secondary, both in terms of chronology and in terms of commercial and aesthetic importance. We need to reverse the terms and think of 'stage to page' as a way of understanding the conception and reception of Shakespeare's drama. Perhaps our nearest contemporary analogy is for the printed play as 'the book of the film'; something parasitic on the film and something to be read after having seen the film, rather than as an autonomous work of art in its own right. Thus the title-pages of Shakespeare's plays in their first publication almost always allude to the circumstances of their performance. *Love's Labour's Lost* (published 1598) tells us the play is 'as it was presented before her Highnes this last Christmas'; *The Merchant of Venice* (published 1600) is advertised 'as it hath beene divers times acted by the Lord Chamberlaine his Servants'; *King Lear* (published 1608) identifies the printed text 'as it was plaid before the Kings maiesty at White-Hall, upon S. Stephens night, in Christmas Hollidaies. By his Maiesties Servants, playing usually at the *Globe* on the *Banck-side*' – and in all these cases the printed text significantly post-dates the earliest performances. And strikingly, Shakespeare's first entry into print is not with drama, but in the genre of poetry. *Venus and Adonis*, his erotic narrative poem in the popular genre of imitations and translations of the Roman poet Ovid, was first published in 1593 and went through fifteen editions before 1638, far outstripping any of Shakespeare's plays in frequency of republication.

Quartos and Folio

Introducing some technical terms at the outset can help us to understand the implications of Shakespeare's publication. *Bibliography* – the study of the printed book – has often looked to outsiders to be dry, dusty, and over-specialised, particularly because its vocabulary is so arcane. Not much of this is directly necessary for our discussion. The term *quarto*, sometimes abbreviated in critical discussions to 'Q' (Q1, Q2 etc indicate first, second and any subsequent quarto editions), refers to a small book, measuring about 22 × 16 cm and made by folding a standard sheet of paper twice. This cheap, pamphlet-style format typically sold for sixpence – rather more than the cheapest entrance to the Globe at one penny. It has been pointed out that print-runs of published drama were typically considerably smaller than spectator capacity at the playhouses. The first play of Shakespeare's to be printed in this format is *Titus Andronicus* in 1594. For the record, the most reprinted Shakespeare plays are *1 Henry IV* (8 quarto editions between 1598 and 1640), *Richard II* (7 editions), *Richard III* (6 editions); given our own reverence for Shakespeare it's salutary to see that now largely-forgotten plays such as Samuel Daniel's *Mucedorus*, Christopher Marlowe's *Dr Faustus*, and Thomas Kyd's *The Spanish Tragedy* are all more widely reprinted in the same period than any of Shakespeare's.

The other major format in which Shakespeare's plays were published is in *folio* (F) form. Folio, too, refers to the size of the book; this time the standard paper is folded once to produce a large, expensive book approximately 45 × 32 cm. The First Folio, published posthumously in 1623, is the first collected edition of Shakespeare's plays. It includes 36 plays, eighteen of which had not been previously published. The most notable absence from the modern canon of Shakespeare's plays is *Pericles* which is not included. Those which have been previously published often appear in the Folio in substantially different versions, something the book's editors, Shakespeare's fellow actors John Heminges and Henry Condell, attribute to the inferiority of the earliest quarto versions: 'where (before) you were abus'd with diverse stolne, and surreptitious copies, maimed, and deformed by the frauds and stealthes of injurious imposters, that expos'd them: even those, are now offer'd to your view cur'd, and perfect of their limbes; and all the rest, absolute in their numbers, as he conceived them'. A second edition of the Folio, including some additional plays now not considered to be Shakespeare's, was published in 1632.

Information about the Folio and Quarto texts and any subsequent editions from which any modern edited version is derived is stored, rather cryptically, in a section of the edition called the *collation*. The Norton and Riverside each have their collation as a series of 'Textual Notes' at the end of each play. In the New Cambridge, Arden 3 and other series, the collation comes on each page, between the play-text and the footnotes, in a thin strip of hieroglyphics such as this example from the beginning of G. Blakemore Evans' edition of *Romeo and Juliet*: '*Actus Primus. Scaena Prima.* F; not in Q2–4, Q1', which tells us that the Latinate act and scene division is present in the Folio text but not the quartos. A good rule of thumb is that the more collation there is, the more work the editor has done to adjudicate between alternative readings or the work of his or her editorial predecessors. If there is a lot of collation, there may be something worth looking at in the early texts. And whereas previously, those early texts of Shakespeare were so precious and so rare that only a few scholars had access to them, online versions (see the 'Where next?' section at the end of this chapter for details) have democratised editing: we can all look at the play texts from which our tidied-up modern editions have been derived, and reopen editorial questions that previously were shared only by an inner circle.

Editing as interpretation

All editors will work with those early texts of their play – the Folio, in all cases, and also quarto texts where these exist – and with what other editors have done with those texts, to produce a coherent and reliable version for modern readers. Typically they will work on standardising spelling, punctuation, and lineation – all of which are discussed below. Editors may provide more or fewer explanatory notes, depending on the market for their particular edition. They may offer an introduction or suggestions for reading. Some editions – the Shakespeare in Production series, for example – annotate the play with reference to the ways in which it has been performed; some, like the Shakespeare Made Easy series, provide a version of the lines in modernised English to help Shakespeare novices; some, like the New Penguin series, have the explanatory notes at the back of the text, making it easier to read the play without constant interruption from footnotes; some, like the New Cambridge, Oxford and Arden 3 series favour extensive on-page annotation.

These aspects may seem incidental, but they can have significant consequences for our reading of the plays. What all this activity amounts to is a series of interpretive acts. Editors interpret the play for us, by the decisions they make and the ways in which they present those to us. By the time we read Shakespeare in an edited text, it has already been interpreted for us, and our own interpretations are inevitably shaped by that prior act of editorial interpretation. Because of this, the concept and practice of 'unediting' have been influential – the idea involves returning to the early texts, because their inconsistencies and silences can be meaningful, revelatory and stimulating in ways that editing smoothes out.

Let's look at a couple of examples. The first is a single and problematic word from *The Tempest*. In this play, Prospero, a magician and deposed duke, lives on an island with his daughter Miranda and his servants Caliban and Ariel. The play has long been associated with contemporary voyages to the so-called New World (it wasn't new to the native Americans who lived there), and, indeed, has as one of its major sources a travellers' account of a shipwreck. (There's more on Shakespeare's use of his sources in chapter 6.) Prospero's former enemies, including the brother who usurped his dukedom, are shipwrecked on his island thanks to a tempest he has conjured. Caliban, dissatisfied with his servitude, joins with two of the servants of the shipwrecked nobles in a plot to overthrow Prospero. In return he promises that he will be useful to his new allies. In the earliest text of *The Tempest*, printed in the Folio in 1623, we have this speech: 'I prethee let me bring thee where Crabs grow; and I with my long nayles will digge thee pig-nuts; show thee a Iayes nest, and instruct thee how to snare the nimble Marmazet: I'le bring thee to clustering Philbirts, and sometimes I'le get thee young Scamels from the Rocke: Wilt thou goe with me?'

This speech as it appears in the Folio differs from the form in which a modern edition will present it in lots of different ways – you might want to compare it with the version in a text you have to hand. An editor will work to modernise spelling here, standardising 'digge' as 'dig', for example. He or she will relineate this prose speech as blank verse, and given the assumptions of nobility or importance that are often attached to verse-speaking, will thereby implicitly elevate Caliban's status at this point, particularly when compared with his drunken companions (there's more on the significance of verse and prose, and a discussion of blank verse, in chapter 4). This is important for readings of the play which have begun to stress Caliban's dignity as a colonised subject, rather than the sub-humanity to which earlier critics shackled him. The editor will probably offer a glossary for the unfamiliar words 'Marmazet' or 'marmoset' (a sort of monkey) and 'Philbirts'/'filberts' (hazelnuts). But then she or he will come to the word 'Scamels'.

No one knows what 'Scamels' are. From the context we can grasp that it is something to eat from the rocks, perhaps a shellfish or mollusc. Much ingenuity has been expended on it, many obscure books of ornithology, marine biology, travel and dialect scoured, and lots of possibilities have been suggested, but no one has answered the question. So what should the editor do? In the Oxford edition, the word is changed, or in editorial-speak, *emended*, to 'seamews' –

on the basis that in certain sorts of seventeenth-century handwriting the word 'seamews' could be misread by the printing-house compositor as 'scamels'. It's an editorial decision which has the advantage that, even if, like me, you don't know what 'seamew' means either, it is a word that can be looked up in the Oxford English Dictionary (it's a seagull). So 'seamews' makes sense – although we might think that if an editor wanted to change 'Scamels' for readers' benefit into something intelligible he or she might as well go the whole way and emend to 'seagulls'. David Lindley, in the Cambridge edition, chooses not to emend the word and leaves it as 'scamels' (2.2.149), thus preserving something of the intrinsic strangeness of Caliban's vocabulary, mixing the exotic 'Scamels' with the then familiar 'filberts'. Perhaps Shakespeare did write 'seamews' and his handwriting was misread by the compositor; perhaps he intended a nonce-word 'Scamels'; perhaps 'Scamels' has a meaning we haven't yet recovered. It's a miniature version of a larger attitude to the text and the role of the editor. By emending, the Oxford editors assert control over the text, replacing an intransigently opaque word with one with an attested meaning. They interpret a word without a known meaning as an aberration which needs to be normalised, by changing it into a word which does have a meaning. By not emending, Lindley leaves the text just beyond understanding, containing things we cannot fully comprehend. And, of course, it's wonderfully appropriate that this word which resists the editorial discourse of mastery should be uttered by Caliban, a character who himself resists the authoritarian control of the bookish (editorial?) Prospero.

The extent to which editors manage the meanings of their texts can also be seen if we look critically at their annotation and footnoting. Footnoting tends to look authoritative, neutral – as if it gives us scholarly information or explanation on which we can build more speculative or creative interpretations. In fact editorial glossing is itself already an act of interpretation. Why, for example, does the Arden editor of *The Two Gentlemen of Verona* feel so sure that the clown Lance's bawdy is 'unintentional' when he pretends that 'this shoe with the hole in it is my mother' (2.3.15)? Or we could take as a more developed example the song which precedes Bassanio's choice of casket in the comedy of *The Merchant of Venice*. Portia's dead father has set as a condition of her marriage that any prospective husband make the correct choice between gold, silver and lead caskets. We have already seen two woefully unpromising suitors fail by choosing gold and silver respectively, and since the choice is the stuff of fairytale it is quite clear to us that the preferred Bassanio must choose the apparently discouraging lead casket. But does Bassanio, too, have inside knowledge? As he is about to make his choice, Portia interrupts him, and the stage direction indicates 'A song the whilst Bassanio comments on the caskets to himself'. M. M. Mahood in her New Cambridge edition notes that the endwords in the first verse of the song 'Tell me where is fancy bred' (3.2) rhyme with 'lead' and that this may therefore be intended as a clue to Bassanio about which casket he should choose. Interestingly, however, she goes on to discount this as a real possibility, since it contravenes their moral characters as, presumably, already and unassailably established: it 'belittles Portia's integrity and Bassanio's insight'. From the discussion in chapter 1, we can see that giving Portia integrity and Bassanio insight in advance of, and separate from, their words and actions in the play is a particular kind of character criticism: here it uses an idea of character to restrict and dictate the text's meanings. If Portia is 'cheating' – circumventing her father's will to exercise some choice in her marriage – this needn't be either a moral lapse or a failure of character consistency. Indeed, in plot terms it makes sense in linking her with Jessica, the daughter of Shylock who also challenges her father's authority by eloping with a Christian. So an editor at once offers us an interpretative possibility – that Portia, the self-styled figure of virtue and wit in the play, has bent the patriarchal rules to get the husband she wants – and at the same time uses her editorial authority in the footnote to close it down.

Editors, therefore, are interpreters. Their own – often scholarly and well-supported, but partial, nevertheless – assumptions, interpretations and attitudes pervade their texts. What an editor does is to interpret, in useful and necessary ways, to be sure, but to interpret nonetheless.

The job of the editor: the example of *Richard II*

One of the major questions for all subsequent editors of Shakespeare is how to take the statement of those first editors Heminges and Condell in their preface to the First Folio. Are the Folio texts always superior, complete, authoritative? What should an editor do in preparing Shakespeare's plays for modern readers and students? Why do we need more editions, and are there any real differences between them? All Shakespeare's plays have already been edited, in that they have been mediated to us by other agents. The elusive and unedited manuscript is, as we have seen, an illusory source of ultimate textual authority. So all the Shakespeare editions we read and study are, effectively, editions of editions. We can start to look at the ways in which the edition has been prepared for us, and how that might affect our interpretation of the play at hand, by working with a single initial example: different editions of *Richard II*, a play about the downfall of King Richard and the ascendancy of his rival, Henry Bullingbrook. Bullingbrook outmanoeuvres Richard who is forced to abdicate; Bullingbrook takes the crown; he orders the murder of Richard, and then expresses his sorrow for his actions.

Having been composed and performed in 1595, *Richard II* was first published in quarto form in 1597. The title-page reads 'The / Tragedie of King Ri-/chard the se-/cond. / As it hath been publikely acted / by the right Honourable the / Lorde Chamberlaine his Ser-/vants.' (The slashes indicate line-breaks: it looks odd to our eyes to break two important words 'Richard' and 'second' across the line.) Then there is a small picture of the blind boy-god Cupid – this is a publisher's mark, rather than anything specific to do with this play – and underneath the place, London, and details of the play's publication: 'Printed by Valentine Simmes for Andrew Wise, and / are to be sold at his shop in Paules church yard at / the signe of the Angel, / 1597.' We can immediately see that something we'd now expect – the name of the author – is missing from the title-page, and the information about performance substitutes for it in the space we might expect to meet Shakespeare's name. The proper names we get are those of the men involved in presenting, either in print or on stage, the play, not in authoring it.

We also get an attribution of genre: it's very clear from the title that this is a tragedy. There's more on genre and structure in chapter 5: but here, titling this a tragedy may shape our reading of its central protagonist. Tragedies are typically structured around the lifespan of the central character: once King Lear, or Cleopatra, or Coriolanus, is dead, the play too is in its dying moments. We scarcely care about Edgar, or Octavius, or Aufidius, the characters on whom the battered and uncertain future of those tragedies seems to rest: they function merely as the mouthpieces for a kind of tragic closure. Thinking of *Richard II* alongside this structure gives us a play resoundingly about the downfall of Richard, rather than a play about the decline of one sovereign and the ascent of his successor. If Richard is the hero of a tragedy, where does that leave Bullingbrook? Is his accession to the throne merely a closing gesture, rather like that in *Hamlet* when the Norwegian prince Fortinbras enters the corpse-strewn Danish throne room, only to have his political victory utterly undermined by the fact that all eyes are still on the dead Hamlet?

The Folio text of 1623 prints the history plays in chronological order, and here *Richard II* bears a slightly different title: 'The Life and Death of Richard the Second'. Much criticism and some performance sequences have followed the implications of this in seeing the play within a sequence, or a series of plays. There's more on the way the Folio develops an idea of serial history in chapter 5: one of its immediate effects is to make *Richard II* less a self-contained tragic play in which an idea of the future dies along with the central character, and more an initiatory movement within a cycle or series of political actions in which one king follows another, one fortune waxes as another wanes, or, to use one of Richard's own metaphors, 'Now is this golden crown like a deep well / That owes two buckets, filling one another, / The emptier ever dancing in the air, / The other down, unseen and full of water' (4.1.184–7). Far from being the equivalent of Fortinbras at the end of *Hamlet*, then, Bullingbrook becomes a worthy, and necessary, opponent of Richard in an historical sequence which sees Richard's reign succeeded by that of Bullingbrook as Henry IV in two plays, *1* and *2 Henry IV*, and, in turn, by his son in *Henry V*.

Richard II appears in another significant early edition, Q4 of 1608. This is important because it includes material not part of the earlier editions: a scene called the 'Parliament scene' in which Richard hands over the crown to his rival in an act so constitutionally extraordinary as to require a new word, 'unkinging'. There has been much scholarly debate about the provenance of this new material, and whether it was left out of the earlier texts or added into the later ones. Most critics suggest that in Elizabethan printings of the play, some form of censorship – perhaps prudence on the part of the publisher, perhaps more active state intervention at a time when all plays had to be licensed for performance by a government agent called the Master of the Revels – was enacted to leave out a potentially seditious depiction of the usurpation of a monarch. We know that towards the end of Elizabeth's long reign, history plays were used covertly to discuss contemporary politics, particularly the question of who would succeed the 'Virgin Queen'. This historical contextualisation is explored in more detail in chapter 7: here it is enough to notice that contemporary events press in on the text of the play.

Even before we get into the first lines of *Richard II*, then, editors have been at work. Andrew Gurr's New Cambridge edition of the play – which takes as its copy-text or preferred early version Q1 – calls it *King Richard II*, thus suspending the early texts' initial generic attribution of tragedy and the readerly expectations this may prompt. Gurr's edition follows the standard livery of all Cambridge's Shakespeare editions: it is part of a prestigious series, identified by author. It proceeds with a full scholarly apparatus of General editorial preface, Contents, List of illustrations, Acknowledgements, Abbreviations and conventions, Introduction. The play begins on page 57; it takes up less than half the length of the book; each page includes explanatory footnotes; there are appendices listing source material, and a reading list. It has a list of characters to introduce the *dramatis personae* before we begin reading. The sense is – and as students of the play we are grateful for this thoroughness – that the play needs a good deal of supporting material to be fully intelligible.

By contrast, Simmes' 1597 quarto, Gurr's copy-text, consists of 38 leaves. There is no character list, no commentary, no advice or instruction on how to

Table 3.1. *Comparing Richard II in its first edition (1597) and the Cambridge text edited by Andrew Gurr*

1597	Gurr, New Cambridge
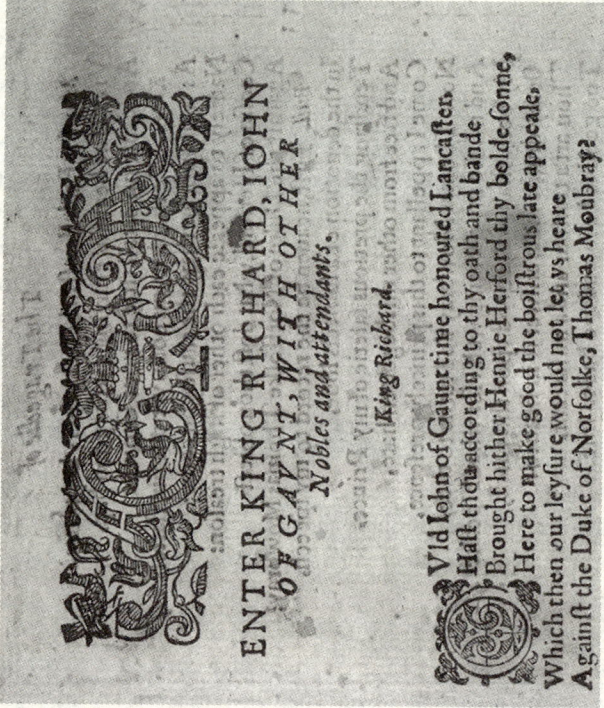	1.1. *Enter* KING RICHARD, JOHN OF GAUNT, *with other Nobles and Attendants.*
	RICHARD Old John of Gaunt, time-honoured Lancaster,
	Hast thou according to thy oath and band
	Brought hither Henry Herford, thy bold son,
	Here to make good the boisterous late appeal,
	Which then our leisure would not let us hear,
	Against the Duke of Norfolk, Thomas Mowbray?

read the play. There are no descriptive stage directions. Looking at the detail of the first lines of the play in the two editions shows us some of the other work done by modern editors.

We can see a number of changes, many of them small ones. Gurr gives us an act and scene number, 1.1, which is not in the quarto text: like most of the quartos the 1597 edition is not divided into acts and scenes, giving a more fluid sense of the run-on between episodes. Gurr regularises the unpunctuated opening line, he modernises spellings such as 'bande' or 'boistrous', he sets the speech out with more space so that the name of the speaker – Gurr opts to call him 'Richard' rather than his title 'King Richard', later 'King', of the quarto – remains adjacent to his indented speech. All this might be thought exactly what a conscientious editor ought to do to smooth out accidentals in the text. We might feel that Gurr's intervention here has merely made it easier for us as twenty-first century readers to begin to approach the play, although we also begin to see that much of the standardised apparatus of the printed play, discussed in more detail below, is actually imposed by editors on the early texts.

Stage directions

Many critics of Shakespeare think it unlikely that such stage directions as exist in the plays are authorial. Perhaps matters of how the play was staged were the business of the stagekeeper or the theatre company as they rehearsed. Because of this, where stage directions are detailed, it may be that they give us particular insight into early performances of the plays, as well as some unexpected interpretative information. *Hamlet* Q1's description of the Ghost dressed in his 'nightgown' sees him enter Gertrude's chamber not in the armour of his public person as in 1.1, but in domestic mode; similarly, Macbeth's first soliloquy in 1.7 when he proposes murdering his sovereign and his house-guest in a speech in which moral and lexical strangeness come together in that neologism (a word unrecorded before this example) 'assassination', is preceded in the Folio text by the mundane domestic detail of 'Enter a Sewer [butler, waiter] and divers Servants with Dishes and Service over the Stage'; something of the magic of theatrical illusion is conveyed in the Folio's detail of Ariel doing Prospero's bidding in *The Tempest*: 'Solemne and strange Musicke: and Prosper on the top (invisible:) [how do you think they did this bit?]. Enter severall strange shapes, bringing in a Banket [banquet]; and dance about it with gentle actions of salutations, and inviting the King, &c. to eate, they depart.' Compellingly, we are getting here a peephole into the Shakespearean performance.

Often, though, stage directions are brief or lack descriptive colour, or they are simply not there. So they are supplied by editors. The Oxford edition notes editorial stage directions with broken brackets; the Riverside and New Cambridge with square brackets. The extent of these interpolations varies. When John Dover Wilson edited the plays in the middle of the twentieth century he supplied a set of novelistic, highly interpretative stage directions to help readers imagine a particular scene. Thus he includes at the head of the first scene of *Richard II* (compare this to the quarto text and to Gurr's edition above): 'A great scaffold within the castle at Windsor, with seats thereon, and a space of ground before it. Enter King Richard, John of Gaunt, with the Duke of Surrey, other nobles and attendants. They ascend the scaffold and sit in their places, the king in a chair of justice in the midst.' It's very detailed, but entirely made up by the editor.

We may feel that the stage directions are literally marginal aspects of the text which do not substantially affect the meaning of the play, and in many cases we may be right. Even small details, however, can make subtle adjustments to our understanding. There's no exit stage direction for Edmund at the beginning of *King Lear*, for example: is he present during the love-test when Lear challenges his daughters to flatter him into their inheritance, and might that be what gives him the idea to plot to divide his own family, or should an editor assume he leaves the stage with his father before the main business begins? Or, to return to the example of *Richard II*, there are no stage directions in quarto or folio texts for the scene in which Richard hands over the crown. We do not know, therefore, whether his declaration that he is giving up the symbols of his office need be accompanied by the gestures which apparently endorse his words. Andrew Gurr's edition does not add in stage directions; the Oxford edition does, and thus gives us:

> Now mark me how I will undo myself.
> I give this heavy weight from off my head,
>   [*Bolingbroke accepts the crown*]
> And this unwieldy sceptre from my hand,
>   [*Bolingbroke accepts the sceptre*]
>   (4.1.192–4)

These additional stage directions commit Richard to enacting his own words – interestingly, they phrase this as a positive action by Bullingbrook (whose name is here edited following the traditions set by the eighteenth-century editor Alexander Pope, who meant it as a compliment to his friend, the then Viscount Bolingbroke) – and thus stage the speech on the page as the moment of the transfer of the symbols of power between former and future king. This is certainly one interpretation of the scene. But Richard's ambivalence to his enforced abdication is another – the speech is immediately preceded by his reply to Bullingbrook's 'Are you contented to resign the crown?' in the tortured, recursive syntax 'Aye – no. No – aye, for I must nothing be / Therefore no 'no', for I resign to thee' (4.1.199–201). (Interestingly, the 1608 quarto – the earliest printed version of this scene – reads 'I, no no I; for, I must nothing bee, / Therefore no no, for I resign to thee': how would *you* have edited that line for a modern reader?) So it is entirely in keeping with the scene – and with aspects of Richard's habitual grandiloquence and his preference, from the opening scene onwards, for words rather than actions, that he might be *saying* he was giving up the accoutrements of power without actually doing so. Here, the added stage directions press one interpretation and effectively exclude others.

Other examples are more substantive. At the end of the comedy *As You Like It*, Rosalind, who since Act 2 has adopted the male disguise of Ganymede, has been reunited with her lover Orlando. She enters to undergo her wedding ceremony. After much gender confusion and homoerotic play during her cross-dressed period, including a wooing scene in which she pretends to be Ganymede *pretending* to be Rosalind, and another in which a hapless shepherdess Phoebe falls for her striking, acerbic Ganymede persona, therefore, the play asserts that heterosexual imperative to which Shakespeare's comedies are traditionally headed: marriage. And almost all editors of the play help this along by adding to the stage direction for Rosalind's entrance. In the Folio we have the stage direction for the entrance in 5.4 'Enter Hymen [the goddess of marriage], Rosalind and Celia.' This unadorned formula 'Rosalind' has been the Folio's stage direction throughout the period Rosalind has been in the role of Ganymede. In the Oxford edition the stage direction adds 'as themselves' – a striking ontological position for anyone, least of all a character in a play – the phrasing also preferred by Michael Hattaway for his New Cambridge edition.

It certainly does make a sort of narrative and thematic sense to have Rosalind return in her women's clothes at this point. Her temporary role as Ganymede can now be set aside; she returns to the (female) person she was at the play's outset, bracketing the freedoms of the Forest of Arden with the 'reality' of heterosexual normativity. But by stating in a stage direction, apparently authoritatively, that she *does* put on her female clothing, the modern editions lose some important element of sexual playfulness. The Folio text leaves open the possibility that she doesn't return fixed into femaleness, that the gender confusion and gender play intrinsic to that pert, knowing title *As You Like It* continues, rather than being finally contained in marriage. This seems even more likely when we remember that Rosalind would have been played by a male actor. After all, the newly married Rosalind reappears to give a cheeky epilogue, flirting wildly with both men and women in the audience: 'My way is to conjure you, and I'll begin with the women . . . If I were a woman I would kiss as many of you as had beards that pleased me, complexions that liked me, and breaths that I defied not' – hardly the demure, gender-fixed behaviour of a blushing bride. And in choosing the name Ganymede, the young male lover of the god Jupiter, the play, or Rosalind herself, toys explicitly with male homosexuality. There's another Folio textual clue which challenges a firmly heterosexual reading to the play's conclusion: in an apparent confusion of male pronouns Hymen discusses the wedding ceremony: 'thou mightst joyne his hand with his, / Whose heart within his bosome is'. Joining two male hands together doesn't seem quite the image of heterosexual union that editors want to see. All 'straighten' one of the 'his' into 'her'. Thus the edited text is at once more normative, more heterosexual, and more prescribed than the first printed version in the Folio.

Speech prefixes

In chapter 1, on 'Character', we saw that the speech prefixes and stage directions in the early texts sometimes name characters in ways alien to modern editions. Thus, no modern editor is so discourteous as to call Edmund in *King Lear* 'Bastard', despite the fact that is his name throughout the apparatus of the early texts, whereas all editors prefer to call the King of Denmark 'Claudius' rather than endorse his ill-gotten gains by each time calling him 'King', as he is in the quartos. One of the ways in which the early texts of Shakespeare may seem to inscribe a different version of character from that of our own psychological presumptions is in the way that character names or designations shift during the play. So Q1 of *Romeo and Juliet* shifts the speech prefix for the character we call Lady Capulet between 'Wife' and 'Mother', which might tell us something about her structural, rather than psychological, role in the play. (Characters as individuals or types are also discussed in chapter 1.)

Something similar, and more culturally chilling, happens to Shylock if we look at *The Merchant of Venice* in the Folio text. Shylock, the Jewish money-lender whose wealth is instrumental in enabling Bassanio to make his wooing visit to Portia discussed above, occupies a complex role in the play and one which we'll come back to in chapter 5 on structure. In Act 4, Shylock ends up in court to get his money back from Antonio, Bassanio's friend and patron, who has borrowed it on his behalf. The term of their bargain was that if the debt was not repaid, Shylock has the right to a pound of Antonio's flesh. But, unrecognised, Portia enters the courtroom dressed as a male lawyer, and manages to outwit Shylock both by legalistic quibbles that there was no mention in the agreement of any blood and by reference to the disadvantaged status of Jews under Venetian law. Shylock's property is confiscated and he is forced to convert to Christianity.

The interpretation of this outcome, and the representation of Shylock throughout the play, has been the occasion for much important criticism. For some commentators he is the comic villain, the spoiling or blocking figure who must be overcome in order for comic values of community and marriage to triumph; for others, the uncomfortable spectacle of Shakespeare's only Jewish character being crushed by the Christians of Venice gives him an almost tragic, or at least sympathetic, status. The early texts can contribute to this debate in some interesting ways. Throughout the play, Shylock is given his proper name in all speech prefixes and stage directions. Until, that is, the trial scene. The Duke's 'We all expect a gentle answer, Jew' (4.1.34) is echoed in the very next word on the next line in the Folio. For the first time Shylock's speech prefix is 'Jew'. Even as he asserts in the scene 'Shylock is my name' (4.1.172), the text has him speak this from the position of 'Jew'. We could argue that here the unspoken words of the text, the speech prefixes which name the protagonists in the courtroom, reveal that this is a cultural struggle not between individuals but between the named Christians and the archetypal Jew; that it is his Jewishness which seems to dominate both Shylock's behaviour and his treatment in the court; that he has become the vengeful, money-grubbing stereotype of anti-semitic slurs. The question of Shylock's cultural identity, and its significance to the play, has become the most pressing issue in readings and productions of *The Merchant of Venice*: there have even been calls for it to be banned because of its problematic relation to the terrible history of anti-semitism which pre- and post-dates it. Here the early texts are engaging with this theme in some interesting ways, ways that are obliterated if editors standardise Shylock's presence in the text.

The job of the editor: the example of *King Lear*

We have seen some of the implications of the sort of editing-as-tidying function, when even apparently unimportant presentational details have an impact on our interpretation of the plays. Finally, let's look at a different and more sustained example, the case of *King Lear*. *King Lear* is the play on which much recent textual theory has focused, because it exists in two substantially variant versions: a quarto text from 1608 entitled a 'true chronicle history of the life

> *Lear.* Breake hart, I prethe breake. *Edgar.* Look vp my Lord.
> *Kent.* Vex not his ghoſt, O let him paſſe,
> He hates him that would vpon the wracke,
> Of this tough world ſtretch him out longer,
> *Edg.* O he is gone indeed.
> *Kent.* The wonder is, he hath endured ſo long,
> He but vſurpt his life.
> *Duke.* Beare them from hence, our preſent buſines
> Is to generall woe, friends of my ſoule, you twaine
> Rule in this kingdome, and the goard ſtate ſuſtaine.
> *Kent.* I haue a iourney ſir, ſhortly to go,
> My maiſter cals, and I muſt not ſay no.
> *Duke.* The waight of this ſad time we muſt obey,
> Speake what we feele, not what we ought to ſay,
> The oldeſt haue borne moſt, we that are yong,
> Shall neuer ſee ſo much, nor liue ſo long.
>
> # *F I N I S.*

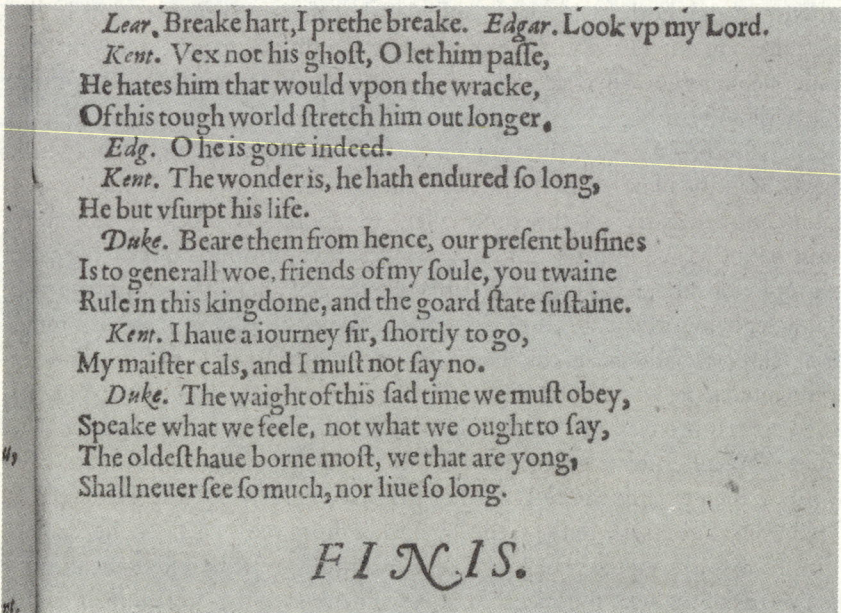

3.1 Ending of *King Lear* Q (1608)

and death of King Lear and his three Daughters', and the text included as *The Tragedy of King Lear* in the 1623 Folio. There are around 300 lines in Q that are not in F, and about 100 lines in F not in Q, as well as hundreds of variants of words, punctuation, or stage directions. Does Lear, for example, express a 'darker purpose' (Q) or 'darker purposes' (F) (1.1.31) as he introduces the disastrous love-test? Given how mysterious his motives are at this point in the play – this is discussed in more detail in chapter 6 on sources – the apparently marginal difference between a singular and a plural may take on considerable significance.

If you read an edition of *King Lear* dating before the mid 1980s, it is likely that the editor has made a selection from quarto and Folio texts according to his or her view of their provenance, authenticity, or literary value. This is known as a *conflated* text: it has the advantage of including all four hundred disputed lines, and the disadvantage that it produces a composite text that never existed until the edition itself. It is based on a presumption that the differences between the texts are the result of accidental or extrinsic factors, and that therefore the specific separate forms of the two early texts are unimportant. However, if you are working from the Oxford or Norton collected editions you will see that

> *Lear.* And my poore Foole is hang'd: no,no,no life?
> Why should a Dog,a Horse,a Rat haue life,
> And thou no breath at all? Thou'lt come no more,
> Neuer,neuer,neuer,neuer,neuer.
> Pray you vndo this Button. Thanke you Sir,
> Do you see this? Looke on her? Looke her lips,
> Looke there,looke there,   *He dies.*
>   *Edg.* He faints,my Lord,my Lord.
>   *Kent.* Breake heart, I prythee breake.
>   *Edg.* Looke vp my Lord.
>   *Kent.* Vex not his ghost, O let him passe,he hates him,
> That would vpon the wracke of this tough world
> Stretch him out longer.
>   *Edg.* He is gon indeed.
>   *Kent.* The wonder is,he hath endur'd so long,
> He but vsurpt his life.
>   *Alb.* Beare them from hence,our present businesse
> Is generall woe : Friends of my soule, you twaine,
> Rule in this Realme,and the gor'd state sustaine.
>   *Kent.* I haue a iourney Sir,shortly to go,
> My Master calls me,I must not say no.
>   *Edg.* The waight of this sad time we must obey,
> Speake what we feele,not what we ought to say :
> The oldest hath borne most,we that are yong,
> Shall neuer see so much, nor liue so long.
>   *Exeunt with a dead March.*
>   ſ ſ 3

3.2 Ending of *King Lear* F (1623)

they print each text separately, so that there is not one but two plays called *King Lear*.

The 'Where next?' section gives an indication of how to follow up some of the critical arguments around the textual history of *King Lear*, and also points out some specific, local points of suggestive comparison between the two versions. Here I want to focus on one important section as an example of the differences between the two plays, and the ways in which those differences are important not just to bibliographers but to anyone who is interested in the notion of tragedy, in dramatic form, in character, in *King Lear*.

As chapter 5 discusses in more detail, tragedy is a particularly end-stopped genre: like comedy, it is defined by its ending, but unlike comedy its ending is peculiarly final. So the ending of a tragedy is a natural focus for our interpretative energy. The ending of *King Lear* in its two versions is doubly significant.

There are a number of points to consider. Here are some for starters:

- In the quarto when does Lear die? There is no stage direction. How might this allow for different possibilities from that in the Folio?
- How do you interpret the shift of the line 'Break heart, I prithee break', from Lear in Q to Kent in F?
- Some critics have argued that Lear dies in the Folio still with the hope that Cordelia is alive: does the text support this? Is it different in the quarto? How does this affect the tragic ending of the play?
- What difference does it make whether 'Duke' (Albany) – senior, noble, tainted by his association with Gonerill – or Edgar, speaks the last lines?
- Does your assessment of these differences materially alter your interpretation of the two texts? Does this have implications for what you would want an editor to do with them in preparing an edition for you to read?

For many critics, the differences between Q and F of *King Lear* are related to the contingencies of performance at different times and in different places. Like the fluid interpretations of the plays on the stage and on film discussed in the previous chapter, that is to say, the early texts of the plays materialise different possibilities and register their thorough-going resistance to singular analysis. Editors have historically taken on the burden of choosing – of second-guessing, of streamlining: that newly democratised process of selection offers one of the most bracing encounters with the plays as they were written, performed and published.

Texts: where next?

- The text of *The Book of Sir Thomas More*, which was never printed and exists only in manuscript, is transcribed online at the University of Virginia – http://etext.lib.virginia.edu/toc/modeng/public/AnoTMor.html. Here the chaotic order of the much-revised original is exactly reproduced, so it is difficult to read: Grigori Melchiori's edited version in the Revels series (Manchester University Press, 1989) works to reconstruct the play and make it more readable, as well as discussing the question of authorship in his introduction; the second edition of the *Oxford Shakespeare* (2005) also prints the complete play; the previous edition only included the 'Shakespearean' speeches, and this change itself is indicative of changed editorial priorities. The most prominent of the speeches attributed to Shakespeare is More's invitation to the rioters to put themselves in the place of those they are attacking:

> Say now the King,
> As he is clement if th'offender mourn,
> Should so much come too short of your great trespass
> As but to banish you: whither would you go?
> What country, by the nature of your error.
> Should give you harbour? Go you to France or Flanders,
> To any German province, Spain or Portugal,
> Nay, anywhere that not adheres to England –
> Why, you must needs be strangers. Would you be pleased
> To find a nation of such barbarous temper
> That breaking out in hideous violence
> Would not afford you an abode on earth,
> Whet their detested knives against your throats,
> Spurn you like dogs, and like as if that God
> Owed not nor made not you, nor that the elements
> Were not all appropriate to your comforts
> But chartered unto them, what would you think
> To be thus used? This is the strangers' case,
> And this your mountainish inhumanity.

- Bibliography, or the study of Shakespeare's texts, can seem arcane and difficult – it's also been transformed in the last twenty or so years, so more recent work tends to be more engaged with matters of literary interpretation, rather than just the quasi-scientific stuff about textual transmission. The essays on 'Printing' in David Scott Kastan's *A Companion to Shakespeare*

(Blackwell, 1999) cover the facts in an engaging way. Leah Marcus' *Unediting the Renaissance: Shakespeare, Milton, Marlowe* (Routledge, 1996), is recommended, particularly on the assumptions behind editorial decisions in *The Tempest, Hamlet, The Merry Wives of Windsor* and *The Taming of the Shrew*. Marcus shows how textual history and the interpretation of the plays are inseparable. Tiffany Stern's *Making Shakespeare: From Stage to Page* (Routledge, 2004) is also recommended as a model of the integration of textual matters with theatre history and dramatic appreciation. In this chapter and elsewhere I've been much influenced by Margreta de Grazia and Peter Stallybrass's elegant and thought-provoking essay in *Shakespeare Quarterly* 44 (1993), 'The Materiality of the Shakespearean Text'. Two indicative and stimulating articles on the revaluation of what textual scholars used, reprovingly, to call the 'bad' quartos – texts considered to be those 'maimed and deformed' ones denounced in the prefatory epistle to the First Folio – are Steven Urkowitz's 'Good News about 'Bad' Quartos' in Maurice Charney (ed.), *"Bad" Shakespeare: Revaluations of the Shakespeare Canon* (Fairleigh Dickinson University Press, 1988) and Random Cloud's 'The Marriage of Good and Bad Quartos' in *Shakespeare Quarterly* 33 (1982).

- Online texts are available from a number of sources:

    The Furness collection at the University of Pennsylvania has a beautifully digitised copy of the First Folio at http://dewey.library.upenn.edu/sceti/, and some other early quartos for browsing. (They also have some worthwhile online tutorials about aspects of printing and editing at http://dewey.library.upenn.edu/sceti/furness/eric/teach/index.cfm)

    The British Library has digitised its 93 quarto texts and has an excellent website where you can compare multiple versions at http://www.bl.uk/treasures/shakespeare/homepage.html

    Michael Best's Internet Shakespeare Editions site has Folio facsimiles and quartos of *Romeo and Juliet, Hamlet, Othello*, and the *Sonnets* at http://ise.uvic.ca/index.html

    Bernice Kliman's hypertext Enfolded *Hamlet*, which enables comparison of a transcribed (i.e. not scanned) Q2 and F *Hamlet*, is at http://www.global-language.com/enfolded.html.

    The University of Virginia Library has mounted transcribed versions of Q1 *Hamlet* at http://etext.lib.virginia.edu/toc/modeng/public/ShaHaQ1.html; Q2 is at http://etext.lib.virginia.edu/toc/modeng/public/ShaHaQ2.html; the complete Folio is transcribed at http://etext.lib.virginia.edu/shakespeare/folio/ – this makes it possible to search the texts, but remember that non-standardised spelling may produce unexpected search results.

- 'Scamels' in *The Tempest* is an example of a textual *crux* – a point of interpretative difficulty. Other famous textual cruces include the Hostess' account of Falstaff's death in *Henry V* for which the Folio text has the incomprehensible line 'for his Nose was as sharpe as a Pen, and a Table of greene fields', which most editors emend, following the eighteenth-century editor Lewis Theobald, to 'and a babbled of green fields' (2.3.14); Q2 *Hamlet*'s 'the dram of eale / Doth all the noble substance of a doubt / To his owne scandle' (1.4.36) – where editors have often emended 'eale' to 'evil' or to 'esill' [vinegar]; the mysterious word 'prenzie' (3.1.93 and 96), often emended to 'precise' in *Measure for Measure*; and Sonnet 129, where the 1609 quarto's 'A blisse in proofe and proud and very wo' was emended by Edmond Malone's edition in the eighteenth century to 'A bliss in proof, and prov'd, a very woe'. Most editions discuss textual cruces; perhaps the most important question to ask is what the variant readings offer to the passage or line's poetic, thematic or associative properties, rather than to strive finally to resolve the matter.
- Looking critically at footnotes may seem difficult, since it's about going head to head with the editor's authority. There's an interesting article by Michael Cordner on the ways in which editors annotate Petruchio and Katherina's first encounter in *The Taming of the Shrew* ('Actors, Editors, and the Annotation of Shakespearean Playscripts' in *Shakespeare Survey 55* (2002), and in her 'Feminist Editing and the Body of the Text', Laurie E. Maguire draws out some of the assumptions behind, for example, the coy or coarse annotating of sexual puns (in *A Feminist Companion to Shakespeare* ed. Dympna Callaghan, Blackwell, 2000). Comparing annotations in two or more editions is a good way to see how a particular editor may be steering our interpretations: how do editors gloss, for example, Malvolio's description of – as he thinks – Olivia's handwriting: 'These be her very c's, her u's, her t's; and thus makes she her great P's' (2.5.72–3). Do they gloss 'cut' as 'cunt', or as 'pudenda', or as 'sexual pun'? What about 'P'? Do they evaluate this pun? Do they tell us whether Malvolio himself is talking dirty, or being made to do so by the play? What would we want them to tell us?
- On Elizabethan censorship, *Shakespeare in Love* (dir. John Madden, 1998), gives us an engaging – and obviously fictional, but nonetheless energetic and involved – portrait of the Master of the Revels, Edmund Tilney (Simon Callow). The standard works on the role of censorship in the drama of the period are Richard Dutton, *Mastering the Revels: The Regulation and Censorship of English Renaissance Drama* (Macmillan, 1991) and Janet Clare, *'Art Made Tongue-Tied by Authority': Elizabethan and Jacobean Dramatic Censorship* (2nd edn, Manchester University Press, 1999). It is often claimed

that *Richard II*'s revolutionary credentials are attested by its performance on the eve of the Earl of Essex's rebellion in 1601: this has a significance for many Shakespearean critics beyond the merely factual, since it represents the literalisation of their interest in politically radical theatre. Two articles on this topic include the sceptical 'Which play was performed at the Globe Theatre on 7 February 1601?' by Blair Worden in the *London Review of Books* (10 July 2003), and Chris Fitter's 'Historicising Shakespeare's *Richard II*: Current Events, Dating, and the Sabotage of Essex' in the online journal *Early Modern Literary Studies* 11.2 (September, 2005) at http://purl.oclc.org/emls/11-2/fittric2.htm.

- Comparing the heterosexualising of *As You Like It* with the history of editing Shakespeare's Sonnets is informative: Margreta de Grazia's important essay 'The Scandal of Shakespeare's Sonnets' is in *Shakespeare Studies* 46 (1993), and reprinted in *Shakespeare and Sexuality*, ed. Catherine Alexander (Cambridge University Press, 2001). On readings of the sonnets which emphasise, rather than suppress, homoeroticism, see Joseph Pequigney, *Such is My Love: A Study of Shakespeare's Sonnets* (University of Chicago Press, 1985) and Jonathan Goldberg's *Sodometries: Renaissance Texts, Modern Sexualities* (Stanford University Press, 1992). There's been some great work on queer sexualities and homoeroticism in Shakespeare's plays – on the relationship between *Twelfth Night*'s Antonio and Sebastian, for instance, or unrequited love as a trigger for Antonio's unexplained melancholy at the opening of *The Merchant of Venice*, or the intensity of the amity between Titania and the mother of the contested changeling boy in *A Midsummer Night's Dream*. For more on these issues, see Valerie Traub, *The Renaissance of Lesbianism in Early Modern England* (Cambridge University Press, 2002) and Mario diGangi, *The Homoerotics of Early Modern Drama* (Cambridge University Press, 1997). You might like to compare the unedited Hymen scene in *As You Like It* with the ending of *Twelfth Night*, in which Viola pointedly does not reassume women's clothes and continues to be called 'Cesario', her male alias, by her new lover Orsino, or with *The Two Gentleman of Verona*, which also concludes with pointed jokes about the still male-clad Julia.

- The textual history of *King Lear* can be traced through the landmark collection of essays in *The Division of the Kingdoms: Shakespeare's Two Versions of 'King Lear'*, edited by Michael Warren and Gary Taylor (Oxford University Press, 1983). Rene Weis edited a useful parallel text edition of Q and F for Longman (1993); the British Library collection of online quartos includes the 1608 *King Lear* (http://www.bl.uk/treasures/shakespeare/

homepage.html); Folio texts can be found on the Furness Collection (digital facsimile) and University of Virginia (transcription) sites listed above.

- Other interesting points of comparison between Q and F texts might include Hamlet's 'To be or not to be' soliloquy, which, in Q1 (1603), is rather different from our (over)familiar version:

> To be, or not to be, I there's the point,
> To Die, to sleepe, is that all? I all:
> No, to sleepe, to dreame, I mary there it goes,
> For in that dreame of death, when wee awake,
> And borne before an euerlasting Iudge,
> From whence no passenger euer retur'nd,
> The vndiscouered country, at whose sight
> The happy smile, and the accursed damn'd.
> But for this, the ioyfull hope of this,
> Whol'd beare the scornes and flattery of the world,
> Scorned by the right rich, the rich curssed of the poore?
> The widow being oppressed, the orphan wrong'd,
> The taste of hunger, or a tirants raigne,
> And thousand more calamities besides,
> To grunt and sweate vnder this weary life,
> When that he may his full Quietus make,
> With a bare bodkin, who would this indure,
> But for a hope of something after death?
> Which pusles the braine, and doth confound the sence,
> Which makes vs rather beare those euilles we haue,
> Than flie to others that we know not of.
> I that, O this conscience makes cowardes of vs all,
> Lady in thy orizons, be all my sinnes remembred.

You might also look at the depiction of the killing of the rebel leader Jack Cade in *2 Henry VI*: in the Quarto (printed as *The First Part of the Contention Betwixt the Two Famous Houses of Yorke and Lancaster* in 1594) the scene is introduced with the stage direction '*Enter* Iack Cade *at one doore, and at the other, maister* Alexander Eyden, *and his men, and* Iack Cade *lies downe picking of hearbes and eating them*', establishing that Cade is at a disadvantage both physically and numerically; the Folio has simply '*Enter Cade*' and then '*Enter Iden*'. It's interesting to compare the presentation of the rebellion, and the possible sympathies of the audience, via these small differences between the texts. Or, alternatively, what difference does it make that the quarto of *Henry V* (1600) has no choruses? Or how does the 12-line Prologue in Q1

Romeo and Juliet differ in the way it frames the narrative from the version we're used to? Or could it be important that Q2 of *Titus Andronicus* (1600) ends with a further four lines to Lucius's speech not found in Q1 or in F: 'See justice be done on *Aron* that damn'd Moore, / By whom our heauie haps had their beginning: / Than afterwards to order well the state, / That like euents may nere it ruinate.'?

与当代作家不同，莎士比亚并没有为我们留下任何剧作的手稿，所以，莎剧的编者就面临着一个极大的考验——他们首先要对16、17世纪印刷出版的莎剧4开本和对开本之间存在的差异做出一个理性的判断：究竟哪些是或代表了剧作家的原意？这是版本研究需要回答的问题。有的时候版本问题很有挑战性，甚至无法取得一致的意见。你觉得作者对《李尔王》结尾处的分析是不是很有说服力？虽然，这一例子很好地说明了当代编者所面临的挑战，但是，是不是也使读者对莎剧版本的可信度产生了怀疑？

Chapter 4

Language

'In a double sense' (*Macbeth* 5.7.50)

After encountering Banquo's ghost sitting at his table, the tortured Macbeth vows to return to the witches, 'for now I am bent to know / By the worst means, the worst' (3.4.133–4). The weird sisters summon up their 'masters' (4.1.62) in the form of three apparitions. The warning of the first, 'beware Macduff' (70), is, however, swiftly overtaken by the apparent comfort offered by the second two apparitions. The bloody child tells Macbeth that 'none of woman born / Shall harm Macbeth' (79–80), and the crowned child announces that 'Macbeth shall never vanquished be until / Great Birnam Wood to high Dunsinane Hill / Shall come against him' (91–3). Macbeth, unsurprisingly, takes these statements as expressions of his literal invulnerability: to him, that none of woman born shall harm Macbeth is simply a more elaborate way of saying that Macbeth shall never be harmed; the impossibility of trees moving up the mound of his castle means that the apparition is promising that he will never be vanquished. That is to say, Macbeth paraphrases the precise terms of the prophecies. And, as the play goes on to reveal, those paraphrases are strikingly inaccurate. The specificity – we might even say the poetry – of the terms of the apparitions' promises was what mattered, and their ostensibly impossible conditions become literally true when Malcolm's forces disguise their approach to Dunsinane by cutting switches from Birnam Wood and Macduff reveals himself to have been born by Caesarean Section just before decapitating Macbeth.

Paraphrasing Shakespeare's language, we might glean from this, is misguided (if not necessarily fatal!), and based on a profound misapprehension of the status of the words on the page. The language of the plays and poems *is the thing itself*, not a vehicle for something else, and therefore it is forever irreducible to paraphrase. The poetry of the witches' apparitions, like the poetry of the texts themselves, simultaneously reveals and occults its own meaning, or, rather, it renders poetry and meaning indivisible. So this chapter will discuss Shakespeare's language by counselling attention to the specifics, a resistance to paraphrase, and a recognition of the enjoyable difficulties of its poetic allusiveness. Sometimes directors cut speeches that seem to be too difficult; sometimes editors gloss them into apparent transparency: both responses have their place, but perhaps they understate the extent to which Shakespeare's language *is*, and irredeemably is, knotty and complex. If we find Shakespeare difficult to understand, it's not that we are stupid but that it is difficult: what I want to suggest are some ways that of becoming more confident with that difficulty.

Did anyone really talk like that?

Simple answer: no. The relation of the language of Shakespeare's plays to the language of his world is a complicated one. Firstly we can recognise that as poetic artefacts, the plays employ forms of heightened language full of rhythmical and metaphorical effects which are separated in intensity from everyday speech. Some of these poetic techniques are discussed below. Audience pleasure at the theatre, at least at the beginning of Shakespeare's career, was derived not from linguistic naturalism, but from what the prologue to Christopher Marlowe's audacious hit *Tamburlaine the Great* called 'high astounding terms'. That listening was the crucial sensory encounter for contemporary theatregoers is registered in the standard locution 'to go *hear* a play' (in, for example, *The Taming of the Shrew*, Induction 2, 130) where we would now expect the verb 'to see'. This act of audition was the encounter with a sense of linguistic estrangement in which poetic conceits, unusual vocabulary, snippets of foreign languages, exotic place names, and classical references combined in aural exhilaration, and in which it is as much the pleasurable sensory experience of the language as its meaning that is important.

What is clear is that Shakespeare's characters do not, in general, talk a language identical with that of Shakespeare's audience, and thus some of Shakespeare's language must have been knotty and difficult for playgoers then as it is now. There are a number of possible causes of this obscurity. First is the state of the language in which Shakespeare wrote. During the sixteenth century, the English language grew exponentially as it coined new words and imported many others from other languages. As David Crystal in *The Cambridge Encyclopaedia of the English Language* tells us, word borrowing is at a peak during Shakespeare's lifetime: from Latin and Greek English borrows technical words like larynx and virus, catastrophe and encyclopaedia, fact and species; from or via Spanish it borrows tobacco, port (wine), cannibal, canoe, mulatto, hurricane (you can see how much these have to do with New World exploration); from or via Italian it borrows argosy, balcony, carnival, lottery, sonnet; from or via French it borrows passport, duel, entrance, moustache and vogue. Both foreign words to fill linguistic gaps, and foreign words as synonyms for extant English words come flooding in, stimulated by increased learning, exploration, printing, and trade. The first English dictionary, compiled by Robert Cawdrey, appeared in 1604, with the title-page, 'A Table Alphabeticall, conteyning and teaching the true writing, and understanding of hard usuall English wordes, borrowed from the Hebrew, Greeke, Latin or French, etc. With the interpretation therof by plaine English words gathered for the benefit and helpe of Ladies, Gentlewomen, or any other unskilful persons. Whereby they may the more easily and better understand many hard English wordes, which they shall heare or reade in Scriptures, Sermons, or elsewhere, and also be made able to use the same aptly themselves.': that repeated juxtaposition of 'hard' and 'English' is an index of the extent to which a rapidly expanding English was developing as a foreign language even to its own native speakers. It was hard for people to keep up. English was becoming a language which had to be learned – and one of the means by which this learning was promoted was the theatre. (It's one of Shakespeare's common comic routines to present for general amusement characters who use words incorrectly, such as Elbow in *Measure for Measure*, Dogberry in *Much Ado About Nothing* or Lance in *Two Gentlemen of Verona*: 'I have received my proportion [portion] like the prodigious [prodigal] son' 2.3.2–3.)

Often Shakespeare responds to the pleasure of this mushrooming vocabulary by using a new word and then glossing it, as in this example from *Timon of Athens* which introduces the unfamiliar word 'decimation' and gives it two glosses, 'tithed death' and 'destined tenth':

> By decimation and a tithèd death,
> If thy revenges hunger for that food
> Which nature loathes, take thou the destined tenth.

                                    (5.4.31–3)

Sometimes new words are necessary for unique situations, so that their linguistic strangeness corresponds to their curious object. When Richard II conducts the ceremony of his own de-coronation, for example, he uses the new word 'unkinged' (*Richard II*, 4.1.219); Macbeth considers Duncan's fate with the new word 'assassination' (*Macbeth* 1.7.2); the ascetic Angelo responds to the unbidden pull of sexual desire with a cluster of unusual words, instructing Isabella to 'Lay by all nicety and prolixious blushes' (*Measure for Measure* 2.4.163) – neither 'nicety' nor 'prolixious' occurs anywhere else in the plays.

In some cases language may have been difficult because of the complexity of a conceit or image which it is hard to encompass at a single hearing. If we look at Richard II's speech on human frailty and kingship in 3.2, for example, we see a dense network of allusions and interconnected words and concepts that can only be fully teased out with time and attention – not perceived in the moment of audition:

> For within the hollow crown
> That rounds the mortal temples of a king
> Keeps Death his court, and there the antic sits
> Scoffing his state and grinning at his pomp,
> Allowing him a breath, a little scene
> To monarchise, be feared and kill with looks,
> Infusing him with self and vain conceit,
> As if this flesh which walls about our life
> Were brass impregnable, and humoured thus
> Comes in at the last and with a little pin
> Bores through his castle wall and farewell king!
> Cover your heads, and mock not flesh and blood
> With solemn reverence.   (*Richard II* 3.2.160–72)

Richard's speech here works with an analogy between the human body, the role of king, and the castle (the scene begins with a reference to the nearby 'Harlechly Castle'). The 'crown' in the first line of the quotation is both the symbol of kingship and the head, just as 'temples' are both the forehead and the physical opulence around the sacred king – but it is another ten lines before we actually get the word 'heads', here implied. 'Mortal' puns on 'human' and 'marked for death', anticipating the triumph of death in the next lines. The personification of 'Death' summons up images of the dance of death – late medieval illustrations of the omnipresence of death, represented as a skeleton, always grinningly at hand as the human world enjoys its foolish luxuries (see 'Where next' for how to follow this up). A sequence of words with connotations of acting – 'antic', 'scene', 'monarchise' (this is the only occurrence of this verb in Shakespeare) – connect with the wider theme of Richard as actor, but antic also suggests a gargoyle or architectural grotesque, thus continuing the association between the built and the human. 'Brass impregnable' is contradicted by the 'little pin' which 'bores' through the wall. The siege of the castle and the breaking of the physical body are elided. There are a sequence of verbal echoes, including hollow, walls, wall, farewell; brass, last, castle; within, king, grinning, pin. And, of course, the death that Richard encounters metaphorically here does in fact come to him later in a prison he again likens to the physical body (5.5.19–21): the speech anticipates this and thus has its poetic and literal fulfilment much later in the play.

It's hard to imagine that any hearer of this speech in the theatre could begin to analyse it in this way: nor would they need to. Part of its real meaning in the play is something we haven't even touched on yet: it dramatises Richard's predilection for the verbal over the active – seen in the play from the opening scene onwards. At the time when he should be marshalling his men against Bullingbrook he is sitting and speechifying. The speech works dramatically as a representation of stasis: precisely what is being said is less important than that the action has stilled to this point as the balance of power shifts, offstage, towards Bullingbrook. So part of the purpose of the elegiac density of the language is to interpolate a curiously poetic passage, requiring slow readerly attention, at a point when the play as drama might expect decisive action. The speech is in part a matter of changing aural tempos in the play, and part of the characterisation of the poet-king Richard's weakening hold on power.

That difficultness or opacity in speech might be part of characterisation or dramatic patterning, a technique of simultaneous disclosure and withholding, can be seen elsewhere. In, for example, the Duke's opening speeches in 1.1 of *Measure for Measure* the strained cadences, contorted word order and stilted vocabulary reinforce, rather than explain, the mystery of his abdication:

> Of government the properties to unfold
> Would seem in me t'affect speech and discourse,
> Since that I am put to know that your own science
> Exceeds in that the lists of all advice
> My strength can give you.   (1.1.3–6)

Similarly, unfamiliar vocabulary in *The Winter's Tale* is used to distance us from its speaker: it's worth, for example, examining Leontes' speech to his son Mamilius as he falls into the vertiginous pit of his own jealousy:

> Can thy dam – may't be? –
> Affection, thy intention stabs the centre.
> Thou dost make possible things not so held,
> Communicat'st with dreams – how can this be? –
> With what's unreal thou coactive art,
> And fellow'st nothing. Then, 'tis very credent
> Thou mayst co-join with something, and thou dost –
> And that beyond commission; and I find it –
> And that to the infection of my brains
> And hard'ning of my brows.   (1.2.139–47)

The syntactic strangeness here – signalled in the modernised edition by the dashes of broken thought patterns – is echoed in the alien lexis. (Considerable editorial work has been expounded on this difficult passage – which is also interesting to look at in its Folio version, bristling with parentheses and different punctuation, such as 'may't be / Affection?' and 'With what's unreal: thou coactive art'.) Leontes stutters out a cluster of words beginning with 'c' in a web of strangeness. 'Credent' appears only four times in Shakespeare's works, on each occasion with a sense of unfamiliarity or effort; the verb 'communicate' is likewise unusual; 'unreal' appears elsewhere once only, in *Macbeth*. These occurrences of 'coactive' and 'co-join' are the only times Shakespeare uses the words. (See 'Where next' for how to perform this sort of frequency analysis.) The passage is thus thick with difficult or strange terms, and, just in case we are nervous that we ought to be able to follow it, the play points this out, in Polixenes' remark 'What means Sicilia?' Why? Clearly, the aberrant nature of Leontes' mental state at this point is conveyed through his peculiar language. But what's more significant is that we as audience members are excluded, distanced, by that language. We can only observe, rather than participate in, Leontes' psychic anguish, and this is of significance not just to this particular passage but to the play of sympathy in *The Winter's Tale*, our exclusion from the truth about Hermione's death (discussed in more detail in chapter 6, 'Sources'), and this tragic-comic play's shifting generic affiliations.

The sense from these examples that the language is not giving up its meaning without a struggle is, therefore, *intrinsic* to that meaning: if we try to ignore the obscurities, or are not confident to identify them as such, or try to explain them away, we miss their significance. Perhaps one of Shakespeare's own coinages gets to the point: in *Antony and Cleopatra* the *neologism* (new word) 'intrinsicate' (5.2.298) intertwines 'intrinsic' and 'intricate': the very qualities of Shakespeare's own linguistic play. (It's no accident that this word is spoken by Cleopatra, whose seductions Samuel Johnson famously used to describe metaphorically what he saw as Shakespeare's weakness for punning and wordplay: 'A quibble was for him the fatal Cleopatra for which he lost the world, and was content to lose it.')

Some of what is unfamiliar about Shakespeare's language, that is to say, is the result of changing patterns of language usage and an evolving grammar and vocabulary; some of what we find difficult would have seemed less problematic to contemporaries. But Shakespeare's language was always poetic, heightened – always at a remove from the everyday – as the Formalists would have it, designedly 'unfamiliar' in order to renew the process of our perception as an object in itself, rather than as a means to an end. Sometimes the dense annotation provided in our modern editions instils in us the simultaneous anxiety that we do not understand Shakespeare *and* that it is vital to understand every word: neither is true. Like the first audiences at the Globe who, in the forward thrust of the performed play, didn't have time to dwell on difficulties but were able to follow the gist of what was happening, sometimes we as readers need to move along the play rather than forever deferring to the footnotes – or try to re-experience the plays aurally, as texts for hearing in the moment as well as, or before, reading.

Playing with language

In these ways, Shakespeare's English both is and is not a part of the English spoken and written around him. But crucially the dense, punning ambiguities of Shakespeare's language do ultimately derive their fertility and inventiveness from the non-standardised state of the English language at the end of the sixteenth century. A non-standardised, free-wheeling, madly expanding language is a source of difficulty, to be sure – but also a great source of verbal liberty and enjoyment.

Take puns: a play on two meanings of a word. Homophone (meaning sounding alike) words such as 'to/two' or 'soul/sole' or 'course/corpse' (which doesn't sound exactly alike to us now but probably did in the early modern period) are not constructed as entirely distinct, because their separate meanings are not collocated under particular separate spellings. Language standardisation in the intervening period has worked to separate out the two words which have no meaningful relation other than a phonic one; and therefore to pun on the two meanings often seems to us a frivolous and silly linguistic activity based on an arbitrary connection between the sounds of words. But standardised spelling is still a long way off in Shakespeare's time – even Shakespeare's extant signatures are all spelt differently – and this allows for a more fluid relation between words that modern English would want to fix as separate – and enables us to think a bit more historically about the joy of the pun.

In an early modern linguistic context, then, in which those homophones are not firmly distinguished by standardised orthographic (spelling) conventions, their interconnectedness may seem less arbitrary and more meaningful. Punning is most often about verbal pleasure. When Feste says that he is not Olivia's fool but her 'corrupter of words', the delight of the metaphor for the playwright son of John Shakespeare, the Stratford glovier, is tangible: 'A sentence is but a cheverel glove to a good wit, how quickly the wrong side may be turned outward' (*Twelfth Night*, 3.1.9–11: it is tempting to see the twins Viola and Sebastian as embodied puns, pleasurably comedic human versions of this reversible glove).

As in that scene between Feste and Viola, the ability to pun together signals a particular kind of personal interconnectedness. Just as the two meanings of a pun have a curiously mismatched quality, so those who use puns can be seen as the human equivalents of this verbal 'odd couple'. When Petruchio and Katherina, for example, parry with a sequence of puns at their first meeting in *The Taming of the Shrew*, we might want to see their quickfire attentiveness to each other's speech as a kind of sexual chemistry, an exchange of wit in which, since neither is a stooge, the awkward equality of their relationship is registered. Like the two senses of the word 'tail/tale', that is to say, the two stubbornly individual characters find a perverse synchronicity in rapid punning sequences like this one:

> PETRUCHIO Come, come, you wasp. I'faith you are too angry.
> KATHERINA If I be waspish, best beware my sting.
> PETRUCHIO My remedy is then to pluck it out.
> KATHERINA Ay, if the fool could find it where it lies.
> PETRUCHIO Who knows not where a wasp does wear his sting? In his tail.
> KATHERINA In his tongue.
> PETRUCHIO   Whose tongue?
> KATHERINA Yours, if you talk of tales, and so farewell.   (2.1.205–12)
> PETRUCHIO What, with my tongue in your tail?

And the fact that the puns here – as so often – are sexualised (the wasp's tail becomes the female tail, the tongue telling a tale flicks suggestively across that tail) relates the unpredictably fricative co-existence of different meanings within the same or related sound sequences to the way in which people, and bodies, rub pleasurably along together. As Viola observes to Feste in *Twelfth Night*, 'they that dally nicely with words may quickly make them wanton' (3.1.12–3), a formulation in which verbal unruliness, comic and sexual timing ('dally'), and promiscuity all coalesce.

If puns in comedy may be seen to displace and to propel the deferred eroticism of its courtship narrative – the punning between Petruchio and Katherina or their more amiable mirrors Beatrice and Benedick (in *Much Ado About Nothing*), for example – then in tragedies their function is somewhat different, but still potentially imaginable in physical terms. In the coalition of bereaved sons – like Malcolm – and bereaved fathers – like Macduff – who defeat Macbeth at the end of that play, young Siward is the final casualty. When in the play's dying moments old Siward (why do they have the same name?) hears of the death of his son, his quibbling response seems inappropriate:

> Why then, God's soldier be he;
> Had I as many sons as I have hairs,
> I would not wish them to a fairer death.
> And so, his knell is knolled.
>
> (5.9.14–17)

Punning on 'hairs' and 'heirs' has a grotesque, distancing quality, even as Siward's wordplay reminds us of one of the play's most insistent themes: succession and dynasty. In place of tragic monumentalising at the moment of death, then, we get this slippery and trivial pun. It is as if the play itself endorses Macbeth's earlier realisation that life – and death – is 'a tale / Told by an idiot, full of sound and fury, / Signifying nothing' (5.5.25–7). In denying us Macbeth's own death onstage – the expected culmination of the tragedy – the play denies death the dignity and focus we might expect. The tragic hero has become 'this dead butcher'; Siward's dead son is a quibble. If the punning blurring of words and bodies had the warmth of sexual contact in the comedies, here it seems to register physical and emotional alienation, not the little 'death' of orgasm of which Elizabethan poets, including Shakespeare, were so (poetically) fond, but the big death, that irretrievable fatal loss. The two senses of the word in the tragic pun do not so much frot playfully together, but rather bleed insidiously into each other, draining away both linguistic and human vitality. Thus the pun, a figure of 'double sense', can itself be understood doubly, both as a positive symbol of unexpected mutality and as a negative image for violently disruptive semantic energy.

Language of the play / language of the person

Just as in the examples from *Richard II* or *The Winter's Tale* above, we might want to argue that Shakespeare's language is used for purposes of characterisation. So Pistol's scrappy grandiloquence in *Henry V*, or Polonius's tedious verbosity in *Hamlet*, or Don Armado's baroque phrasing in *Love's Labour's Lost*, or Justice

Shallow's repetitions in *2 Henry IV* become ways of representing a kind of idiolect – the individual person's register and habits of speech. Some critics have argued that this is more evident in Shakespeare's seventeenth-century plays – Frank Kermode sees a decisive shift from *Hamlet* onwards – and that in the first half of his career Shakespeare is more concerned with flashy verbal patterning than with character realism. It's an idea that separates out that layer of the language which is apparently controlled by the character and that which exists apparently independently of them. Is it the character, or the play, that seizes on a particular metaphor at a particular moment? Sometimes there is a mismatch for modern readers between verbal rhetorical patterning and its emotional content: it can be difficult to judge whether a piece of highly-wrought verse is an index of sincerity – as, for example, in the Duchess of York's keening lament in *Richard III*:

> She for an Edward weeps, and so do I;
> I for a Clarence weep, so doth not she.
> These babes for Clarence weep, and so do I;
> I for an Edward weep, so do not they.
> Alas, you three, on me, threefold distressed,
> Pour all your tears; I am your sorrow's nurse,
> And I will pamper it with lamentation.

> (2.2.82–8)

Such verbal patterning in different contexts can register the opposite of sincerity, as in the protestations of love by Gonerill and Regan in the first act of *King Lear*, or Claudius's calculated unctuousness at the beginning of *Hamlet*.

But there are some important ways in which the language spoken by the dramatic characters seems to be less their own and more that of Shakespeare the poet or dramatist. (This is parallel to the discussion of Lady Macbeth's 'child' in chapter 1, 'Character'.) Checking word frequency, for example, can give us a thermal picture of the verbal hotspots in a play, and concordances or searchable online texts are extremely useful in this regard. So we might see a significance in the frequency of the word 'crown' in *Julius Caesar*, as the lexis registers the threat to the republic of Caesar's apparent monarchist ambitions, or note the oblique but insistent eroticism of the repeated word 'bed' in *Othello*, or references to time in *Macbeth* – Shakespeare's shortest tragedy, or the word 'eye' in *A Midsummer Night's Dream*, with its focus on perception and sight. These are not preoccupations of a particular character, but verbal tics of a whole playworld. Similarly, clusters of related imagery contribute powerfully to the mood and tone of the plays. For example, animal imagery in *King Lear* gives a sense of an inhuman world: the Fool notes, seeing Kent in the stocks, 'Horses are tied by the heads, dogs and bears by th'neck, monkeys by th'loins, and men by the'legs' (2.4.7–9); images of ill-fitting clothing convey the misfit between Macbeth and his regal role; *Troilus and Cressida* shares with its near contemporary, *Hamlet*, a disgusted, cynical focus on images of food, consumption and disease. Identifying the language of the play replaces people with words as the focus of our critical attention.

Prose and verse

Flicking through Shakespeare we can see that one of the most obvious distinctions in the arrangement of his language is that between prose and verse. Put simply, you can spot verse – even when it's only single lines – by the fact that the letters down the left hand margin are capitalised and the line does not always reach the right hand margin. Sometimes verse lines have punctuation at the end, sometimes they do not. Sometimes a verse line is divided between speakers, and most modern editions will indent the speech so that the full line is visually evident, as in this example from *King Lear*:

> LEAR Now by Apollo –
> KENT   Now by Apollo, king.
>   Thou swear'st thy gods in vain.
> LEAR   O vassal! Miscreant!
>   (1.1.154–5)

Sharing lines of verse can create intricate relations between speakers: each is listening to the other, extending their interaction into a continued metrical whole. It is particularly good for expressing erotically charged exchanges, for example in the scenes in *Measure for Measure* when Isabella pleads with Angelo for Claudio's life, or when Cressida and Diomedes talk under Troilus' bitter surveillance in 5.2 of *Troilus and Cressida*. Where an edition has included line numbering for ease of reference, a verse line divided between different speakers will count as a single line for purposes of counting.

Prose, by contrast, does not have a capital letter at the beginning of each line and continues to the right hand margin. This rather pragmatic distinction between prose and verse might seem unsatisfactory, and there have been many attempts to elevate the division into something apparently more meaningfully sustained. None has really worked. Prose isn't always associated with lower-class characters, although this is sometimes asserted: the Gardener in 3.4 of *Richard II* speaks blank verse, as does Caliban in *The Tempest*; nearly everyone in *The Merry Wives of Windsor* – citizen wives and husbands, Justice, parson, servant, Falstaff, housekeeper, suitor – speaks prose, as do the knights Sir Toby Belch and Sir Andrew Aguecheek in *Twelfth Night*. Prose isn't less rhetorical or less full of poetic imagery, nor even less rhythmical: the famous counter-example to this claim is Shylock's wonderfully powerful speech in *The Merchant of Venice*:

> I am a Jew. Hath not a Jew eyes? Hath not a Jew hands, organs,
> dimensions, senses, affections, passions? Fed with the same food, hurt
> with the same weapons, subject to the same diseases, healed by the same
> means, warmed and cooled by the same winter and summer as a
> Christian is? If you prick us, do we not bleed? If you tickle us, do we not
> laugh? If you poison us, do we not die? And if you wrong us, shall we not
> revenge? If we are like you in the rest, we will resemble you in that.
>
> (3.1.46–53)

In its use of rhetorical devices including *apostrophe* (address to an absent person or abstraction); *anaphora* (repetition of the same word or words at the beginning of successive clauses or sentences); *gradatio* (building up of an argument to a climax); *isocolon* (parallel syntactic structures) and the related *parison* (parallel sentences side by side); and *quaesitio* (repeated questions), Shylock's speech is as carefully and artfully wrought as any piece of verse. (See 'Where next?' for details on rhetorical terms.)

Linguistic shifts: *1 Henry IV*

While it is difficult to make a sustained distinction, other than a formal one, between Shakespeare's use of prose and of verse, moments which shift from one to the other call attention to both forms. As an example, let's look at the opening act of *1 Henry IV*. The play opens at court, as the king voices the parlous state of the nation:

> So shaken as we are, so wan with care,
> Find we a time for frighted peace to pant,
> And breathe short-winded accents of new broils
> To be commenced in strands afar remote
>
> (1.1.1–4)

Henry's opening speech is over 30 lines long and the whole scene's length of 107 lines comprises only nine speeches. This is a scene in which sense of urgency in the 'short-winded accents' is belied by the apparently ordered linguistic sequence, as the speakers complete their lines in measured and explicatory verse. The next scene introduces us to a very different cadence. Falstaff asks 'Now, Hal, what time of day is it, lad?', and the Prince answers in prose: 'Thou art so fat-witted with drinking of old sack, and unbuttoning thee after supper, and sleeping upon benches after noon, that thou hast forgotten to demand that truly which thou wouldst truly know. What a devil has thou to do with the time of day?' (1.2.1–5). The more casual world of the tavern and its relation to the court is exemplified in this shift of rhythm. Short, interrupted speeches between the Prince and Falstaff give a sense of easy-going and boisterous friendship, in which shared wordplay serves to establish the rapport between the characters.

The linguistic contrast between the first two scenes of the play conveys the dynamic – between public and private, between political and domestic, between verse and prose – which the Prince must negotiate during the course of the play. But lest we feel anxious about the outcome of this dialectic, we are reassured with an early aural indication of Hal's ability to straddle both worlds – his bilingualism. After he and Poins have set up the trick they intend to play on Falstaff, the Prince is left alone on stage. Cue a soliloquy – in blank verse:

> I know you all, and will a while uphold
> The unyoked humour of your idleness.
> Yet herein will I imitate the sun,
> Who doth permit the base contagious clouds
> To smother up his beauty from the world,
> That when he please again to be himself,
> Being wanted, he may be more wondered at
> By breaking through the foul and ugly mists
> Of vapours that did seem to strangle him.
>
> (1.2.155–63)

It's all under control, Hal is telling the audience: I'm not really sullying myself in this unworthy tavern world. I can slum it in prose, but blank verse is my real princely tongue. The rhythmic contrast with the forgoing lines of the scene is a marked one, just as on the page this stands out from the preceding prose and eases us into the next scene in which the king speaks blank verse. Hal's ultimate allegiance – linguistic and moral – is always to his father.

What is important in the example from Act 1 of *1 Henry IV* is not, therefore, the intrinsic connotations of either blank verse or prose, but the arresting interplay between them. It's like the moment when the Old Shepherd and his son pick up the abandoned baby Perdita in *The Winter's Tale* (3.3): the debased verse of the court scenes which has concluded with Antigonus leaving Perdita to her Bohemian fate is supplanted, perhaps renewed, by their prose exchanges. We are in a different world, physically, emotionally – and linguistically. Or consider the difference between Brutus' prose defence of the killing of Caesar and the verse *tour de force* of Antony (*Julius Caesar*, 3.2). Or Beatrice – who has previously only spoken prose – shifting into verse when she hears of Benedick's love for her in Act 3 of *Much Ado About Nothing*. Or the sudden shock of how far Lady Macbeth has declined, offstage, when she emerges in her sleepwalking scene speaking prose, or, in the same play, the delicate emotional shifts in 4.2, the scene at Macduff's castle, when the domestic prose informality between Lady Macduff and her son is sandwiched, tenderly, vulnerably, between the verse of political dictat.

Shakespeare's verse

All introductions to Shakespeare will give some account of *blank verse*, the unrhymed iambic pentameter line made up of five iambs, or two-syllable units following a pattern of unstressed/stressed beats. Often the verse is 'scanned', or marked up, to register this beat. So we might take a 'standard' line such as 'But soft, what light through yonder window breaks' (*Romeo and Juliet*, 2.2.2), and see that the stresses come regularly on 'soft', 'light', 'yon', 'win' and 'breaks'. So far so good. But things quickly get rocky. Firstly, scanning is an art not a science: it's open to interpretation, to different inflections at different moments in the history of pronunciation and from different actors. So the opening line of *Twelfth Night*, 'If music be the food of love, play on' (1.1.1) would seem to have a standard scansion with stressed beats of 'mu', 'be', 'food', 'love', 'on'. An actor might, however, want to deliver the line by inverting the final unit (called a *foot*), to stress 'play', or 'play on' (two stressed syllables are called a *spondee*).

Secondly, as with many poetic effects, the management of pace, rhythm and meaning through regular blank verse quickly becomes monotonous. Once we have learned to recognise it, that is to say, we are also taught that it, like festivity in Claudius' Denmark, is 'more honoured in the breach than the observance' (*Hamlet*, 1.4.16). It is not, therefore, this standard rhythm that is of most interest: rather, we need to become alert to variations from it and to points of linguistic shifting where the difference in cadence marks like a change of linguistic tempo. So here I am interested in the moments when rhythm changes – and in how we can attune our ears to these shifts. Sometimes the rhythmic shift is a matter of varying the iambic line – as when Richard of Gloucester opens the play in which he will seize the crown, *Richard III*, by seizing the standard metre: 'Now is the winter of our discontent' (1.1.1), the play's famous opening, begins not with the unstressed/stressed iamb, but with its opposite, the trochee (stressed/unstressed); Richard's usurpation of the throne which occurs late in the play (the title *Richard III* is curiously inappropriate) is anticipated from its first moment by his masterly usurpation of linguistic mastery. Juliet, impatient for Romeo's return so that they can consummate their marriage, also begins her soliloquy with a trochee, as if her very words are hasty for (metrical) fulfilment: 'Gallop apace, you fiery-footed steeds' (*Romeo and Juliet*, 3.2.1). Sometimes rhythmic variation works by running the sense of the speech across the end of the line, or by placing a punctuation stop, or *caesura*, in the middle of a line for emphasis. A short, 'unfinished' line can also be powerful in its interruption of a pattern, as when Iago meditates:

> The Moor is of a free and open nature,
> That thinks men honest that but seem to be so,
> And will as tenderly be led by th'nose
> As asses are.
> I have't. It is engendered. Hell and night
> Must bring this monstrous birth to the world's light.
>
> (*Othello* 1.3.381–6)

The short line scripts a pause, a silence, a gap: a metrical image of Iago's inscrutable inner privacy even at a moment of soliloquy when he seems most confiding in the audience. Verse form and meaning are here inseparable.

Linguistic variation: *A Midsummer Night's Dream*

Let's develop this with reference to *A Midsummer Night's Dream*, a play with a number of interesting linguistic features, including the fact that more than half of its lines are rhymed. For the most part it is the two pairs of lovers, Demetrius, Lysander, Hermia and Helena who use rhyming speeches, and this makes a metrical analogue to their symmetries and pairings throughout the play, as the love-potion applied by Puck gives their couplings the quality of a formal dance exchanging partners. We might look at the first encounter between erstwhile friends Helena and Hermia in this regard:

> HERMIA I frown upon him; and yet he loves me still.
> HELENA O that your frowns would teach my smiles such skill!
> HERMIA I give him curses; yet he gives me love.
> HELENA O that my prayers could such affections move!
> HERMIA The more I hate, the more he follows me.
> HELENA The more I love, the more he hateth me.
>
> (1.1.194–9)

It is clear that the coupling of lines in end-rhyme is emphasised by their syntactic parallels (the rhetorical figures of *isocolon* and *parison* identified in Shylock's prose speech above). The back-and-forth of the dialogue expresses both the selfishness of love and its interchangeability: each line is poetically dependent on the other, just as each of the various permutations between the lovers is dependent on the excluded ones. Whereas most comedies seek to suppress the absurdity of the love at first sight convention – we need to believe that Orlando's wrestling really makes Rosalind fall for him, otherwise we have no commitment to the comic teleology – here in *A Midsummer Night's Dream* the pleasures of its artificiality are paraded through rhyme.

As with *1 Henry IV*, it is changes of linguistic cadence that are significant. *A Midsummer Night's Dream* moves through the blank verse of Theseus' court to the comically short-winded rhyming lines of *Pyramus and Thisbe*, the inset play rehearsed by Peter Quince and his scratch troupe of amateur actors: 'The raging rocks / And shivering shocks / Shall break the locks / Of prison gates' (1.2.24–7). It engages the incantatory rhythms of the fairies – 'over hill, over dale, / Thorough bush, thorough briar, / Over park, over pale, / Thorough flood, thorough fire' (2.1.2–5) and the prose of the mechanicals. The best way to get used to these shifts is to speak the verse aloud: you don't have to be a great actor to do so! We can see that Shakespeare manages these different groups of characters by giving them quite distinct linguistic properties, thus conveying the shifts between human and fairy worlds and between consciousness and magic. We might relate these changes of tempo to the play's quality of musicality, as expressed in numerous related musical works by Mendelssohn, Purcell, and the 1930s jazz-musical with Louis Armstrong as Bottom, *Swingin' the Dream*. Something of the incongruity of the interplay between worlds is conveyed as Titania welcomes the ass-headed Bottom to her bower in Act 3. Titania is being punished by Oberon for her cussedness regarding the disputed changeling Indian boy, and her punishment is what many critics have seen as the demeaning sexual humiliation of her amorous love for the bestially transformed weaver Bottom. This may be true, but it is also the case that Titania retains her regal verse throughout: whatever else she does, she does not partake of Bottom's habitual prose. The distinction of cadence allows us to assess their relationship and the play's treatment of Titania at this point. Strikingly, *A Midsummer Night's Dream* ends not with the reinstatement of the authoritative linguistic pattern of Duke Theseus but with the whispery cadences of the woodland. Puck, Oberon and Titania all speak in rhymed couplets of seven or eight syllables, sustaining the magical qualities of the play into its final speeches, as Puck dares us to banish the illusion by acknowledging the end of the entertainment: 'Give me your hands, if we be friends, / And Robin shall restore amends' (5.1.415–6). Theatre, like magic, is a matter of conjuring through language.

The point of these suggestions is, cumulatively, to suggest that analysis of Shakespeare's language does not proceed in isolation from analysis of Shakespeare's anything else. In fact, that 'anything else' is always and already linguistic. Chapter 2, on 'Performance', discussed the significance of the verbal to Shakespeare's theatre, in which dramatic effects we might now expect to be visual – set design, lighting, props – were largely conveyed through spoken language. Rhythm, rhetoric and register – and that resistance to paraphrase – are all crucial to the specifics of this spoken language. So too is pleasure.

Language: where next?

- The Formalists' proposition about literature as language made unfamiliar can be found in the selection from Viktor Shlovsky in *Modern Literary Theory*, eds. Philip Rice and Patricia Waugh (Edward Arnold, 4th edn, 2001).
- The woodcuts in Hans Holbein's *Dance of Death*, first published in 1538, are available online at http://www.godecookery.com/macabre/holdod/holdod.htm. The illustration 'The King', in which the skeletal figure of Death offers a cup to a sumptuously dressed monarch sitting at table, is particularly relevant to Richard's imagery. For more on the iconography of death in the period, Michael Neill's *Issues of Death: Mortality and Identity in English Renaissance Tragedy* (Oxford University Press, 1997) is subtle and suggestive.
- Modernised texts of Shakespeare available on the internet are often of uncertain editorial provenance. One good searchable site is http://www.it.usyd.edu.au/~matty/Shakespeare/; searchable folio texts (unmodernised transcriptions, which makes searching a little unpredictable) are available at http://etext.virginia.edu/shakespeare/folio/. David and Ben Crystal's book *Shakespeare's Words* (Penguin, 2004) has an accompanying website with searchable database at http://www.shakespeareswords.com/.
- Identifying moments when the tempo within or between scenes shifts is most easily done by looking at a collected edition of Shakespeare such as the Norton or Riverside (an individual play text doesn't have enough text on a single page opening for this purpose), and seeing the play unfold in long sweeps. Then it's easy to spot rhythmic changes, where long speeches give way to quick interchanges (single line interchanges are called *stichomythia*)

or broken or shared lines, and where prose and verse abut. *Antony and Cleopatra* would be a good place to start.

- Caroline Spurgeon's *Shakespeare's Imagery and What it Tells Us* does a great job of identifying image clusters, although her explanations for them often seem unnecessarily biographical (she interprets the shared imagery of *Troilus and Cressida* and *Hamlet*, for example, as evidence that the two plays are written 'at a time when the author was suffering from a disillusionment, revulsion and perturbation of nature'; one of her sections is titled 'his sympathy for snails', as if we can see through to Shakespeare's own most bizarre personal penchant by a quantitative assessment of his imagery). Frank Kermode's *Shakespeare's Language* (Penguin, 2001) is adept in making word frequency illuminate the central preoccupations of the plays, although he has relatively little to say about the plays before *Hamlet*. On rhyme, and for stimulating linguistic analysis across a range of plays Simon Palfrey's *Doing Shakespeare* (Arden, 2005) really sparkles. One way of thinking creatively about Shakespeare's manipulation of rhythm is to consult actors' guides: Cicely Berry's *The Actor and his Text* (Virgin, 1987) has a great chapter on 'metre and rhythm' and offers some interesting exercises to think about the language physically as well as poetically. On the history of the English language I've drawn on David Crystal's *The Cambridge Encyclopedia of the English Language* (Cambridge University Press, 1999).

- There is a useful list of rhetorical terms at the back of *Reading Shakespeare's Dramatic Language: A Guide*, eds. Sylvia Adamson et al. (Arden, 2001). George Puttenham's Elizabethan version of something similar is available in *Sidney's 'The Defence of Poesy' and Selected Renaissance Literary Criticism*, ed. Gavin Alexander (Penguin, 2004) and online via the Elizabethan E-Texts site at http://www.sourcetext.com/sourcebook/e-texts.htm.

- The idea that musical adaptations of Shakespeare may give us some kind of analogy for their linguistic effects could be followed up with reference to, for example, Kenneth Branagh's widely disliked but still stimulating *Love's Labour's Lost* film of 2000, in which something of the play's set-piece verbal acrobatics is conveyed by their translation into musical numbers (could this be done for other plays?), or the particular affinity between musicals and the early, more linguistically patterned comedies (e.g. in *Kiss Me Kate* (*The Taming of the Shrew*) or *The Boys from Syracuse* (*The Comedy of Errors*)), or the treatment, say, of Shakespearean soliloquies in operas such as Verdi's *Otello* or *Macbeth*, or *Romeo and Juliet* translated into *West Side Story* or as the ballets by Prokofiev or Tchaikovsky, Even the soundtrack to a modern film version like Baz Luhrmann's *Romeo and Juliet* (1996) can say something about the linguistic variation within the play itself: how might we begin to compare, say, the interplay between poetic formality and emotional spontaneity as the lovers compose a sonnet at their first meeting in 1.5.92–105), and that of patterned pop lyrics such as these, from Gavin Friday's 'Angel', at the same point in the film: 'Angel, hold on to me / Love is all around me / Angel, hold on to me / Oooh, come closer / To me, don't go / Don't leave me'? Is it even a tenable comparison to place Shakespeare alongside pop lyrics? Or is the comparison with another 'high' art form like opera more appropriate? Why, or why not?

凡是读过莎士比亚英文原作或观看过英国皇家莎士比亚剧院演出的都有一个共同的体会：莎剧的语言难度很大，特别是对21世纪非英语国家的读者和观众来说。文艺复兴时期的英语既受到古希腊古罗马语言和文化的影响，也与欧洲其他国家的语言和文化相互渗透、相互影响。当时尚未定型、处于演变过程中的英语为剧作家提供了一个极好的发展空间，但也为后来的读者和观众增添了理解上的难度。在分析《麦克白》中女巫的三条预言时，作者用了这样一句话，"The Language of the plays and poems is *the thing itself*."。你是如何理解这句话的？你同意这个说法吗？在莎士比亚的其他剧作中是不是也体现了这样一个原则？

Chapter 5

Structure

Finding the heart of the play

Try a trick. Gather together the pages of the text of your chosen play – not including any introduction or prefatory material – and try, as accurately as you can, to open the play in the middle. Look at where you are. Who is on stage? What is going on? What is the effect of the scene to the development of the plot? It doesn't always work, but often the chronological mid-point in a play gives us something central: an event, a tableau, an encounter, which we might construct as in some way pivotal.

Here are some examples. In *Romeo and Juliet*, for example, the centre-point of the play is the death of Mercutio, brawling with Tybalt. We might see this first death in the tragedy as a signal that things cannot now go well; the death of this jesting character who dies on a joke – 'ask for me tomorrow, and you shall find me a grave man' (3.1.89–90) – marks the end of the lightness with which the Montague/Capulet feud has been temporarily leavened. Chapter 6 considers Shakespeare's use of his sources in more detail, but it is interesting to note here that Mercutio is one of Shakespeare's most substantial additions to his sources: what would the play be like without him, and why, having invented him, does Shakespeare have to kill him off at this point? Another death marks the midpoint of *Julius Caesar*, round about the point in 3.2 where Mark Antony brings in the body of the assassinated Caesar, while Brutus, one of the conspirators responsible for Caesar's death, explains why this has happened. We could see this moment as a crucial fulcrum as power, authority, and the ability to shape events shifts from Brutus to Mark Antony, thus presaging the eventual defeat of Brutus and encapsulating in miniature the play's unsettling ability to shift perspectives and sympathies, so it is hard to know with whom we should ally our own view. In the middle of *Measure for Measure* is a curiously unsettling – unsettling because it raises vast issues to which the play never returns – encounter in prison between Claudio and his sister Isabella. Claudio is awaiting his execution; Isabella tells him the price of his freedom, her virginity, is too high. He accepts this initially, then the realisation of his imminent death hits him:

> CLAUDIO Death is a fearful thing.
> ISABELLA And shamèd life a hateful.
> CLAUDIO Ay, but to die, and go we know not where,
>   To lie in cold obstruction, and to rot,
>   This sensible warm motion to become
>   A kneaded clod, and the delighted spirit
>   To bathe in fiery floods or to reside
>   In thrilling region of thick ribbed ice,
>   To be imprisoned in the viewless winds,
>   And blown with restless violence round about
>   The pendent world or to be worse than worst
>   Of those that lawless and incertain thought
>   Imagine howling; 'tis too horrible.
>   The weariest and most loathèd worldly life
>   That age, ache, penury, and imprisonment
>   Can lay on nature, is a paradise
>   To what we fear of death.   (3.1.116–32)

This little kernel at the heart of the play is a bit of the almost contemporaneous play *Hamlet*; Claudio, isolated from a comic social world in his prison cell (remember Hamlet's 'Denmark's a prison' (2.2.234)?), stares into the abyss of tragedy. The effort of being so tragic – he is a Hamlet without the stamina – seems to exhaust Claudio's character, though, and we never hear him speak again during the play. The awareness of death – and an uncomfortable, thoroughly unChristian concept of death – can't, however, be taken back: the play, like Claudio, never recovers from this terrible knowledge, and this may be seen as one of the reasons it has often been allocated out of the category of comedy to which the Folio attributes it, into a new designation called 'problem play'. Comedies seem not to know about death, and comic characters who come close to it – Sebastian in *Twelfth Night*, Egeon in *The Comedy of Errors*, Hero in *Much Ado About Nothing* – tend to get the better of it.

In the middle of *The Merchant of Venice*, in 3.1, we hear that the eponymous merchant Antonio's ships have been wrecked and that therefore he will not be able to repay his bond to the Jewish moneylender Shylock. It is also the point at which Shylock hears of his daughter's spending spree with her Christian husband, and these two pieces of news come together to fuel Shylock's savage covenant of revenge. Shylock is at his most human – recognising sentimental, rather than monetary, value in a turquoise 'I had [. . .] of Leah when I was a bachelor. I would not have given it for a wilderness of monkeys' (3.1.96–7) – and his most vengeful: 'If you tickle us, do we not laugh? If you poison us, do we not die? And if you wrong us, shall we not revenge?' (3.1.50–2). The litany of similarities between Jew and Christian in Shylock's famous 'hath not a Jew eyes?' speech comes down to endorsing not love or commonality but mutual hatred and destruction. As such this central scene poses Shylock as the challenge to the romantic comedy of the play.

The point of this analysis of the middles of plays is that here we can often see a moment of generic struggle. Shakespeare's plays were allocated by his first editors into three categories or *genres*: comedies, tragedies and histories. In fact, the title of the first collected edition, the Folio of 1623, is *Mr. William Shakespeares Comedies, Histories, & Tragedies*. Since then we have been exercising much critical energy on defining these genres, on deducing from the plays included in each category what is essential to comedy, tragedy or history. Many templates have been offered; most carry with them a long list of exceptions or shoehornings which undermine rather than consolidate the definition. When the playwright Thomas Heywood wrote in 1612 that 'Tragedies and comedies . . . differ thus: in comedies, *turbulenta prima, tranquilla ultima*; in tragedies, *tranquilla prima turbulenta ultima*: comedies begin in trouble and end in peace; tragedies begin in calms and end in tempest' he may have made the only tenable distinction. If things end up better than when you started out, at least for the central characters, the world is a comic one; it's a tragedy where they are getting worse. The middle point of the play, according to these chiastic (*chiasmus* – a rhetorical figure of balance in which repeated terms are reversed) definitions, might be thought to be crucial in establishing which way things are going. Instead of looking, then, at the endings, when genre seems to be fixed through marriages or deaths, it's interesting to look at the moments in the middle when genre is being negotiated, when it is in the process of being made.

Shakespeare's genres: dynamic, not static

In many of these mid-points, that is to say, what we see is a battle over the genre of the play: a tussle about how things are going to work out. Most introductions to genre begin with definitions from notable theorists from Aristotle onwards; most are subsequently discomforted by their apparent misfit with Shakespeare's own employment of those genres. (See 'Where next' for some early modern definitions of genre.) I'd prefer to emphasise the ways in which Shakespeare seems to use his plays to comment on, rather than merely to occupy, generic categories and generic expectations.

Thus, Mercutio is the comic hope for an alternative to the hatreds of *Romeo and Juliet*: it's symbolically significant, therefore, that he's killed by Romeo's clumsy attempt to intervene in the fight. Shylock, a minor character in *The Merchant of Venice* who appears in only five scenes, is, nevertheless, always threatening to take it over. When Portia arrives at the Venetian courtroom disguised as the lawyer Balthazar, she is fighting for the play as comedy; Shylock, whetting his knife on the sole of his shoe, is trying to wrest it from the comic. When, as in Jonathan Miller's stage production (available on video directed by John Sichel (1974): see chapter 2 for more discussion of Shakespeare in performance), the part of Shylock is taken by a tragic actor – Miller cast Laurence Olivier – this generic uncertainty is even more pronounced. Portia's got to get rid of Shylock by the end of Act 4 because Act 5 belongs to the tragic hero. She does so, but Act 5 of *The Merchant of Venice* is a curious and uncomfortable affair, with a distended charade about the rings, and Shylock's spendthrift daughter Jessica and her new husband Lorenzo ominously trading abused-wives-in-mythology stories, all overshadowed by Shylock's unmentioned fate. We could see, therefore, both *Romeo and Juliet* and *The Merchant of Venice*, as negotiating potential generic conflict, personifying a literary-critical discussion into an encounter between different protagonists on the stage. The same might be true of history plays: take *1 Henry IV*, for example, Hotspur is a character from a chivalric chronicle history, Falstaff from a London comedy, Prince Hal from something approaching the modern *bildungsroman*, or narrative of maturation. Their encounters are thus points at which different generic possibilities rub up against each other as the play dramatises its own negotiation of generic markers.

Table 5.1. *Aspects of comedy and tragedy*

Comedy	Tragedy
Titles suggest a mood, a time, or something flippant	Titles focus on an individual – or, less often, two individuals
Movement is towards marriage and social cohesion	Movement is towards isolation and social breakdown
Ends in marriages	Ends in deaths
Suggests a future beyond the play in renewed social bonds	Little sense of a future beyond the end of the play
Tendency to dialogue	Tendency to soliloquy
Female characters prominent and active	Male characters prominent and active
Transfer to a different location is full of possibility for change	Transfer to a different location intensifies old problems
Puns tend towards fecundity and sexual innuendo	Puns tend towards nihilism and the impossibility of communication
Choices are maintained, events are less predestined (what Susan Snyder calls 'evitability')	Sense of inevitability or inescapability about the sequence of events

Tragedy and comedy

I have tried to suggest so far that genre is produced dynamically in Shakespeare's plays, and that it is a topic for negotiation rather than for slavish conformity. When Desdemona momentarily revives at the end of *Othello* there is a tiny window of generic opportunity: perhaps she is not dead, perhaps the tragedy can be averted (it can't). When a 'green and gilded snake' (4.3.103) and a 'lioness, with udders all drawn dry' (4.3.109) converge dangerously on a sleeping man in the Forest of Arden in *As You Like It*, there's a sudden sense that this wood may not be so hospitable and comically transformative as it had seemed (perhaps it's time to go home). That is to say, therefore, that all plays combine elements we might want to consider as 'tragic' or 'comic', and it is the effect and the style of these combinations that is important, rather than some external definition of Shakespearean genre.

Because comedy and tragedy have often been seen to be at opposite ends of the generic spectrum, it can be useful to identify how the plays negotiate our expectations of these definitive forms (we will return to history below). Table 5.1 gives a template for the ways in which comedy and tragedy have tended to be distinguished.

While it's interesting to set out these generic differences, it's also clear that all of Shakespeare's plays partake of elements from both columns. We could trace in *Measure for Measure*, for example, the shift between the comic dominance of a female character – Isabella – and that of a male character – the Duke, even as the play negotiates the marital conclusion of comedy and the threat of the tragic conclusion of death. We could identify moments of soliloquy in comedy – Viola's in *Twelfth Night* – or their absence in a tragedy such as *Timon of Athens*. From this list, we can see that tragedy and comedy tug on the same rope and make use of the same tropes, to different effect. The interplay between these elements and these expectations is what makes Shakespeare's plays work.

At the end of his career, Shakespeare works on a number of plays – including *The Winter's Tale*, *Cymbeline*, and *The Tempest* – tended to be seen by recent scholars as a group, sometimes dubbed 'late romances', in which comic and tragic elements are intermingled. Thus *The Winter's Tale* gives us a jealous husband, rather like Othello, who accuses his wife Hermione of infidelity with his best friend Polixenes, banishes his infant daughter, and repents of his rashness only on hearing his wife has died, at the end of Act 3. The next act is set after the passage of sixteen years: in a pastoral landscape the alienated princess is approaching marriage, and this comic coda to the tragedy brings about resolution and restitution at the end of the play. It is clear that this structure juxtaposes tragedy and comedy in an explicit way, but what should also be clear to us is that this is a typical technique throughout Shakespeare's works, rather than one confined to this later period.

Tragedy – expanding the genre

Let's return to tragedy to examine this characteristic juxtaposition of generic expectations. The Folio catalogue lists eleven plays in its category 'Tragedies': *Coriolanus, Titus Andronicus, Romeo and Juliet, Timon of Athens, Julius Caesar, Macbeth, Hamlet, King Lear, Othello, Antony and Cleopatra* and *Cymbeline*. *Troilus and Cressida*, which comes immediately before *Coriolanus* in the body of the book, may also have been intended as a tragedy, but it is not listed in the catalogue. Since at least A. C. Bradley's *Shakespearean Tragedy*, first published in 1904, however, critical discussion has tended to focus on *Macbeth, Hamlet, King Lear*, and *Othello* as if these are the 'real' or 'true' or 'tragic' tragedies, and thereby suggesting that the remaining plays are insufficiently tragic to be worthy of the designation. But since the compilers of the Folio seem not to have been troubled by this kind of comparative evaluation, and to have preferred the inclusive plural 'tragedies' to the offputtingly formal 'tragedy' – sometimes critics even give it a capital letter, as if it's a proper noun – it is useful to remind ourselves of the challenges to our assumptions about tragedy that this broad definition offers.

Perhaps here we could begin with a tragedy which has caused critics the most aesthetic difficulty until very recently: *Titus Andronicus*. First published in 1594, *The Most Lamentable Roman Tragedy of Titus Andronicus* takes place in ancient Rome during the fourth century BC. Tamora, captive Queen of the Goths, pleads with the Romans for the life of her son Alarbus, but he is sacrificed and she plans a deadly revenge against her captor, the renowned Roman warrior Titus. Tamora's other two sons, Chiron and Demetrius, rape Titus' daughter Lavinia and mutilate her, cutting off her hands and tongue so that she cannot reveal the names of her attackers. Aaron, Tamora's Moorish (black African/Muslim – the word could suggest either or both) lover, kills two of Titus' sons and tricks Titus into chopping off his own hand, and driven mad by his suffering, Titus plans revenge on Tamora, her husband Saturninus the emperor, and Aaron, and devises a horrific plot with his brother Marcus and son Lucius. Titus kills Chiron and Demetrius, and serves their bodies in a pie to their unwitting mother, then kills Tamora and then Lavinia. Saturninus kills Titus, then is killed by Lucius who becomes the new emperor. Aaron is sentenced to death, but the fate of the baby born of his adulterous affair with Tamora is uncertain.

As this brief synopsis of events suggests, *Titus* is undoubtedly a tragedy of sensation, and of serial sensation, rather than a tragedy of introspection. It begins with solemn ritual – the crowning of the emperor, the welcoming of the triumphant Titus 'laden with honour's spoils' (1.1.36), the burial of his 'valiant sons' – and degenerates into muddle and irascible murder. Within the course of the long opening scene, then, which lasts for the whole of the first act, the horror and barbarity which lies below the surface of Rome's civilised rites is exposed. (Julie Taymor's excellent, disturbing film of the play, *Titus* (1999) is highly recommended: it begins strikingly by juxtaposing the random juvenile violence of a modern child playing with toy soldiers and a menacingly closely choreographed and stylised march of the Roman legions marching through the ruined Coliseum on their return from battle.) No one in the play is untainted by the prevailing atmosphere of corruption and violence. There is no hero. Titus may be the play's eponymous character, and he has been a heroic Roman soldier, but when we see him in the play he has no shred of this greatness. Taymor casts a post-Hannibal Lector (*Silence of the Lambs* dir. Jonathan Demme, 1991) Antony Hopkins as Titus, drawing on a mixed legacy of classical acting and Hollywood sociopath to characterise the central character as an opaque, dangerous and unpredictable figure.

Related to Titus' lack of moral or personal greatness is the lack of sympathy the play generates. The insistent use of alienating devices, particularly laughter, keeps us from identifying with the characters, and its proximity to a kind of black comedy is one of the play's most generically unsettling features. Its gruesome insistence on dismemberment, both actual and metaphorical, brings it close to self-parody. Seeing his mutilated daughter, Titus asks 'What accursèd hand / Hath made thee handless in thy father's sight?' (3.1.66–7), and the joke is yet young. Images of dissection come thick and fast in this central scene. 'I'll chop off my hands too' (72), ''tis well Lavinia, that thou hast no hands; / For hands to do Rome service is but vain' (79–80). Father and son argue over who will sacrifice a hand to Aaron as ransom for the other Andronici. 'Lend me thy hand' (186), Titus asks Aaron, who responds by cutting off Titus's. Titus instructs his daughter 'Bear thou my hand, sweet wench, between thy teeth' (281). Figures of speech which use parts of the body seem to continue the litany of vivisection, as the play's very language enacts its characters' self-destructive fantasies of revenge on the human body. Bowels, stomachs, tongues, heads: all become grotesquely animated as testaments to violence and destruction. Such wordplay disturbingly mocks any impulse towards empathy: the only possible audience response is, like Titus's 'ha ha ha' (263) – a queasy or disconcerted laughter.

Writing of his performance of Titus with the Royal Shakespeare Company under the direction of Deborah Warner in 1987–8, Brian Cox emphasises the play as a 'tightrope between comedy and tragedy' which is, above all, 'ludicrous'. This element of the ludicrous is what is exiled from most tragedies – and what brings *Titus Andronicus* into the absurdist style of twentieth-century dramatists such as Beckett or Pinter. Far from prompting empathy, catharsis – those noble tragic emotions – what *Titus* seems to offer its audience is a disturbing kind of mirror, not to its spiritual or emotional side, but to its visceral one. This tragedy challenges the automatic association between Shakespearean tragedy and such related and valorised cultural forms as soliloquy, humanity, and poetry: Titus is not an interior tragic protagonist who struggles with his finer feelings, and indeed he is always being jostled from the central role in his own play by the diabolic energies of Aaron. Rather, *Titus Andronicus* suggests that what we enjoy about tragedy is the perverse pleasure of seeing other people suffering, and that this tragedy, far from bringing empathy and final catharsis, dramatises alienation, distance, and the cruelty of the onlooker. We do nothing to stop Lavinia being raped, mutilated and ultimately murdered. In fact, we pay to watch.

For centuries, critics were so disgusted by this savagery and meaningless brutality that they comforted themselves with the idea that it was not, in fact, by Shakespeare – the opposite of the desire to attribute to him those liberal sentiments of *The Book of Sir Thomas More* (see chapter 3, 'Texts', for this discussion). The man who could write the sublime, humane tragedies of *Hamlet* and *King Lear* could not, surely, even as a young man, have written this gruesomely unwholesome cocktail of sex, mutilation, and madness. More recent critics, however, have returned to the play to find in it the troubling aesthetics of violence as envisioned by a film director such as Quentin Tarentino (*Reservoir Dogs*, 1992, *Pulp Fiction*, 1994, *Kill Bill 1*, 2003), a triumphantly modern, camply excessive, darkly ironic representation of unpalatable truths about human violence, suffering, and inherent barbarism. So it's a play which makes blanket statements about Shakespeare's tragedies being elevated or noble or psychological impossible to sustain, and which may encourage us to look at brutal aspects of other plays – the blinding of Gloucester in *King Lear*, Hamlet's casual attitude to Polonius' body, the final Folio stage direction in *Coriolanus* in which the chant 'Kill, kill, kill, kill, kill him' is followed by '*Draw both the Conspirators, and kils Martius, who falles, Auffidius stands on him*' – as central rather than marginal to their metaphysical concerns. Tragedy's savage affiliation with bloodsports – the spectacle of bear-baiting which was one of the Shakespearean theatre's closest commercial rivals – here challenges more cerebral assumptions. By taking a wider view of what plays were included as tragedies, we start to push at the generic boundary and to approach some sense of the range of what was considered tragic by the plays' first audiences.

Comedy – expanding the genre

There are fourteen plays designated 'Comedies' in the Folio catalogue: *The Tempest, The Two Gentlemen of Verona, The Merry Wives of Windsor, Measure for Measure, The Comedy of Errors, Much Ado About Nothing, Love's Labour's Lost, A Midsummer Night's Dream, The Merchant of Venice, As You Like It, The Taming of the Shrew, All's Well That Ends Well, Twelfth Night*, and *The Winter's Tale*. As in the 'tragedies' category, however, discussion of comedy has tended to elevate a few central plays as supreme generic examples and to have difficulties with the others, or has tended to subdivide the genre into 'happy' or 'dark' or 'problem' or 'early' comedies or 'romances'. Just as *Titus Andronicus* pushes at our associations of tragedy, so too *All's Well That Ends Well* pushes at the definition of comedy in some usefully expansive ways.

All's Well That Ends Well, often categorised as a problem play along with *Measure for Measure* and *Troilus and Cressida*, written about the same time at the beginning of the seventeenth century, throws down a challenge to comic assumptions in its very title. Is indeed 'all's well that ends well'? Is anything which looks like a comedy at its conclusion a comedy, no matter what has gone before? In *All's Well* we have a device common to many of Shakespeare's comedies: a woman actively pursuing her own desires in choosing a partner. We see this when Hermia prefers Lysander over Demetrius at the beginning of *A Midsummer Night's Dream*; when Julia dresses in male clothing to secure her errant lover Proteus' affections in *Two Gentleman of Verona*; and when Rosalind in *As You Like It* and Viola in *Twelfth Night* take similar sartorial steps to pursue their relationships with Orlando and Orsino respectively.

In *All's Well* the woman is Helena, but what is different about this play from the other comic narratives of female romantic agency is the extent of the putative groom's resistance. Helped by her late father's ointments, Helena, a woman of modest background, has cured the king of a singularly unpleasant and long-standing medical complaint which has foxed all his physicians. She replies to his expansive offer of reward: 'then shalt thou give me with thy kingly hand / What husband in thy power I will command' (2.1.189–90). Helena has already chosen her partner: Bertram, the Count of Rousillon. But Bertram is not amenable to this, notwithstanding her miracle-working with the king: 'I cannot love her, nor will strive to do't' (2.1.137). He is forced to go through the wedding ceremony, but vows 'I'll to the Tuscan wars, and never bed her' (2.3.250). Bertram sends a message to Helena: 'When thou canst get the ring upon my finger, which never shall come off, and show me a child begotten of thy body that I am father to, then call me husband; but in such a "then" I write a "never"' (3.2.50–3). The rest of the play shows us Helena's drive to meet this riddling challenge. She interposes herself between her husband and Diana, a woman he urges 'give thyself unto my sick desires' (4.2.35), and in a version of the bed-trick we also find in *Measure for Measure*, substitutes herself for Diana in the sexual encounter he arranges, garnering his ring into the bargain. Bertram is made to see that he has been bested and that the terms of his bargain have been fulfilled, and he accepts Helena as his wife.

Part of the generic difficulty here is with tone. *All's Well* shares with other so-called 'problem plays' a register steeped in the satiric imagery of commerce and disease. The king's own condition only literalises a predominant tone of sexualised sickness, and Helena cannot heal the play's debased linguistic world as she does its ruler. While all comedies work to regulate and sublimate sexual desire into socially acceptable marital unions – perhaps the neatest summation of this equation is Touchstone's quaintly rhyming proposal 'Come sweet Audrey, we must be married or we must live in bawdry' (*As You Like It*, 3.4.73–4) – *All's Well* is disturbingly frank about this process, as it transforms Bertram's adulterous lust for Diana into the means by which his unwelcome marriage is ratified. And while other comedies tend to pair a feisty woman with a man who may not be her equal – witness Orlando's daft sonnets in *As You Like It*, Orsino's self-indulgent love-melancholy in *Twelfth Night*, the insipid interchangeability of Lysander and Demetrius in *A Midsummer Night's Dream*, Proteus' unreliability in *Two Gentlemen of Verona*, the fortune-hunter Bassanio in *The Merchant of Venice* – the incompatibility between the principals in *All's Well* is of a different order of magnitude. In fact, the critical quarrel over this rebarbative play has tended to coalesce around whether Helena or Bertram is the more disagreeable. Audiences and readers have found it difficult to endorse Helena's quest since Bertram's evident unwillingness – and unworthiness – mean that, unlike her comic predecessors, her desires forfeit their narrative sympathy. *All's Well* isn't one of the much-enjoyed 'festive' comedies associated with the rhythms and rituals of the carnival calendar; it isn't a 'feel-good' romance; its final moments can offer us only a provisional version of its apparently certain title, as both Bertram and Helena begin their final speeches with 'If' and the King offers, tentatively, 'all yet seems well, and if it end so meet, / The bitter past, more welcome is the sweet' (5.3.322–4).

The Folio's inclusion among the comedies of *All's Well*, a play ending in marriage or at least marital acknowledgement, works to unsettle certain expectations about comic mood or tone. Or perhaps it gives us retrospective warrant to unearth some of the suppressed darkness which is intrinsic to many of the comedies – and to the genre of comedy itself. Perhaps *All's Well* legitimates and refocuses our attention on what's potentially terrifying about comedy, a borderline insane world in which isolation or incompleteness – what Antipholus of Syracuse fears in *The Comedy of Errors* with 'I to the world am like a drop of water / That in the ocean seeks another drop, / Who, falling there to find his fellow forth, / Unseen, inquisitive, confounds himself' (1.2.35–8) – is the threat from which all are desperately running. Twins search maniacally for their missing half, unlikely couples prefer the uncertain yoke of marriage to the lonely alternative, characters lose themselves and their familiar world, entering into a strange landscape where men grow asses' heads and the greenwood births hungry lionesses, and where, as Feste notes melancholically at the end of *Twelfth Night*, 'the rain it raineth every day' (5.1.369). When Puck encourages us to think, as *A Midsummer Night's Dream* concludes, 'you have but slumbered here' (5.1.403), we might briefly recognise the playworld as a nightmare from which it is a relief to awake, but from which lurid fragments continue to flash into our waking consciousness.

History: is this a fixed genre?

The genre of 'histories' is a distinctive aspect of the Folio's categorisation. Although the title 'history' appears on a number of quarto title-pages, it seems to be used with its earlier sense of 'story' – not necessarily factual – alongside the more modern meaning of 'record' or 'chronicle' in examples such as *The most Excellent Historie of the Merchant of Venice* (1600) and *The History of Henrie the Fourth* (1598). Plays the Folio lists under 'Histories' were first published as tragedies, as, for example, *The true Tragedie of Richard Duke of Yorke* (1595, printed as *The Third Part of King Henry VI* in the Folio) or *The Tragedy of King Richard the third* (1597). By 1623, however, the genre had settled around the plays of medieval English history printed in chronological order: plays based on Roman history, or, like *Macbeth*, on the history of other countries, were not included in the category.

As this suggests, 'histories' seem to be generically derived from their source material: they are histories primarily because of their relation their external sources, rather than because of their internal shape or narrative form. And out of this relation to an ongoing narrative of English history we can see some quite specific structural decisions being made. Thus perhaps *Richard II* and *Richard III* might be seen as what *Hamlet*'s Polonius pedantically called 'tragical-historical'; the chorus structure of *Henry V* gives it an epic quality and, in the last act, the play works overtime to re-invent itself as a romantic comedy with a long wooing scene between the victorious Henry and the vanquished French princess Katherine; both parts of *Henry IV* employ comic devices and episodes, in particular the character of Falstaff who does indeed reappear in his own comedy, *The Merry Wives of Windsor*.

If genres are settled by a play's conclusion, then Shakespeare's decisions about how to cut the material he found in Raphael Holinshed's prose *Chronicles of England*, his major source for the history plays, are illuminating. In *Richard II*, for example, there are presentiments of the civil war – the Wars of the Roses – which followed Richard's deposition. The Bishop of Carlisle, for instance, prophesies that if the lawful king Richard is dethroned 'The blood of English shall manure the ground / And future ages groan for this foul act' (4.1.137–8); and, indeed, reading across the history plays as if they were a serial that grim forecast comes true. (Of course, what within the world of the *play* is a prediction, that unrest will follow Bullingbrook's coronation, is for the *audience* an already known sequence of past events: the Bishop prophesies what has already happened.) But there is no hint of the prophecy coming immediately true in the play itself. When Macbeth kills Duncan, another lawful king, the ramifications are instantly felt: 'the night has been unruly . . . Lamentings heard i'th'air, strange screams of death' (2.3.46–8). *Macbeth*'s depiction of the overthrow of a sovereign places the transfer of power at the beginning of the play and anatomises its political and psychological consequences; *Richard II*'s places the transfer at the end of the play and has therefore little interest, or little time, for the repercussions. Comparing these two structures with that of *Julius Caesar* – where, as we saw above, the transfer of power occurs at the play's midpoint – shows Shakespeare's differing emphases.

But by not showing any retribution falling on Bullingbrook within the play, Shakespeare may be subtly radicalising his depiction of political and monarchical succession. Contrary to contemporary orthodox opinion – one sermon 'against rebellion' appointed by the authorities to be preached in every church reminded congregations how God had punished 'Lucifer [. . .] who by rebelling against the majesty of God, of the brightest and most glorious angel is become the blackest and most foulest fiend and devil' – *Richard II* seems to show that there is no immediate punishment for overthrowing the king, 'the figure of God's majesty, / His captain, steward, deputy, elect' (4.1.125–6). We have to wait until *1 Henry IV*, the play in which Bullingbrook's own compromised authority is explored, for that. And while the Folio catalogue, and the modern tradition of performing multiple history plays in sequence, may suggest that's not a long time to wait, the evidence for the first audiences seems to be different: some months, as a minimum, separated performances of *Richard II* and *1 Henry IV*.

By ending *Richard II* when he does, therefore, Shakespeare's formal shaping of the play has thematic and interpretative implications. So too does the structuring of *1 Henry IV* by means of a series of parallels – between court and tavern, verse and prose, Prince Harry and Hotspur, Falstaff and King Henry, past and future, or that remarkable shift from martial to marital at the end of *Henry V*, or the sequence of repetitions and recapitulations which mark the *Henry VI* plays. We might imagine that the narrative material from which the history plays are drawn would limit Shakespeare's imaginative freedom; what we see instead is that it is how he structures these plays, what shapes he chooses to cut from a long narrative sweep, that is of particular interest. If history is a genre curiously bolstered from texts outside itself – its relation to its particular source material – it also has a special narrative freedom. The way in which Shakespeare structures his history plays draws attention both to larger generic forms and to the specific interaction of the building blocks of individual scenes.

Structuring scenes: *Much Ado About Nothing*

The most shocking scene in *Much Ado About Nothing* comes in Act 4. The callow, inexperienced Claudio has been tricked by the malevolent Don John into believing that his bride Hero has been unfaithful to him. He denounces her at the altar; she swoons in an apparently mortal fit. What's more terrifying is that her father Leonato immediately sides with Claudio, responding to the shame of his daughter's 'foul tainted flesh' (4.1.136) with the wish 'Do not live, Hero' (116). The friar who was to officiate at the marriage steps forward, and, with Hero's cousin Beatrice, proposes a plan: 'Your daughter here the princes left for dead, / Let her awhile be secretly kept in, / And publish it, that she is dead indeed.' (195–7). This, the friar asserts, will 'quench the wonder of her infamy' (232). Being brought to a realisation of what he has lost will make Claudio repent his harsh treatment.

Wait a minute! Problems in love, a friar, a young bride pretending to be dead . . . haven't these people ever seen *Romeo and Juliet*? (*c.* 1594; printed in 1597, and by 1599 widely known). How can this romantic comedy manage a fistful of elements previously associated with tragedy, and simultaneously reassure its audience that Hero's disgrace is a temporary setback, rather than a complete reversal of the play's comic mood?

The answers to this question take us to Shakespeare's handling of structure: the ways in which he deploys existing narrative patterns or genres, and the effective internal architecture of these larger compositions. In the first place, Shakespeare generates a false or premature conclusion to *Much Ado About Nothing* which, precisely because we know has come too soon, we know cannot be final. There's time for things to be put right. Comedies always dramatise impediments to coupledom – 'the course of true love never did run smooth' (1.1.134), as Lysander observes at the opening of *A Midsummer Night's Dream* – due to the opposition of families, or the apparent incompatability of social status, or the fact that the female partner passes unrecognised in male clothing; Claudio's rejection of Hero is just a rather pointed version of this generic trope of deferral. We might compare this to the death of King Lear (discussed in chapter 3, 'Texts'), when the internal clock of the playgoer or reader knows that there is no going beyond this point; there is no time left. Or a different point of comparison with *Much Ado About Nothing* might be its tragic counterpart in *Othello* – another play in which male jealousy disrupts, this time fatally, heterosexual union – where the couple's happiness, expressed so beautifully in Othello's 'it is too much of joy' comes too early, at 2.1.189. There is time for Iago's mischief to take hold; the miniature comedy of the first scenes of the play has spent itself too quickly. The reunion of the couple after the storm in Cyprus should be the play's triumphant conclusion, rather than this tempting-fate provisionality.

So there is time for Hero's broken marriage to be put right. And Shakespeare also cauterises this misogynistic scene of sexual jealousy – a dark complement to the play's valorisation of male bonding – by the way in which he places it amid other scenes. In chapter 1, on 'Character', we saw how Shakespeare writes for particular actors, and one example was the comic player Will Kemp whose name appears in the early texts of *Much Ado About Nothing* as the speech prefix for the character of Dogberry. Dogberry is a good-natured but pompous constable charged with the security of Messina's streets, and, like many of Shakespeare's comic characters, he has a tendency to mix up his words, in, for example, his attempt at proverbial wisdom: 'comparisons are odorous [odious]' (3.5.13). This form of verbal humour associated with the lower classes – we seem to be laughing *at*, rather than *with*, Dogberry – offers us the unintended obverse of the punning with which Beatrice and Benedick's exchanges sparkle: if we look at Kenneth Branagh's sunny 1993 film of the play, we can see that Dogberry, played by Michael Keaton, seems to be acting in a different style, even a different play, from the other characters. Shakespeare uses this tonal difference to inoculate the scene of Hero's disgrace. The most serious and potentially tragic scene in the play is bracketed off by two scenes with Dogberry and his associates and their terrible puns. The tension is managed; we have a reason to laugh after the stress of the interrupted wedding scene; but more importantly, there is a sense that the dark elements of the play are contained in a reassuringly comic envelope, unable to seep out and taint its overall mood. Dogberry and his fellow watchmen are the means, unwittingly, by which Don John's calumnies come to light, but they are also the guarantors that his spitefully uncomic view of the world cannot prevail. Dogberry, perhaps, is the Mercutio who does not die, just as Hero is the Juliet who survives the pretence of death to be reunited with her husband.

Juxtaposing scenes, activating ironies: *Henry V*

Much Ado About Nothing, then, works by juxtaposing scenes so that their meaning is mutually constituted. We can see a different example of this in Act 4 of *Henry V*. Here, Shakespeare employs the device of a chorus whose descriptive, rhetorical, exhortatory speeches preface each of the five acts. The Chorus to Act 4 is charged with describing the French and English military encampments the night before the battle of Agincourt, and a long speech invokes the difference between the two sides. The French, confident of victory, are eager for morning's light; the 'poor condemnèd English, / Like sacrifices, by their watchful fires /

Sit patiently and inly ruminate / The morning's danger.' (4.0.22–5). Amid this demoralised army moves King Henry, full of comfort to his men. He 'bids them good morrow with a modest smile, / And calls them brothers, friends, and countrymen' (33–4). Everyone 'plucks comfort from his looks' (42); that 'little touch of Harry in the night' (47) is the English secret weapon; an ethics of companionship and solidarity morally as well as militarily opposed to the presentation of the foppish French.

So the Chorus – who might be seen as a kind of spin-doctor or propagandist for Henry – presents an image of his selfless devotion to his men as they keep watch through the night. But Shakespeare compromises, or allows us to compromise, that initial presentation by the way he structures the ensuing scenes. Having *told* us about Henry moving among his troops, the scene now *shows* us. First Henry encounters Pistol, and, in disguise, tells him his name is 'Harry *le roi*'. Then he meets a group of three soldiers, John Bates, Michael Williams and Alexander Court. In chapter 1, on 'Character', we saw that often Shakespeare's characters are not so carefully or consistently named as are these three soldiers. Something about the detail of their names seems to suggest that they are not merely examples or mouthpieces – not like, for example, Plebeians 1, 2, and 3 in 3.2 of *Julius Caesar*. Rather their names give them a kind of individual dignity, and thereby serve to magnify their role in the play.

So the scene is set up for the King to show off his comforting looks, to give good cheer to his men. But that is not what happens. In fact Henry gets into an unseemly row with these stoic English soldiers whose sense of their imminent death transcends the propaganda of the Chorus. What, they ask the newcomer, might the King think of their chances in the battle? The disguised King pleads for the essential humanity of the King in a wonderfully circular argument: 'I think the King is but a man as I am' (4.1.97); the soldiers are unmoved by this, and continue to articulate the question the play can neither suppress nor answer. Is Henry's campaign in France just? Henry's long speeches argue that 'Every subject's duty is the king's, but every subject's soul is his own' (4.1.159–60): the king cannot be held responsible for the immortal souls of soldiers killed in his wars, any more than the father is responsible for a son who is killed on his errand, or a master responsible for a servant murdered on business. Henry and Williams cannot agree on this, and their quarrel turns to deferred violence as they vow to fight each other after the battle. Bates' 'Be friends, you English fools, be friends! We have French quarrels enough' (197–8) highlights the inappropriateness of this behaviour – and implicitly contrasts it with the idealised solidarity conjured up by the Chorus' speech only minutes ago. What Henry notably does not do here is to answer the question 'if the cause be not good' (4.1.123); instead of reassuring the men by arguing for the rightness of his cause, he instead challenges the assumption that their deaths are the responsibility of the king.

Henry then withdraws into a soliloquy – his only soliloquy of the play – and it is a lament about the burden and loneliness of office familiar from the history plays (and familiar to more recent leaders, too: Prince Charles cites it in his collection of favourite bits from Shakespeare published as *The Prince's Choice*, marvelling at the dramatist's 'insight into the mind of someone born into this kind of position'). Kingship is but 'ceremony', Henry rehearses, but in a comparison between the king and the commoners he seems entirely to forget the worries of the unsleeping soldiers he has just left:

> No, not all these, thrice-gorgeous ceremony,
> Not all these, laid in bed majestical,
> Can sleep so soundly as the wretched slave
> Who, with a body filled and vacant mind,
> Gets him to rest, crammed with distressful bread;
> Never sees horrid night, the child of hell,
> But like a lackey from the rise to set
> Sweats in the eye of Phoebus, and all night
> Sleeps in Elysium.   (4.1.239–47)

That Henry identifies the untroubled lives of those not burdened with office with sleep must surely be connected to his night-time encounter with Bates, Williams and the silent Court. Far from sleeping, these ordinary men are frightened, worried for their own lives in a desperately unequal conflict far from home and beyond their understanding or control. But it seems that Shakespeare wants those men and their ongoing challenge to Henry's moral authority to echo in Henry's own soliloquy here. As Henry thinks about himself, he caricatures the 'wretched slave' in a manner rather different from his gestures of brotherhood. If we read it alongside the preceding dialogue, that is to say, it has a different implication from when read extracted from its careful position in the play. There are lots of other great juxtapositional ironies in this act – there are some suggestions for taking it further in 'Where next?' at the end of this chapter.

Showing v. telling

One aspect of the sophistication of Shakespeare's construction of Act 4 of *Henry V* is the friction between the two modes of showing and telling, or, as theories of narrative would put it, between *mimesis* and *diegesis*. Why doesn't Shakespeare show us what Claudio sees at the window and interprets as Hero's infidelity in *Much Ado About Nothing* (and why *do* we see what Claudio does in Branagh's 1993 film)? Why do we hear from Gertrude about the death of Ophelia in such lyrical detail (and, similarly, why do such different films as Olivier's 1948 version and Almereyda's 2000 one show it to us)? Why does Shakespeare withhold the wonderful scene of Perdita's reconciliation with her father in *The Winter's Tale* (discussed in chapter 6, 'Sources'), or Petruchio's outlandish arrival at the church in *The Taming of the Shrew*, or the way in which Isabella persuades Mariana to the friar-Duke's bed-trick plan in *Measure for Measure*, or the meeting between Oberon and Titania in which the changeling boy is surrendered so that Bottom can be returned to his proper form in *A Midsummer Night's Dream*? Why aren't we allowed to see for ourselves whether Caesar rejects the public's proffered crown with regret or conviction at the opening of *Julius Caesar*, when offstage cheers tantalise us with what is being withheld from our view? Although there may on occasions be practical reasons why it is difficult to show a particular scene, for the main part actions are withheld for a thematic purpose: it serves to characterise the tellers, or to submit unseen events to different interpretations, or to pace events for us. Thus, that we hear from the Duke of York about the entry of Richard and Bullingbrook into London towards the end of *Richard II* rather than seeing it for ourselves, is a response to the practical difficulty of representing horses on stage, a development of the Yorks as barometers of changing opinion in the play, and a representation of the ethical difficulty of judging the relative merits of Richard and Bullingbrook as king. It's a moot point whether any Shakespeare play depends on a specifically *visual* denouement, despite the increasing popularity and theatrical possibility of visual spectacle during his career.

The management of showing and telling might stand as a literal version of Shakespeare's management of structure more generally. By highlighting certain generic expectations and pushing others into the background, making visible certain connections and obscuring others, the plays engage their audiences in several active matrices: between this play and others, between this play and expectations about the kind of play, between this scene and the ones which precede or follow it, between the shown and the hidden. Shakespeare's structure is therefore always dynamic rather than inert, actively produced from moment to moment.

Structure: where next?

- Other middles to look at might be *Othello* (the so-called 'temptation scene' in which Iago persuades Othello of his wife's infidelity); *Hamlet* (the performance of the 'Murder of Gonzago'); *King Lear* (the scene on the heath in the storm); *The Winter's Tale* (the fateful trial of Queen Hermione). How might this structure be affected by the placing of the interval in a modern theatrical performance? And what, too, about plays where this trick doesn't really work? Might they be presenting an alternative structure?

- On that negative relation between comedy and death, writing of the newly fashionable genre of 'tragicomedy' in the preface to *The Faithful Shepherdess*, John Fletcher proposes that 'A tragic-comedy is not so called in respect of mirth and killing, but in respect it wants deaths, which is enough to make it no tragedy, yet brings some near it, which is enough to make it no comedy, which must be a representation of familiar people, with such kind of trouble as no life be questioned.' Some critics have suggested that *Measure for Measure* and *All's Well That Ends Well* – and perhaps *The Winter's Tale* – should be included in this genre. But it's not entirely true that comedies cannot encompass death: *Love's Labour's Lost* ends with the promised marriages deferred because of the death of the Princess's father. The conclusion is self-conscious about its relation to comic protocols. The witty Berowne is commissioned to charitable works 'With all the fierce endeavour of your wit / To enforce the painèd impotent to smile' (5.2.839–40) to which he replies 'To move wild laughter in the throat of death? – / It cannot be, it is impossible' (841–2). In a final exchange we have Berowne's rueful 'Our wooing doth not end like an old play; / Jack hath not Jill. These ladies' courtesy / Might well have made our sport a comedy' (860–2). What is the effect of this deferred comic ending?
- One way to write about Shakespeare and structure would have been to set the plays against definitions of tragedy and comedy: I chose not to do that, but here are some excerpts from contemporaneous discussion of genre so that you can if you want:

Tragedy:

(1) 'The high and excellent Tragedy, that openeth the greatest wounds and showeth forth the ulcers that are covered with tissue; that maketh kings fear to be tyrants, and tyrants manifest their tyrannical humours; that, with stirring the affects of admiration and commiseration, teacheth the uncertainty of this world, and upon what weak foundations gilden roofs are builded.' Philip Sidney, *An Apology for Poetry* (c. 1581)

(2) Classical tragedy shows 'the disastrous miseries of man's life and so out of that melancholic vision, stir horror, or murmur, against Divine

Providence'; contemporary tragedies show 'God's revenging aspect upon every particular sin, to the despair, or confusion, of mortality.' Fulke Greville, *The Life of Sir Philip Sidney* (*c.* 1611)

(3) 'If we present a tragedy, we include the fatal and abortive ends of such as commit notorious murders, which is aggravated and acted with all the art that may be, to terrify men from the like abhorred practices.' Thomas Heywood, *An Apology for Actors* (1612)

Comedy

(1)   . . . persons, such as Comedy would choose,
        When she would show an image of the times
        And sport with human follies, not with crimes.
        Except, we make 'em such by loving still
        Our popular errors, when we know th'are ill.
        I mean such errors, as you'll all confess
        By laughing at them, they deserve no less.

        Ben Jonson, Prologue to *Every Man in his Humour* (1600)

(2) 'the moving of laughter is a fault in comedy, a kind of turpitude, that depraves some part of man's nature, without a disease. As a wry face without pain moves laughter, or a deformed vizard, or a rude clown dressed in a ladies habit and using her actions, we dislike and scorn such representations which made the ancient Philosophers ever think laughter unfitting in a wise man.' Ben Jonson, *Timber, or Discoveries* (1640)

(3) comedy serves 'to recreate such as of themselves are wholly devoted to melancholy, which corrupts the blood; or to refresh such weary spirits as are tired with labour, or study, to moderate the cares and heaviness of the mind, that they may return to their trades and faculties with more zeal and earnestness, after some small soft and pleasant retirement.' Thomas Heywood, *Apology for Actors* (1612)

For more definitions and discussions of Renaissance genres, see Barbara K. Lewalski (ed.), *Renaissance Genres: Essays on Theory, History, and Interpretation* (Harvard University Press, 1986), and Brian Vickers (ed.), *English Renaissance Literary Criticism* (Oxford University Press, 1999). More specifically on Shakespeare are Lawrence Danson's excellent *Shakespeare's Dramatic Genres* (Oxford University Press, 2000) and Susan Snyder's 'The Genres of Shakespeare's Plays' in Margreta de Grazia and Stanley Wells (eds.), *The Cambridge Companion to Shakespeare*, in part a distillation of her *The Comic Matrix of Shakespeare's*

Tragedies (Princeton University Press, 1979). Also recommended are the three volumes of Cambridge Introductions to Shakespeare's Tragedies, Comedies and Histories (Janette Dillon, *The Cambridge Introduction to Shakespeare's Tragedies* (Cambridge University Press, 2007); Penny Gay, *The Cambridge Introduction to Shakespeare's Comedies* (Cambridge University Press, 2007); and Waren Chernaik, *The Cambridge Introduction to Shakespeare's History Plays* (Cambridge University Press, 2007).

- Jonathan Bate's Arden 3 edition of *Titus Andronicus* (1995) is a landmark in the critical rehabilitation of the play, and his Introduction discusses its tarnished reputation. Brian Cox describes his performance as Titus in Deborah Warner's production in *Players of Shakespeare* (eds. Russell Jackson and Robert Smallwood, Cambridge University Press, 1993). Indicative recent essays on the play include Gillian Kendall, 'Lend Me Thy Hand': Metaphor and Mayhem in Titus Andronicus', *Shakespeare Quarterly* 40 (1989); Albert H. Tricomi, 'The Aesthetics of Mutilation in *Titus Andronicus*' in Catherine Alexander (ed.), *Shakespeare and Language* (Cambridge University Press, 2004); and Deborah Willis, 'The Gnawing Vulture': Revenge, Trauma Theory, and *Titus Andronicus*', *Shakespeare Quarterly* 53 (2002). There are stimulating chapters on the play in Cora Kaplan's *Roman Shakespeare: Warriors, Wounds and Women* (Routledge, 1997), Cynthia Marshall's *The Shattering of the Self: Violence, Subjectivity and Early Modern Texts* (Johns Hopkins University Press, 2002) and Pascale Aebischer's *Shakespeare's Violated Bodies: Stage and Screen Performance* (Cambridge University Press, 2004). Julie Taymor's film *Titus* (advertising taglines: 'The fall of an empire is nothing compared to the descent of man'; 'if you think revenge is sweet. . . . taste this') is available on DVD; Peter Brook's darkly violent *King Lear* (1971) is a good comparison in its stress on brutality (rather than, or as well as, say, nobility or philosophy or self-discovery) as a constituent of tragedy, as is Roman Polanski's *Macbeth* (also 1971).
- On *All's Well That Ends Well*, Susan Snyder's Oxford University Press edition (1993) has a great introduction on the play's generic affiliations. Other indicative recent criticism includes David Scott Kastan, '*All's Well That Ends Well* and the Limits of Comedy', *English Literary History* 52 (1985); Alexander Leggatt, 'In the Shadow of *Hamlet*: Comedy and Death in *All's Well That Ends Well*' in *Re-Visions of Shakespeare: Essays in Honor of Robert Ornstein* (ed. Evelyn Gajowski, University of Delaware Press, 2004); and Susan Snyder, 'The King's Not Here': Displacement and Deferral in *All's*

Well That Ends Well, *Shakespeare Quarterly* 43 (1992). One way to trace the increased interest in the darkness within Shakespeare's comedies is through performance: recent productions of *Twelfth Night* have been more sensitive to Malvolio's treatment, for example – Trevor Nunn's 1996 film is a good example. Kate Chedgzoy's *Measure for Measure* (Northcote House, 2000) is good on that play's contemporary relevance. I discuss some of the issues of genre and their critical history in the volume *Blackwell Guides to Criticism: Shakespeare's Comedies* (Blackwell, 2004).

- On the way Shakespeare juxtaposes scenes, you might consider the construction of Act 1 of *1 Henry IV*. How are the two worlds of court and tavern characterised, and why does Prince Henry's soliloquy come so early in the play (also discussed in chapter 4, 'Language')? What's happening in *Titus Andronicus* when Lavinia is dragged offstage by her rapists Chiron and Demetrius, and the next scene sees her brothers Quintus and Martius falling into a pit described as a 'subtle hole . . . Whose mouth is covered with rude-growing briers / Upon whose leaves are drops of new-shed blood . . . A very fatal place it seems to me' (2.3.198–202): could we see Lavinia's violation being literalised here, and what are the gender/familial implications of this displacement? Or have a look at the interplay between Roman and Egyptian scenes in *Antony and Cleopatra*, and the close, almost cinematic cutting in Acts 3 and 4 (particularly when compared with battle sequences in the earlier English history plays). The example of *Henry V* discussed in this chapter could be taken further: how does Henry's promise that 'he today that sheds his blood with me / Shall be my brother; be he ne'er so vile / This day shall gentle his condition' (4.3.61–3) fit with his description of the English casualties 'none else of name, and of all other men / But five and twenty' (4.8.97–8)? When does Henry give the order for the French prisoners to be killed? Why, precisely at the moment of Henry's triumph in France, does Fluellen remind us that the king, like Alexander, killed his best friend Falstaff?

- If you are interested in narrative theory and on the elaboration of the distinction between 'showing' and 'telling', Paul Cobley's *Narrative* in Routledge's New Critical Idiom series (2001) is a lucid place to start. Other fruitful showing/telling points might be the murder of Duncan in *Macbeth* – compared, perhaps, with the onstage killing of Julius Caesar or Richard II. Is it unshowable? How does Macbeth's description of the body work? Or the role of Gower, a 'teller', in *Pericles* – which bits of his story are shown, and which related? Or the conversion of Duke Frederick at the end of *As You Like It*: is it more, or less, convincing by being told rather than shown? How might we compare Shakespeare's structuring of *The Tempest* – where the history of Prospero's exile and arrival on the island some twelve years previously is told in the lengthy second scene, with that of the contemporaneous play *The Winter's Tale*, in which the first three acts are separated from the last two by the figure of Time indicating the passage of sixteen years, thus establishing a structure based on showing rather than telling?

在探讨莎剧结构的时候，经常发现在全剧的中心位置，某个事件、某个戏剧场景对剧情的发展有着举足轻重的作用。这种情况不仅存在于莎士比亚的悲剧之中，也存在于他的喜剧和历史剧中。

莎士比亚笔下的悲剧、喜剧、历史剧和悲喜剧的最大特点，就是不恪守亚里士多德为这些剧种写下的定义。就像莎士比亚的悲剧中往往有喜剧成分、他的喜剧中常有悲剧倾向一样，他的历史剧中既有喜剧因素，更有悲剧的成分。这种创新精神在很大程度上恰恰是戏剧天才的最真实的表现。作者在本章的结尾处谈到了 showing 和 telling 之间的关系，是不是所有的剧作家都面临同样的抉择？莎士比亚在这方面有什么独到之处？

Chapter 6

Sources

Antony and Cleopatra and Plutarch

At some time during 1606–7, when he was writing his tragedy *Antony and Cleopatra*, Shakespeare must have been sitting at a table with a copy of Thomas North's translation of the classical Greek historian Plutarch as *The Lives of the Noble Grecians and Romans* (1579), open at page 981, the life of Marcus Antonius. We can see that a section of North's prose, about two-thirds of the way down the right-hand leaf, caught his eye. North is describing how Mark Antony fell in love with Cleopatra:

> Therefore when she was sent unto by divers letters, both from Antonius himself, and also from his friends, she made so light of it, and mocked Antonius so much, that she disdained to set forward otherwise, but to take her barge in the river of Cydnus, the poop whereof was of gold, the sails of purple, and the oars of silver, which kept stroke in rowing after the sound of the music of flutes, hautboys, citherns, viols, and such other instruments as they played upon in the barge. And now for the person of her self: she was laid under a pavilion of cloth of gold of tissue, apparelled and attired like the goddess Venus, commonly drawn in picture: and hard by her, on either hand of her, pretty fair boys apparelled as painters do set forth god Cupid, with little fans in their hands, with the which they fanned wind upon her. Her Ladies and gentlewomen also, the fairest of them were apparelled like the nymphs Nereides (which are the mermaids of the waters) and like the Graces, some steering the helm, others tending the tackle and ropes of the barge, out of the which there

113

came a wonderful passing sweet savour of perfumes, that perfumed the wharfside, pestered with innumerable multitudes of people. Some of them followed the barge all alongst the rivers side: others also ran out of the city to see her coming in. So that in the end, there ran such multitudes of people one after another to see her, that Antonius was left post alone in the market place, in his Imperial seat to give audience: and there went a rumour in the peoples' mouths, that the goddess Venus was come to play with the god Bacchus, for the general good of all Asia.

Shakespeare famously cuts and reshapes this evocative description into the unexpectedly lyrical account by the cynical Roman Enobarbus to his fellow soldiers:

> MAECENAS She's a most triumphant lady, if report be square to her.
> ENOBARBUS When she first met Mark Antony, she pursed up his heart upon the river of Cydnus.
> AGRIPPA There she appeared indeed, or my reporter devised well for her.
> ENOBARBUS I will tell you.
> The barge she sat in, like a burnished throne
> Burned on the water. The poop was beaten gold;
> Purple the sails, and so perfumèd that
> The winds were lovesick with them. The oars were silver,
> Which to the tune of flutes kept stroke, and made
> The water which they beat to follow faster,
> As amorous of their strokes. For her own person,
> It beggared all description: she did lie
> In her pavilion – cloth of gold, of tissue –
> O'er-picturing that Venus where we see
> The fancy out-work nature. On each side her
> Stood pretty dimpled boys, like smiling Cupids,
> With divers-coloured fans, whose wind did seem
> To glow the delicate cheeks which they did cool,
> And what they undid did.
> AGRIPPA   O, rare for Antony!
> ENOBARBUS Her gentlewomen, like the Nereides,
> So many mermaids, tended her i'th'eyes,
> And made their bends adornings. At the helm
> A seeming mermaid steers. The silken tackle
> Swell with the touches of those flower-soft hands
> That yarely frame the office. From the barge
> A strange invisible perfume hits the sense

> Of the adjacent wharfs. The city cast
> Her people out upon her; and Antony,
> Enthroned i'th'market-place, did sit alone,
> Whistling to th'air, which but for vacancy,
> Had gone to gaze on Cleopatra too,
> And made a gap in nature.   (2.2.195–228)

We can see how the vocabulary reverberates between North and Shakespeare: Cydnus, barge, poop, 'cloth of gold of tissue', Nereides, perfume, wharf, tackle, Cupids, pretty boys, mermaid, city, flutes, marketplace, purple, silver oars, stroke, wind, Venus, helm, gentlewomen. This level of lexical dependency makes it immediately clear that Shakespeare's description owes a great debt to North's.

But it is this evident similarity between the two passages that, paradoxically, allows us to identify something we might want to call distinctly 'Shakespearean'. We can see that Shakespeare has done something different with this material: different in intensity and in effect. For the most part those shared words are nouns; Shakespeare adds a number of adjectives – 'burnished', 'beaten', 'divers-coloured', 'dimpled', 'silken' – to a passage which has relatively few, thus thickening its sensuality, and heightening its erotic charge. Verbs and attributes appropriate to humans are repeatedly given to inanimate objects: it is the winds that are 'lovesick', the water 'amorous', a version of melodrama in which desire is laterally displaced from humans onto the surrounding environment. Whereas North has the people 'follow' and run to see this tableau, Shakespeare makes the city itself expel its citizens. He extends North's device of *ekphrasis* – a rhetorical figure denoting a self-contained set-piece description, sometimes of a work of art – into hyperbole and the impossibility of representation, from 'commonly drawn in picture' to 'o-er-picturing'. For Enobarbus there is something about Cleopatra which 'beggared all description': even in the act of evocative description, there is that 'gap' between representation and object, unlike North's workmanlike introduction 'and now for the person of herself'.

We can see, too, how the iambic line (for more on this, see chapter 4, Language) imparts its own musculature to the scene, as Enobarbus switches from the prose of barrack-room gossip into the verse of unwilling infatuation. The unfilled half-line after 'I will tell you' takes on the quality of an expectant pause. The words at the end of each line are given subtle emphasis by their placement; 'the tune of flutes kept stroke' in a line that enacts its own rhythmic assertion; the repeated 'id' sounds in s*id*e, Cup*id*, d*id*, un*did did* chime with the d's of dimpled, delicate, divers, wind to tighten North's looser aural syntax in 'with the which they fanned wind upon her' with its muffling 'th' and 'ch' sounds. The difference between North's Antonius 'left post alone' and Shakespeare's Antony – the added detail of his insouciant whistling is nicely done, a tiny hint of the pride that features so strongly in his later suicide – abandoned by the very air, enthroned and solitary, is striking. The passage in North ends with a gesture of equivalence between the great lovers as Venus and Bacchus; it's a small but telling testament to Shakespeare's insistence on Cleopatra in a tale he sees not as 'The Life of Marcus Antonius', as in North, but *Antony and Cleopatra* – that the focus remains on her throughout Enobarbus' speech. Like the disappearing Egyptian crowds, that is to say, we too are looking at Cleopatra even when, as now, she is not on stage – as always, she is stealing the scene from the Romans, and from Antony. The play itself enacts Antony's own fascination with Cleopatra that it at once defames and desires; like Antony we are always chafing to return from the sterile rigour of the Roman scenes to the pleasurable cadences of Egypt.

Originality: was Shakespeare a plagiarist?

Perhaps the question of originality needs to be taken head on at this point. Does our view of Shakespeare's creativity take a knock when we discover that almost every one of his plays follows a major extant source and that only *A Midsummer Night's Dream*, *The Merry Wives of Windsor* and *The Tempest* could claim to have a Shakespearean plot? Some of those sources are, like North's translation of Plutarch, or like Holinshed's monumental history of England used for the history plays, evidently open on the table before him as he works; others, such as the old play *King Leir* discussed below, or the survivors' story of a shipwreck on Bermuda which provides some details and stimulus for *The Tempest*, show an influence which may have been transmuted through memory. Whereas for modern writers this level of indebtedness might well be seen as a failure of imaginative resource, a paucity of that gift of inventive originality which forms one of our most sustained current aesthetic categories, for a writer in the late sixteenth century making use of previous literary models and texts was a validated cultural activity. ('Originality' does not even take on its meaning of 'freshness of style or character, esp. in a work of literature or art' (*Oxford English Dictionary*) until the late eighteenth century.)

Nor does Shakespeare attempt to hide his source material. He alerts us to the debt to Chaucer at the beginning of *Two Noble Kinsmen*, and he has another medieval poet, Gower, onstage as a narrator in *Pericles*. Indeed, he even uses a source as a stage prop on one occasion. In his tragedy *Titus Andronicus*, Shakespeare uses the Ovidian story of the ravished Philomel as an analogue to the story of Titus' daughter Lavinia. The story is a kind of challenge to Chiron and Demetrius, her rapists, who use it as an instruction book for their crimes, determining not to be caught out like Philomel's attacker Tereus by adding their own touch of cutting off Lavinia's hands so that she cannot reveal their names. The source also may be seen to dictate Titus' action in eventually killing Lavinia, whose prototype Philomel and also Lucrece, die because of their shame at being raped: Titus alludes to the pattern, although a different example, when he asks Saturninus: 'Was it well done of rash Virginius / To slay his daughter with his own right hand / Because she was enforced, stained, and deflowered?' (5.3.36–8). The source material is thus woven into the verbal fabric of the play and into the characters' motivations and actions. Shakespeare has read his Ovid – but so too have Saturninus, Titus, Chiron, Demetrius and Lavinia. Ominously for the future, Rome's children (like their counterparts in Elizabethan grammar schools), too, are reading Ovid, and here the source is brought deliberately onstage. Young Lucius brings on a copy of Ovid among his schoolbooks, and it is this which offers Lavinia the prompt to reveal the names of her attackers. Studies of *Titus Andronicus* have tended to be preoccupied by its bloodiness (as discussed in chapter 5, 'Structure'), but its unusually dense engagement with its source also renders the play curiously literary, a self-consciously written kind of a text, meditating on its own relation to the literary past via its allusions to its source material. Rather like pop artist Andy Warhol's iconic screenprints such *Marilyn*, *Elvis*, or *Campbell's Soup Cans*, that is to say, *Titus Andronicus* is archly self-conscious about its own derivativeness.

Ringing the changes, making small alterations to an existing story, retelling the familiar in a slightly unexpected way: these were the hallmarks of the writer brought up on the Elizabethan grammar school's diet of rhetorical textbooks and translation in and out of Latin, and in and out of different metrical patterns. The Elizabethans enjoyed familiar stories and genres. 'Imitation', learning from other writers and imitating previous literary and stylistic models, was a high status artistic endeavour. As Shakespeare's contemporary playwright Ben Jonson put it, drawing appropriately on classical authorities including Horace and Seneca, the poet must

> be able to convert the substance or riches of another poet to his own use.
> To make choice of one excellent man above the rest, and so to follow
> him till he grow very he, or so like him as the copy may be mistaken for
> the principal. Not as a creature that swallows what it takes in crude, raw,

or undigested, but that feeds with an appetite, and hath a stomach to concoct, divide, and turn all into nourishment. Not to imitate servilely, as Horace saith, and catch at vices for virtue, but to draw forth out of the best and choicest flowers, with the bee, and turn all into honey, work it into one relish and savour; make our imitation sweet; observe how the best writers have imitated, and follow them.

It's Shakespeare's task of digestion or blending, and the interplay between copy and principal, recognisability and difference, with which the study of his sources is primarily concerned.

In his study *The Anxiety of Influence*, the critic Harold Bloom has given us an influential paradigm for conceptualising the ways in which poets respond to the legacy of their literary forebears. 'Strong poets', Bloom contends, have 'the persistence to wrestle with their strong precursors, even to the death'; the 'battle between strong equals, father and son as mighty opposites, Laius and Oedipus at the crossroads' is what quickens literary genealogy and the creative mind of the poet. While Shakespeare is explicitly excluded from Bloom's study – because of his 'absolute absorption of the precursor' (only Marlowe is judged a worthy 'strong equal' to Shakespeare) – Bloom's concept of the writer's violent struggle with literary tradition is nevertheless an illuminating frame for Shakespeare's different use of his source material.

Shakespeare at work: the intentional fallacy?

That image of Shakespeare copying and changing North's *Lives* gives us a precious, almost fetishistic glimpse, perhaps, of the playwright at work. We saw how 'Shakespeare's hand' in *The Book of Sir Thomas More* (chapter 3, 'Texts') was a sort of secular relic, and source study may seem to offer a similar fantasy of closeness as if by comparing Shakespeare's work with that of his sources we recover that moment of composition, and gain a kind of insight into Shakespeare's creative mind. And while the language of authorial intention – the idea that we can and should assess from the evidence of the text in front of us the author's intention, a critical manoeuvre sometimes called 'the intentional fallacy' – is usually a smokescreen for critics' own interpretations, it does sometimes make a furtive hermeneutic return in source study.

If, for example, we take *Measure for Measure*, at the heart of which is the story of Angelo, the corrupt governor who tries to get Isabella to have sex with him to release her brother Claudio from jail, we can see this basic story structure in a number of folkloric traditions before Shakespeare. Because he uses it for the contemporaneous play *Othello*, Shakespeare's immediate source is likely to be the Italian Geraldi Cinthio's *Hecatommithi*, a collection of prose stories first published in 1565. In Cinthio's story, the woman Epitia is the central character in the play. Her sixteen-year-old brother is in prison for raping a woman, and his offer to marry his victim has not commuted the death sentence hanging over him. Epitia consents to sex with the official in order to save her brother. When all is revealed, he is forced to marry her, and then she successfully pleads for his life. Again, we can see Shakespeare's evident debt to this story, but with some key differences.

Firstly, Cinthio's character is in prison for rape. Shakespeare makes it clear that Claudio is not a habitual fornicator, and that he considers Juliet 'is fast my wife' (1.2.128), and her reply to the Duke's 'Love you the man that wronged you?' – 'Yes, as I love the woman that wronged him' (2.3.25–6) tells us and him that her pregnancy is the result of mutual and consensual love-making, not coercive violence. Shakespeare's change blurs a moral absolute, making Claudio much more sympathetic than he might have been were he guilty of rape, and thus made the severity of Angelo's interpretation of the law seem all the more unreasonable. Secondly, Shakespeare has made his Isabella into a nun, or at least a novice nun. Our sympathy towards her religious scruples about sex with Angelo is a key axis in this unflinchingly interrogative play – can we agree with her strong statement 'more than our brother is our chastity' (2.4.186)? Isabella is not simply a woman of upright moral character but one about to devote herself to strict religious principles – another, we might say, of the extremists in Shakespeare's play. For her, to give up her body is to give up her soul. Thirdly, Shakespeare develops the character of the Duke, who, in the disguise of a friar observes much of what is happening and plots to engineer his complicated moral and marital denouement (discussed at the beginning of chapter 2, 'Performance'). In the sources, the Duke figure returns at the end as the classical *deus ex machina* – the fantastical and authoritative personage who enters the stage at the end to bring about the final conclusion. By retaining him throughout as 'a looker-on here in Vienna' (5.1.313), Shakespeare implicates the Duke in the seedily sexualised world of the city, even as he mystifies his motives.

All three of these changes – substituting of consensual sex for rape, making Isabella into a nun, and developing the role of the Duke – could be said to bring moral questions to the fore of Shakespeare's drama, and the evidence that these have been introduced deliberately makes it difficult to explain them away as somehow incidental or irrelevant to the plot. We are on safer critical ground arguing that Shakespeare *intends Measure for Measure* to raise moral questions (although we still need to question the relevance of the search for intention), rather than to provide answers, when we can trace such a range of purposive, intentional changes to the source material.

The source bites back: *Romeo and Juliet* and *The Winter's Tale*

This image of Shakespeare making purposive and intentional changes to his source material suggests that the writer is supremely in control of his material: Bloom's strong poet meets the seven-stone literary weakling. Indeed, source studies have tended to be distorted by an implicit assumption that pre-eminent among Shakespeare's changes to his sources is the change from 'not very good' to 'genius'. But there are examples of sources which remain immanent in Shakespeare's plays, or, to put it another way, they don't just roll over but put up a fight however he attempts to subdue them.

Romeo and Juliet might be a good example here. Although the story of the parted lovers and the apparently fatal draught of potion has a number of antecedents, Shakespeare's immediate source is a long narrative poem translated by Arthur Brooke from Italian via French as *The Tragicall History of Romeus and Juliet* (1562). Brooke's popular poem tells how the two lovers, forbidden to meet because of their families' feuding, take advice from Juliet's nurse and a friar, and eventually die within minutes of each other after Juliet is believed dead. So far, then, so familiar. But there are some highly significant Shakespearean twists to Brooke's narrative.

Although Brooke's poem presents the lovers sympathetically, his prefatory material is sternly didactic in tone. The Preface tells the reader that 'every example ministreth good lessons to the well-disposed mind' – arguing that the mind disposed to good can learn a welcome lesson either from positive examples – what they ought to do, or from negative ones – what they should never do:

> And to this end, good reader is this tragical matter written, to describe unto thee a couple of unfortunate lovers, thralling themselves to unhonest desire, neglecting the authority and counsel of parents and friends, conferring their principal counsels with drunken gossips and superstitious friars (the naturally fit instruments of unchastity) attempting all adventures of peril for the attaining of their wished lust, using auricular confession (the key of whoredom and treason) for furtherance of their purpose, abusing the honourable name of lawful marriage, to cloak the shame of stolen contracts, finally, by all means of unhonest life, hasting to most unhappy death.

Table 6.1. *Prologues to Arthur Brooke's* Romeus and Juliet *and Shakespeare's* Romeo and Juliet

Brooke's *Romeus and Juliet*	Shakespeare's *Romeo and Juliet*
Love hath inflamed twain by sudden sight.	Two households, both alike in dignity,
And both do grant the thing that both desire.	In fair Verona (where we lay our scene),
They wed in shrift by counsel of a friar.	From ancient grudge break to new mutiny,
Yong Romeus climbs fair Juliet's bower by night.	Where civil blood makes civil hands unclean.
Three months he doth enjoy his chief delight.	From forth the fatal loins of these two foes
By Tybalt's rage, provoked unto ire,	A pair of star-crossed lovers take their life;
He payeth death to Tybalt for his hire.	Whose misadventured piteous overthrows
A banished man he 'scapes by secret flight.	Doth with their death bury their parents' strife.
New marriage is offered to his wife:	The fearful passage of their death-marked love,
She drinks a drink that seems to reave her breath.	And the continuance of their parents' rage,
They bury her, that sleeping yet hath life.	Which but their children's end nought could remove,
Her husband hears the tidings of her death.	Is now the two hours' traffic of our stage;
He drinks his bane. And she with Romeus' knife,	The which if you with patient ears attend,
When she awakes, her self (alas) she slayeth.	What here shall miss, our toil shall strive to mend.

The strong message here is that Romeus and Juliet, far from being tragic or innocent, are rather silly, libidinous, wayward, disobedient – and, crucially for the Protestant readers of Brooke's English version, Catholic.

We can see immediately that Shakespeare has abandoned this moralistic framing. He hasn't, however, altogether jettisoned the idea of prefatory material: *Romeo and Juliet* begins with a Prologue, written in the fourteen-line sonnet form, which has its counterpart at the head of Brooke's poem. Comparing the two can open up some big issues for Shakespeare's play and for his alterations to his source (table 6.1).

There are lots of points of difference to discuss here: here are some suggestions for starters:

- How do the two prologues frame the story of the lovers within the context of the feud?
- To whom, or to what, does each attribute the tragic events?
- Are there differences in the presentation of love versus sex?
- Which, and how much, detail does each offer the reader?
- How do Brooke and Shakespeare each make use of the sonnet form?
- Does the fact that both play and poem begin by sketching out what's going to happen tell us anything about the literary tastes of their first audiences?
- In the 1623 Folio text of *Romeo and Juliet* there is no Prologue (see chapter 3, 'Texts', for more detail on Shakespeare's earliest texts). How would the play be different without it?

In Shakespeare's play, the children's actions are ennobled, especially by contrast to the bigotry of their families. The feud between Montagues and Capulets seems so pointless as to have no moral authority, and the play encourages us to follow the lovers and to identify our narrative hopes with them. By implicitly supporting children against parents, the play challenges an accepted social hierarchy, the necessary obedience of children to their parents, particularly over the issue of their marriage. The Prince ends the play by turning on the patriarchs of the two feuding families: 'see what a scourge is laid upon your hate' (5.3.292). In addition, as was discussed in chapter 5 on structure, Shakespeare introduces a new character – Mercutio. Perhaps Mercutio, Shakespeare's major supplement to his inherited story, bears the burden of trying to change that script. Perhaps we could see him as Shakespeare's challenge to the solemn tragedy of Brooke's story – a character of wit and satiric deflation whose purpose is to undermine Romeo's melancholic pretensions towards tragedy. With his death, that comic energy is gone, and the trajectory of tragedy, already sketched in the source, becomes irresistible. We might see Mercutio then as Shakespeare's attempt to wrest his material out of its generic frame. The death of Mercutio, you'll remember, is by accident, almost due to a lapse in authorial concentration as he takes his eye off the theatrical ball and thus fails to control Romeo's habitual rashness in rushing between the swordsmen: perhaps this might be read as the playwright's failure fully to master his story and to rewrite its ending. All he can do is write some puns around Mercutio's death to remind us of what has been squandered.

It's interesting how much Shakespeare's prologue to *Romeo and Juliet* stresses fortune – the inevitability of what happens. The lovers are 'star-crossed', and 'misadventured', the family loins are 'fatal', bringing forth death instead of life. We could wonder where this inevitability comes from; it's not present in the sonnet in Brooke, although we could argue it is implicitly present in his narrative construction of bad deeds being punished in a world overseen by a just God. In Shakespeare's play who is controlling this plot? Why is it all so fated from the outset? One answer to this might be that the source is controlling the plot. However much else Shakespeare can change, he can't, as the death of Mercutio might attest, change the ending. One way, therefore, of conceptualising Shakespeare's relation to his sources is that the sources retain something of their initial integrity: they cannot be fully transformed and assimilated into their new dramatic lodgings. While Shakespeare can change details, for instance – some of these are suggested in the 'Where next' section at the end of this chapter – he doesn't change the outcome. In *Richard III*, for example, there may be a certain amount of admiration of Richard III's machiavellian energy, and his nemesis Richmond may be dramatically stymied by being so very lacklustre, but that's as far as Shakespeare can go: Richmond is still going to win at the battle of Bosworth Field. Shakespeare's *Romeo and Juliet* may seem to buck the moralistic gloss of Brooke's source poem, but his play still ends in tragedy for the lovers. If children go against their parents' wishes, that's to say, we may pity them, but they still have to die: there is no possibility for Shakespeare's lovers to escape the bigotry of Verona and live in happiness in that trailer park Baz Luhrmann's film (1996) imagines as the play's Mantuan exile.

This pull of the source may help explain some of the strangeness of the ending of the late play *The Winter's Tale*. The first half of Shakespeare's play tells how Leontes, King of Sicilia, becomes convinced that his pregnant queen Hermione has been having an affair with his best friend Polixenes, king of Bohemia. Only when he has banished his new-born daughter and heard of the death of his wife and his son does Leontes realise the enormity of his passionate jealousy. The second half of the play introduces us to the daughter, Perdita, who has been brought up by a shepherd in Bohemia, and who has fallen in love with the disguised son of Polixenes, Florizel. When Polixenes hears of his son's entanglement with an apparently unworthy woman, the couple flee to Sicilia to escape his anger and throw themselves on the mercy of his erstwhile friend Leontes. It is revealed that Perdita is Leontes' lost daughter, Polixenes and Leontes are reconciled through the union of their children, and, in a final *coup de theatre*, Hermione is revealed to have been alive all this time after all. Much of this follows the contours of Robert Greene's prose romance *Pandosto. The Triumph of Time* (1588), in which Pandosto = Leontes, Bellaria = Hermione, Fawnia = Perdita, Dorastus = Florizel, and Egistus = Polixenes. But Shakespeare's ending of the story is rather different.

In Greene's *Pandosto*, when Dorastus (Florizel) and Fawnia (Perdita) arrive at Pandosto's court, the king, 'contrary to his aged years, began to be somewhat tickled with the beauty of Fawnia' (he doesn't know at this point that she's his longlost daughter), and his 'frantic affection' for her grows despite his efforts to deny it. Fawnia, however, rejects his advances summarily: 'I had rather be [Dorastus'] wife and a beggar, than live in plenty and be Pandosto's concubine.' Pandosto, 'broiling at the heat of unlawful lust', has Dorastus imprisoned. Hearing of this, Egistus commands Pandosto to kill Fawnia as an unworthy bride for a prince and to return his son to him. Pandosto wants to be reconciled with Egistus, and decides to follow his instructions, but then Porrus, Fawnia's foster-father, reveals the jewels and seal found with her, and Pandosto recognises her as his lost daughter. All seems to be reconciled, but Pandosto cannot enter into the rejoicing and marriage celebrations '(calling to mind how first he betrayed his friend Egistus, how his jealousy was the cause of Bellaria's death, that contrary to the law of nature he had lusted after his own daughter), moved with these desperate thoughts, he fell into a melancholy fit, and to close up the comedy with a tragical stratagem, he slew himself'.

Greene's phrasing is interesting: Pandosto's suicide turns a comedy into a tragedy. Shakespeare's ending seems to reverse this, and to turn a tragedy into a comedy. By keeping Leontes alive at the end, by miraculously returning Hermione to him, and by evading the issue of the king's incestuous desire for his unrecognised daughter, Shakespeare wrests the tragedy of the opening acts into apparently comic redemption for both generations. But we might look a little more closely at what is going on in the play to see the faint but undeniable outline of those darker forces.

Shakespeare's late plays, of which *The Winter's Tale* is one, are preoccupied with the relationship between fathers and adult or near-adult daughters. It's arguable that all these relationships bear the slight traces of incestuous desire. Thus we have Prospero and Miranda in *The Tempest* and paternal aggression to the threats to her chastity in the form of Caliban and Ferdinand, Cymbeline and Innogen in *Cymbeline* where the wicked stepmother is jealous of the king's natural daughter, and, most prominently, Pericles and Marina. *Pericles* begins with an explicit scene of father–daughter incest at Antioch. Presenting himself as a suitor to the king's daughter, Pericles has to answer her riddle in order to win her hand: 'I am no viper, yet I feed / On mother's flesh which did me breed. / I sought a husband, in which labour / I found that kindness in a father. / He's father, son, and husband mild; / I mother, wife, and yet his child. / How this may be, and yet in two, / As you will live resolve it you' (1.1.65–72). Unfortunately, it's not rocket science. But Pericles' fear for his own life means he can neither confront the incest nor refuse to answer the riddle. Instead he escapes and is condemned to a long series of sea voyages, at the end of which he is reunited with his own lost daughter, Marina, who is another sexual anomaly: a chaste prostitute who has brought one of the brothel's clients, the governor of Mytilene, to repent his ways and propose marriage to her.

So we know that Shakespeare's long interest in father–daughter relationships, from comedies such as *As You Like It* or *The Merchant of Venice* through a tragedy such as *King Lear*, reaches a particular intensity in these late plays. But we also know that, reading Greene's *Pandosto*, Shakespeare has chosen to omit this dynamic between Leontes and Perdita. Or at least he has structured the play to suppress – or perhaps, as a more psychoanalytical vocabulary might have it, to sublimate – incestuous desire. If we read carefully, however, we might see Leontes' first encounter with Perdita marked by this taboo. The young couple's entrance follows a discussion between Leontes and his conscience/keeper/confidante Paulina about Hermione's beauty, in which Paulina extracts from the king a promise that he will not remarry without her permission. When he sees Perdita, then, Leontes' mind is on his queen, but he is full of praise for Florizel's young bride's beauty, and 'sorry / Your choice is not so rich in worth as beauty' (5.1.212–3). When Florizel says that his father will grant Leontes anything, the king's hypothetical wish is not for the couple's marriage but for himself: 'I'd beg your precious mistress' (222), which earns from Paulina the reproving 'Your eye hath too much youth in't' (224).

There is no further discussion between father and daughter. It is almost as if the play stares into the face of Pandosto's incestuous desires, and is too frightened to go further. The scene in which Leontes recognises Perdita as his daughter is recounted, not shown (there's more on telling, as opposed to showing, in chapter 5 on 'Structure'). And most extraordinarily of all, Hermione is revealed to be alive: she returns to claim Leontes, to mop up that 'youth' in his eyes, to divert sexual desire back into marriage and away from incest. Lest this seem an improbable causality, let's look at the way Shakespeare structures his ending, particularly in relation to his previous plays.

Perhaps one of the reasons Shakespeare is so popular is that he makes us, the audience, feel smart. His plays are crucially dependent on dramatic irony, the technique by which audiences know more than the characters on stage. We know that both sets of twins are hurtling around Ephesus in *The Comedy of Errors*, even though it takes a while for the Antipholuses and Dromios to work it out, and much of our pleasure in the play derives from watching the comic misunderstandings proceeding from their ignorance. We know that Viola in *Twelfth Night* and Rosalind in *As You Like It* are women disguised as men; we know that Iago means no good to Othello; we know that Macbeth has killed

Duncan; we know that the merry wives are playing a trick on their Windsor husbands. The plays are always structured to put us ahead of the game. Late in his career, therefore, in *The Winter's Tale*, there is no reason for us to doubt the truth of Paulina's terrible announcement in 3.2: 'The Queen, the Queen, / The sweet'st, dear'st creature's dead' (199–200). Leontes exits the scene saying 'Prithee bring me / To the dead bodies of my queen and son' (233–4); since, as we find out later, Hermione is not really dead, this request is an impossibility, but nothing in the lines alerts us to this discrepancy. Of course, Paulina could wink to the audience, or she could overplay her already histrionic lines in the scene to give us a clue that this is all a performance to punish Leontes' fatal jealousy – but this isn't scripted. Antigonus, Paulina's husband who is charged with depositing the infant Perdita far from Sicilia, even sees the ghost of Hermione in a dream, an apparent corroboration of her death, since, in, for example, *Richard III* or *Julius Caesar*, ghosts, even those in dreams, are of people we know to be dead. So, contrary to the usual structure, dramatic irony is suspended. We know no more than Leontes. The play tells us Hermione is dead, so Hermione is dead.

It is only after Perdita's reappearance at court that we hear anything to prepare us for Hermione's 'revival'. One of the gentlemen discussing the reunion of father and daughter mentions that Paulina is about to reveal a statue of Hermione, and his interlocutor concurs: 'I thought she had some great matter there in hand, for she hath privately twice or thrice a day, ever since the death of Hermione, visited that removed house' (5.2.103–6). It's a rather late indication of what is to come, patched into a narrative which has little need of Hermione given that its terminal energies are now focused towards the next generation's recovery of what their elders have lost. So maybe the strangeness, the unexpectedness, of Hermione's return, unlike her still-dead counterpart Bellaria in Greene's *Pandosto*, should be seen as part of Shakespeare's wrestling with his source, and with that troubling incest he is trying to banish from his comic ending. The hasty and belated way in which Hermione's survival is reintroduced as a possibility might indeed give us a glimpse of Shakespeare effortfully at work – but working to flex his own writerly muscle on his source material. He needs to quash the incest story, and he does it by providing another mate for Leontes. Perhaps it's relevant to introduce one of Seneca's metaphors for the process of imitation. The writer's own work shouldn't be quite identical to its predecessors: 'I would not have you resemble him as a child resembles his father.' It's striking that a play so concerned with paternity, with the resemblances between father and son (and, here especially, mother and daughter) should also be so involved in matters of intergenerational literary relationships. Source study here becomes inextricable from the thematics of the play: as in

Titus Andronicus, we can read a self-conscious meditation on the relation to the source in the fantastical ending of *The Winter's Tale*.

The strong poet? *King Lear*

So far the sources we have looked at are clearly sources for Shakespeare – but may not be sources for his first audiences. Since we don't know with any certainty how far the reading public in the period overlapped with the theatre-going public, we can't know whether spectators at early performances of, say, *The Winter's Tale* were mentally comparing it with their recollection of the thirty-year old prose romance *Pandosto*, and we can be fairly sure that no one in the Globe was following North's Plutarch with their finger as the first Enobarbus delivered his eulogy on Cleopatra. Thus *Pandosto* and the *Lives* serve as what we might categorise as sources for *composition*, rather than sources for *reception*. To make a modern analogy, we might think about the example of a modern film – say Franco Zeffirelli's *Hamlet* (1990). Zeffirelli has clearly read *Hamlet* in order to make his adaptation, but the majority of the cinema-going public probably hasn't. The only demographic fact we know about people who go to the cinema is just that – that they go to the cinema. So their 'sources' for Zeffirelli's *Hamlet* are more likely to be previous films – perhaps Mel Gibson's *Lethal Weapon* trilogy (Zeffirelli apparently identified Gibson as a potential Hamlet having seen him playing a scene as a zany cop with suicidal tendencies in *Lethal Weapon* (dir. Richard Donner, 1987)), or Glenn Close (Gertrude) as the psychotic bunny-boiling *femme fatale* in *Fatal Attraction* (dir. Adrian Lyne, 1987) – and it is interesting to think how these associations might shape audiences' reading of these characters in Zeffirelli's film. (There's more on this, and on the related idea of 'fantasy casting', in chapter 2, 'Performance'.)

So what we know about audiences for *King Lear*, first performed in 1605–6, is that they went to the theatre. And since *King Lear* is unusual among Shakespeare's plays in having a previous play, rather than prose or poetry, as a substantial source, we might be able to assume that at least some members of the audience were familiar with that play, the anonymous *The True Chronicle Historie of King Leir and his Three Daughters* published in 1605, three years before the first printed text of Shakespeare's play. This text of Shakespeare's, incidentally, trumpets in huge type that this is by Shakespeare – it's the first time in the publishing history of Shakespeare's plays that the author's name has had first billing, presumably to differentiate it from its near namesake (see chapter 3, 'Texts', for more on this topic, and for some discussion of Shakespeare's own double vision of *King Lear*). If *Romeo and Juliet* and *The Winter's Tale* seem to carry within them the ghostly outline of their sources, a sense of struggle with the precursor, this creative *agon* (conflict) is submerged in the process of composition. *King Lear*, on the other hand, gives us an example of Shakespeare changing the ending of his sources to dramatically violent effect – and what is important about this transformation is that it is a dynamic part of the play's reception.

King Leir, the source play, begins with a long speech from Leir:

> Thus to our grief the obsequies performed
> Of our (too late) deceased and dearest Queen
> Whose soul I hope, possessed of heavenly joys,
> Doth ride in triumph 'mongst the Cherubins;
> Let us request your grave advice, my Lords,
> For the disposing of our princely daughters,
> For whom our care is specially employed,
> As nature bindeth to advance their states,
> In royal marriage with some princely mates.
> For wanting now their mother's good advice,
> Under whose government they have received
> A perfect pattern of a virtuous life:
> Lest as it were a ship without a stern
> Or silly sheep without a Pastor's care;
> Although our selves do dearly tender them,
> Yet are we ignorant of their affairs:
> For fathers best do know how to govern sons.
> But daughters' steps the mother's counsel turns.
> A son we want for to succeed our crown,
> And course of time hath cancelled the date
> Of further issue from our withered loins:
> One foot already hangeth in the grave,
> And age hath made deep furrows in my face:
> The world of me, I of the world am weary,
> And I would fain resign these earthly cares
> And think upon the welfare of my soul,
> Which by no better means may be effected
> Than by resigning up the crown from me
> In equal dowry to my daughters three.

We can see from this opening speech that Shakespeare has made a number of changes. Firstly, this king Leir's behaviour is precisely situated as a response to the death of his wife. His clearly articulated feeling is that without a mother to look after and advise them, his daughters are vulnerable, and this prompts him to settle them with husbands. His own sense of his own age has been exacerbated by the death of his wife. He mourns the fact that he has no son, and that he is past begetting one. He wants to withdraw from political life, to prepare his soul for his own death, and to divide the kingdom equally between his daughters. Government of the state – even the word 'government', and the metaphor of the ship, commonly used of state politics – has been devolved onto government of the family, upset by the queen's death. All this psychologically and politically plausible motivation is given at the outset in this long introductory speech.

When we compare this with Shakespeare's Lear, we can see how radically different, in terms of being radically underexplained, his king's behaviour is. Shakespeare's play begins not with the aged king setting out his reasons, but with courtiers discussing which of his sons-in-law he prefers 'in the division of the kingdom' (1.1.3–4). Lear's queen is evidently not part of the play: we never get any mention of her. (The 'Where next' section gives some suggestions about how this pattern of excised or marginalised mothers in Shakespeare might be further explored.) And nowhere do we discover why, at this particular point, he has decided to take this cataclysmic step: critics and performers have been divided about whether it represents an early sign of the senility with which he is increasingly afflicted during the play. We are not sure in Shakespeare's play whether Lear ever intends to divide his kingdom equally – his invitation to Cordelia to 'draw / A third more opulent than your sisters' (1.1.80–1) suggests that this pie has already been cut in her favour. We can intuit that the problem of succession for Shakespeare's Lear is that there is no son – and Lear's misogyny is clear in lines such as 'Down from the waist they're centaurs, / Though women all above. / But to the girdle do the gods inherit; / Beneath is all the fiend's. / There's hell, there's darkness, there is the sulphurous pit, burning, scalding, stench, consumption' (4.5.120–5), but that is not stated so clearly.

Shakespeare thus makes mysterious certain motivations in his play that the anonymous play of *King Leir* renders more explicit. Making motivations more blurred is a key aspect of Shakespeare's engagement with his sources – in the source for *Othello*, for example, Cinthio's *Hecatommithi*, we are told clearly that the Iago character, called simply 'Ensign', plots to destroy 'the Moor', Othello because he 'fell ardently in love with Disdemona'. Shakespeare's refusal to perpetuate this simple causal dynamic has led to one of the most-asked characterological questions in Shakespeare's works: why does Iago do what he does – and in looking at the sources we can speculate that the prompting of this question is crucial and perhaps intentional to Shakespeare's design for his play. Similarly the sources for *Hamlet* make it clear that the Hamlet character feigns madness as a cloak for his active revenge strategy; Shakespeare's Hamlet's intent

'To put an antic disposition on' (1.5.172) is less clearly motivated, and slides more seriously into 'real' madness than do his counterparts in the sources.

Other changes to the source make certain aspects of Shakespeare's design clear. In the second scene of *King Leir* we hear a private conversation between the two older sisters about how they hate their favoured younger sister: 'All the court hath work enough to do / To talk how she exceedeth me and you.' Even though they go on to do terrible things in the play, there is a sneaking sympathy for them which is structurally different from the way Shakespeare introduces his three sisters. Gonerill and Regan's first speeches in Shakespeare's play are their obsequious, public, and highly rhetorical responses to Lear's love-test, and hence we have no access to them other than via their self-interest; this is contrasted with the introduction of Cordelia who seems to address us directly, confiding private, sincere thoughts in the asides punctuating her sisters' inflated speeches. Comparing Shakespeare's introduction of his characters and the scenario with that of the writer of *King Leir* can help sharpen our sense of his structure – discussed in more detail in chapter 5. If in the case of Lear's own motivations, Shakespeare has made his character less readable than his counterpart in the sources, in the case of the wicked daughters he seems to have done the opposite, simplifying their characterisation.

The most significant change, however, is at the end of the play. In common with every other Lear story before Shakespeare's – there's more on these in the 'Where next?' section at the end of this chapter – the old play of *King Leir* ends with the reconciliation of Leir and Cordella, and the defeat of Gonorill and Ragan's forces at the hands of Cordella and her husband, the king of Gallia. Resigning his throne with gratitude to his son-in-law, 'For it is yours by right, and none of mine', Leir recognises that Cordella always loved him:

> Ah, my Cordella, now I call to mind,
> The modest answer, which I took unkind:
> But now I see, I am no whit beguiled,
> Thou lovedst me dearly, and as ought a child.

Leir has got what he wanted – has abdicated his throne in favour of the son he never had – the King of Gallia whom he calls 'my son'. There is no sense that it was his foolish and impossible wish to abdicate that caused all the disturbance – rather it was the unnaturalness of his two eldest daughters which set everything at variance, and their deaths mean order is restored. In Shakespeare's play, by contrast, the suggestion is that it is Lear's abdication which causes all the upset, and that this situation cannot be retrieved except by Lear's death, the proper way for the throne to pass to another. As with the unkinged Richard in *Richard II* who is left untidily alive as his successor Bullingbrook ascends the throne,

Lear can't be left hanging about while someone else takes over the kingdom – the succession and the new order can only be ratified by the death of the old monarch – a way, perhaps, of saying that kings simply can't abdicate.

But Lear is not the only, nor for many readers and viewers of Shakespeare's play the most shocking, casualty of the play. When he enters in 5.3 bearing Cordelia in his arms, this poignant stage image registers some of the emotional weight of a reverse pieta. Something has gone terribly wrong. Cinderella must not die. Like Lear himself, the audience is in disbelief. In none of the sources for the play does Cordelia pre-decease Lear: in all of the previous Lear stories the favoured younger daughter is preserved, rewarded, and becomes queen after his death. Here the strong poet quite clearly takes on the full momentum of the received story and deliberately and significantly changes its ending. It is hard, given this shift from the sources, to deny the bleakness, the unredeemed quality, of Shakespeare's play, his cruel refusal to allow the comforting fiction of the fairy-tale which shapes both the plot and our expectations of its conclusion. By perverting this expectation of redemption, Shakespeare's play challenges any easy equivalence of tragedy, justice, and morality. The scene of Lear and Cordelia's reconciliation at the end of Act 4 becomes, in retrospect, a structural device for ratcheting up the despair at the end of the play. The death of Cordelia shows us the strong poet doing literary press-ups, one-handed, taking control of the source material and exulting in his mastery. When Kent asks, bewildered by the sight of the aged king bearing the lifeless body of his favoured daughter, 'Is this the promised end?' (5.3.237) he speaks as much for the audience as for the characters left at the play's bitter conclusion.

Shakespeare's negotiation of his sources thus engages a dialogue at once conscious and submerged: between the playwright and his predecessors, and between the playwright and his audience. Sources do not answer questions about Shakespeare's plays; rather, they tend to reveal that the prompting of questions, rather than the supplying of answers, is crucial to his dramatic praxis.

Sources: where next?

- If you have access to a university or college library, the standard collection of Shakespeare's source material is Geoffrey Bullough's 8-volume *Narrative and Dramatic Sources of Shakespeare* (Routledge, 1957–75). Bullough reprints the sources and begins the work of processing the differences in introductory essays arranged by play. Many individual play editions of Shakespeare – the New Cambridge, Arden or Oxford editions – include source material in appendices. There are some good online source sites: Thomas North's translation of Plutarch's *Lives of the Noble Grecians and Romans*, used by Shakespeare for *Antony and Cleopatra*, *Julius Caesar*, and *Coriolanus* is available and searchable via the Perseus Project: http://www.perseus.tufts.edu/cache/perscoll_Renaissance.html#text1; the Furness collection at the University of Pennsylvania has digitised its copy of Raphael Holinshed's *Chronicles of England* (1587), used by Shakespeare for the history plays and for *King Lear*: http://dewey.library.upenn.edu/sceti. Other sources are linked to from the excellent gateway 'Mr William Shakespeare and the Internet' at http://shakespeare.palomar.edu/sources.htm.

- Harold Bloom's book *The Anxiety of Influence* outlines his argument about 'strong poets': the introduction to the second edition (Oxford University Press, 1997) develops his idea that Shakespeare, notwithstanding his writerly rivalry with Marlowe, stands apart from this literary narrative. (The most stimulating account of Shakespeare's relation to Marlowe throughout his career is in Jonathan Bate, *The Genius of Shakespeare*, Picador, 1997.) Another, less Oedipal and less masculinist, version of this genealogy is in W. Jackson Bate's *The Burden of the Past and the English Poet* (Chatto and Windus, 1971). On the 'intentional fallacy', a term coined by W. K. Wimsatt and Monroe Beardsley in their 1946 essay of the same title, see Seán Burke (ed.), *Authorship, from Plato to the Postmodern: A Reader* (Edinburgh University Press, 2000) and Andrew Bennett's concise and clever *The Author* in Routledge's New Critical Idiom series (2005).

- Other significant characters Shakespeare has added to his plays include Paulina in *The Winter's Tale*, Enobarbus in *Antony and Cleopatra*, Lucio in *Measure for Measure*, Falstaff in *1* and *2 Henry IV*, the Fool in *King Lear*. He keeps Queen Margaret alive for *Richard III* when her real life counterpart was already dead. What function do these characters perform in their plays? By contrast, some of the characters removed by Shakespeare from his sources include Hero's mother in *Much Ado About Nothing* (there's a trace of her ghostly presence in the 1600 quarto text's opening stage direction '*Enter Leonato gouernour of Messina, Innogen his wife, Hero his daughter, and Beatrice his neece, with a messenger*', usually emended by editors), or the child born to Iago and Emilia in the sources for *Othello*: to what effect have these characters been omitted?

- To read more of *King Leir*, see the online transcribed text at http://pages.unibas.ch/shine/kingleir.html. Marina Warner discusses *King Lear* briefly as a Cinderella-type story in her study *From the Beast to the Blonde: On Fairy Tales and their Tellers* (Chatto and Windus, 1994); Jane Smiley's *A Thousand Acres* (1992), filmed by Jocelyn Moorhouse in 1997, retells a version of the *King Lear* story from the point of view of Ginny/Gonerill. It is interesting to compare the version from which Shakespeare departs with the similar adaptations made in the eighteenth century to Shakespeare's play. Samuel Johnson's distress at the death of Cordelia meant that he could not reread the play's ending, and he observed that the popular rewriting by Nahum Tate (1681), in which Cordelia survives to marry Edgar, answered the need for justice in tragedy: 'a play in which the wicked prosper, and the virtuous miscarry, may doubtless be good, because it is a just representation of the common events of human life: but since all reasonable beings naturally love justice, I cannot easily be persuaded, that the observation of justice makes a play worse' (see my *Blackwell Guides to Criticism: Shakespeare's Tragedies*, Blackwell, 2004, for this and more on pre-twentieth century Shakespeare commentary); there's an accurate online text of Tate's version at http://andromeda.rutgers.edu/~jlynch/Texts/tatelear.html. But if Shakespeare's changes to the *Lear* sources seem to go against 'justice', his alterations to the history of Scotland he uses for *Macbeth* do the opposite: out of a story of dog-eat-dog infighting, Shakespeare sanctifies Duncan's rule and makes Macbeth's regicide an act of evil rather than of politics. Holinshed's *Chronicles of Scotland*, Shakespeare's source for *Macbeth*, is available in a digitised facsimile from the Furness Collection at http://dewey.library.upenn.edu/sceti.

- On mothers in Shakespeare we might think about Hero's shadowy mother, discussed above, alongside the absence of mothers from *As You Like It*, *Two Gentlemen of Verona*, *A Midsummer Night's Dream*, *1 Henry IV*, *Othello* – or the representation of Volumnia in *Coriolanus* or Gertrude in *Hamlet*, or the chorus of bereaved mothers in *Richard III*, or the issue of the Macbeths' childlessness discussed in chapter 1, 'Character'. In his biography of Shakespeare (1998) Park Honan proposes that Mary Arden, Shakespeare's mother, was overprotective of her baby son born during plague years in Stratford (fun and suggestive, but approach such biographical speculation with caution!); an essay by Mary Beth Rose asks 'Where are the Mothers in Shakespeare: Options for Gender Representation in the English Renaissance' (*Shakespeare Quarterly*, 42, 1991); Janet Adelman takes a more psychoanalytic look in her wonderful *Suffocating Mothers: Fantasies of Maternal Origin in Shakespeare's Plays, 'Hamlet' to 'The Tempest'* (Routledge, 1992).

对莎士比亚剧作故事来源的研究为我们揭示了戏剧大师的创作方式：以经典作品或广为流传的通俗故事为蓝本，对故事中的情节、人物或事件做些改动，用一种更有激情的方式来重述，就产生了莎翁笔下独特的戏剧故事，它们往往比原作更有激情、更有感染力，当然也有更强的生命力。你觉得作者对莎士比亚的《罗密欧与朱丽叶》和布鲁克的长诗的对比有说服力吗？

Chapter 7

History

Politic picklocks: interpreting topically

Ben Jonson's play *Bartholomew Fair* (1614) begins with a prologue scene, in which the audience is drawn into a legal bond with the play, its actors and author, and the obligations of each party are drawn out in wonderful mock-legalese. Here's an example:

> the foresaid hearers and spectators [. . .] neither in themselves conceal, nor suffer by them to be concealed, any state-decipherer, or politic picklock of the scene, so solemnly ridiculous as to search out who was meant by the Gingerbread-woman, who by the Hobby-horse man, who by the Costermonger, nay, who by their wares; or that will pretend to affirm, on his own inspired ignorance, what Mirror of Magistrates is meant by the Justice, what great lady by the Pig-woman, what concealed statesman by the Seller of Mousetraps, and so of the rest.

Don't overinterpret, this part of the 'contract' tells the audience (although presumably the injunction not to find real-life parallels for the characters in the play is designed to prompt exactly that speculation). Don't be a 'state-decipherer' or a 'politic picklock'. Your job is to enjoy the play for what it is. Sometimes a Gingerbread-woman is just a Gingerbread-woman.

Unlike Jonson, Shakespeare doesn't include explicit commentary on his own dramatic art: he doesn't give us any prologues on his didactic aims, or address his audience in so direct a way. But the idea that contemporary audiences tended towards topical interpretation, tended to read dramatic characters and scenes in terms of real-life personages and events, is a useful one to consider in relation to Shakespeare. We are so used, following – coincidentally – Jonson again, to seeing Shakespeare as 'not of an age, but for all time' (from the eulogy 'To the Memory of my beloved, the author Mr. William Shakespeare: And what he hath left us' published in the First Folio in 1623), that we often overlook the immediate context in which his plays were produced and consumed. That is to say, we value aspects we see as 'timeless' – recognisable emotions, or quotable poetry – over those which might have their roots more directly in the cultural or political milieu of their first performances. And since plays in the period had only a limited number of performances over the course of a few weeks, and that they were largely performed in what we would now call 'modern' (i.e. Elizabethan, rather than Roman, medieval etc.) dress, they were particularly likely to reflect on, or be interpreted in the light of, current affairs. Sometimes this is a matter of a particular local reference: when the steward Malvolio convinces himself that his employer Olivia favours him despite the disparity in their status, he adduces an example which probably relates to some contemporary gossip about a similar cross-class liaison: 'The Lady of the Strachy married the yeoman of the wardrobe' (2.5.34–5). On other occasions the topicality is more oblique: how might Prospero's dominance over his island kingdom in *The Tempest* engage with contemporary discussions about nascent English colonisation, or how might it affect responses to the plebeians if we connected the disturbances about food prices with which *Coriolanus* begins with the similar riots in the Midlands in the months preceding the play's composition?

Of course, historical reading – one of the dominant modes of current Shakespearean scholarship – demands special subtlety of interpretation. Contrary to what we might think from a surface reading of Shakespeare's plays, the Elizabethans were not more likely to give birth to twins, nor to deliver long soliloquies at points of particular stress, nor were Elizabethan women much, apparently, in the habit of dressing as men, nor was love at first sight any more common than it is now. The high body count at the end of a tragedy such as *Hamlet* does not reflect a more violent era or a more casual attitude to murder. In fact the associations of 'reflection' are, as many critics have noted, always inadequate for the reciprocal and nuanced relations between a literary work and the culture producing and consuming it. Shakespeare's plays are not documentaries, and we need to beware of assuming that the plays represented 'real life' for their earliest audiences. The case of *Romeo and Juliet* is a cautionary one: it was long assumed that because Juliet is married at fourteen, the age of marriage must have been, in general, rather lower in Elizabethan England than it is in Britain today. This apparent historical 'fact' was then used to support an interpretation of the play in which the youth of the central couple is relatively unremarkable. But demographic research by historians has revealed that in fact the average age of marriage in the late sixteenth century was well in the twenties for both partners, so marriage at fourteen would indeed have seemed anomalous. What does this mean for the play? Well, it activates a range of meanings, including perhaps that Juliet would have been considered still a child, and that the role of the Nurse might seem more relevant, perhaps that her father's decision to marry her to Paris might have seemed harsh, perhaps that the play was always more about adolescent sexuality than the iconic grand passion our culture has harnessed to it.

So, while we can't see *through* Shakespeare's plays to the culture that produced and consumed them – Shakespeare's plays are milkily resistant to this sort of transparency – reading Shakespeare's plays in their historical moment can generate some unexpected piquancy, or make sense of apparently opaque references. Just as Hollywood films now are a long way from most of our lives – all action heroes and extreme drama and perfect teeth – we can still see that their plots, characters and structures play out contemporary cultural narratives about gender roles, the individual against the system, the threat from the 'other', the valorisation of survival, the need for excitement and suspense. We'll see that Shakespeare's plays engage with his contemporary world in some similar ways.

History plays: political Shakespeare?

Perhaps it is most obvious to begin with a group of plays explicitly concerned with political life: Shakespeare's English history plays. During the 1590s, history was one of the dominant literary genres – in prose, poetry and drama – a popular cultural form, therefore, not necessarily a personal interest of Shakespeare's. History provided a means of relating the present to the past and future, it was an important element in the establishment of English national and religious identity, and, crucially, it allowed for the veiled discussion of current political issues. Thus the exiled Jesuit priest Robert Parsons adduced examples from history to illustrate his argument that the line of royal succession might be altered by the people in certain circumstances (he wanted to argue for the claims of a Spanish princess to the post-Elizabethan English throne); for John Foxe history proved the inevitable justness of the Protestant faith (good people in the Catholic past had been proto-Protestants, had it been available to them); for the Florentine political philosopher Niccolo Machiavelli, history showed how politics was the result of human, rather than divine, actions (God didn't seem especially to have reserved his protection for morally good rulers); examples from history gave John Stubbs the misguided confidence to advise Queen Elizabeth against marrying a French nobleman, arguing that French and English royal marriages in the past had always turned out badly (he had his writing hand cut off for his trouble). History, therefore, was never firmly in the past, but instead offered a curious temporal amalgam with its moral exemplars and warnings and its cycles of repetition, echo, prophecy, prefiguring, expiation, and the extended, sometimes mysterious, mechanisms of cause and effect.

History was not, then, a matter of recovering the truth of the past, but of constructing a contingent truth for current pragmatic purposes. It was always politically loaded and subjectively laced, and for these reasons, therefore, the writing of history was topical and immediate – sometimes explicitly. In the Chorus to Act 5 of *Henry V*, the audience at the Globe in 1599 is invited to imagine the joyful and triumphant return of Henry to London bringing victory at Agincourt, and their imagination is piqued with a contemporary parallel:

> As, by a lower but by loving likelihood
> Were now the general of our gracious empress,
> (As in good time he may) from Ireland coming,
> Bringing rebellion broachèd on his sword,
> How many would the peaceful city quit,
> To welcome him?   (5.0.29–34)

The 'general of our gracious empress' is the Earl of Essex, sent in the spring of 1599 by Elizabeth to quell the Earl of Tyrone's rebellion in Ireland. Ireland had been a thorn in the side of the Tudor administration for years, and this became acute in the last decade of the sixteenth century, when London poured money, troops and supplies across the Irish Sea in prosecuting an unwinnable war one historian has memorably dubbed 'England's Vietnam'. The Chorus thus makes a parallel between Henry's campaign in France and Essex's in Ireland, and a range of other references to Ireland in the play, not found in the sources, reinforce the simile. The play gives us Captain Macmorris, Shakespeare's only Irish character, Pistol's apparently Gaelic remark 'Colin o custure me' (4.4.3), the references to 'kern of Ireland' and 'foul bogs' (3.8.49–53), and Henry's promise to Katherine that 'England is thine, Ireland is thine, France is thine' (5.2.217–8). In the Folio text of 1623 (the Irish material would be a good point of comparison between Q, 1600, and F: see chapter 3, 'Texts', for more discussion) Queen Isabel of France greets the victorious Henry as 'brother Ireland' (5.2.12): editors often describe this as an error and emend, as does Andrew Gurr in his New Cambridge edition, but in the context of that much-desired victory in Ireland, it seems an error more Freudian than casual. So, thinking about the first performances of the play, probably during early summer 1599, we can see Henry's miraculous victory over France as a projection of, a vicarious fulfilment of, contemporary hopes for Essex's success in Ireland. The play is performing then something of the same social or cultural function as, for example, Laurence Olivier's film version did in another war-torn context in 1944 (discussed in more detail in chapter 2, 'Performance').

History plays: Shakespeare as propagandist?

If we read *Henry V* in this way, does that make Shakespeare a propagandist? Much of the discussion about the way Shakespeare's plays engage with contemporary issues has been distorted by a desire to discern Shakespeare's own politics in the plays, and to argue for these politics as either conservative or radical. Thus the English history plays, including *Henry V*, have long been interpreted as a kind of veiled commentary on the political milieu of the 1590s. For conservative critics they have seemed collectively to present an orthodox view that the deposing of a king – in *Richard II* – is a terrible crime for which generations of expiation must be served before the guilt is cleared and the new dynasty – the Tudors – can take over at the end of *Richard III*. For critics who have wanted to co-opt Shakespeare for a different politics, on the other hand, the history plays have seemed to enact the cyclical *realpolitik* of individual pragmatism: kings rise and fall in their turn, outside any grand moral schema; the structure of the individual plays temporarily freeze-frames, rather than resolves, the historical process.

In fact it's probably more accurate, and more fruitful, to interpret Shakespeare's historical plays as documents of changing contemporary views of historical narrative and of causation, rather than as ideologically committed political drama. They prompt questions, rather than provide answers. Shakespeare isn't writing for the authorities, neither ideologically nor practically. And just as Shakespeare's sources and his culture mobilised a range of ways of thinking about historical events, from the Providentialism of the medieval church – 'things happen according to God's will' – to the radical human-centred historiography of Machiavelli – 'things happen because humans make them so', so too different characters and different plays give us different views of why things happen. Thus Bedford begins *1 Henry VI* lamenting over the coffin of Henry V and demanding that 'Comets, importing change of times and states, / Brandish your crystal tresses in the sky, / And with them scourge the bad revolting stars / That have consented unto Henry's death' (1.1.2–5), offering a cosmic correspondence between worldly events and heavenly phenomena;

arch-individualist Richard Duke of Gloucester delights in his megalomania in *Richard III* with the assertive first-person pronoun 'I do the wrong' (1.3.324); Henry IV counsels his reprobate son that his power is dependent on the popular perception of the king's separateness from the people, and tells the Prince of Wales that 'thou hast lost thy princely privilege / With vile participation' (*1 Henry IV*, 3.2.86–7); Henry V greets news of his victory at Agincourt by acknowledging divine assistance: 'O God, Thy arm was here! / And not to us, but to Thy arm alone / Ascribe we all' (4.8.98–100). (In the account of the English defeat of the French in *Henry V*, Shakespeare has apparently deliberately de-emphasised from his source material the technological superiority of the English longbows, and the human battle tactics in which sharpened stakes were used to arrest the French cavalry in order to strengthen this providential interpretation.)

If tragedy, as the discussion of the prologue to *Romeo and Juliet* in chapter 5 suggests, is in part about answering the question of agency, history shares its interest in the intersection between human and metaphysical action. And it, too is engaged with the issue of consequences. What happens if you usurp a monarch, as does Bullingbrook in *Richard II* (answer: wait and see). What happens if, like King John, you plot to kill your innocent rival for the throne and twit the papal legate (answer: your 'bowels crumble up to dust' (5.7.31) when you are poisoned by a vengeful monk). We could not without wilfully ignoring counter-evidence attribute to Shakespeare a single view of historical causation or consequence, nor a particular political position, but we can see reiterated through the history plays an interest in the questions, rather than the answers.

What is also clear is that the history plays' fascination with rebellion and with the transfer of power owes something to contemporary concerns with the ageing and childless Elizabeth's unknown successor. The unspeakable – literally, in that it was punishable by death – question of who would take the throne after Elizabeth's death is transmuted into the various jockeyings for power that we see throughout the history plays' sustained avoidance of stable or long-term government. (As the product of a decade during which most living English people would have known no other ruler than Elizabeth, this is particularly striking.) Instead of portraying political stability, the history plays are insistently curious about and attentive to the struggle for power. Thus, for example, the Bullingbrook who takes the throne at the end of *Richard II* and immediately expresses concerns about his absent son, emerges at the beginning of the next play already besieged and threatened: 'So shaken as we are, so wan with care' (*1 Henry IV* 1.1.1), without even the shortest honeymoon period as monarch. When the noblemen shift sides to back Bullingbrook in *Richard II* we see how an oligarchy bends in the political wind; when the rebels plot to partition a conquered England between them in *1 Henry IV* there's a rehearsal of one possible future political scenario in which the nation is divided between rival factions; when the citizens of Angiers are commanded to recognise first John and immediately after, Arthur, as their rightful king in Act 2 of *King John*, the possibility of competing successors is obliquely raised. All of these could be seen as dramatic responses to cultural uncertainty, or as ways of vicariously anticipating the post-Elizabethan world order.

By the end of the 1590s the Elizabethan Privy Council had taken control of the genre of history, requiring that all works of English history should be authorised before publication. Probably Shakespeare's shift to Roman history with *Julius Caesar* (1599), registers this increased state control – and allows him more explicitly to explore the question of what makes a good leader. It's no coincidence that in this first play to turn away from the regal infighting which has dominated the English histories, the political crime for which Caesar is assassinated is the desire – perhaps – to be crowned king and to replace the republic with a monarchy: as Brutus muses, 'He would be crowned: / How that might change his nature, there's the question' (2.1.12–3). But the interest in who governs and in dynasties continues. The Roman plays, in taking as their setting different eras of Rome's development, dramatise different models of government from elective empire in *Titus Andronicus*, the republic and its aftermath in *Julius Caesar*, and the system in which an unwilling Coriolanus is persuaded to sue for the popular vote to become a consul. All of these systems propose some political involvement by the citizenry, although for the most part the people are seen to be easily manipulated by their social superiors, as over the body of Caesar in the middle of *Julius Caesar*. It's interesting to compare the presentation of the Roman plebeians with the relatively infrequent depiction of their English equivalents in the history plays: Jack Cade and his rebels in *2 Henry VI*, perhaps, or the common soldiers in *Henry V*. No version of perfect government emerges from the plays, no ideological or narrative *telos* (aim, ultimate purpose) can be easily discerned. But what we can see is a series of plays which keep returning to pick at this scab of Elizabethan political life.

Hamlet as history play?

And this is the case not just with the plays most obviously about immediate historical events. In the context of the English history plays which preceded it, it's interesting to look at *Hamlet*'s relation to its contemporary culture. *Hamlet* may be *the* play above all others that has been thought to evade the historical circumstances of its initial composition, in its apparent anticipation of modernity in Hamlet's own tortured exploration of selfhood. Thus Michael Almereyda's film (2000) of the play set in a modern corporation called Denmark Inc. (discussed in chapter 2, 'Performance') is only an extreme version of a widespread critical tendency to see Hamlet, and *Hamlet*, as contemporary not with the end of the sixteenth century but with an always relative 'now'. By valorising *Hamlet* as a tragedy, we have focused on the internal agonies of its central protagonist, rather than on the political consequences of his situation – and, notably, those productions of the play which have been most concerned with a tragic Hamlet – Laurence Olivier's 1948 film is a good example – have tended to cut his successor Fortinbras entirely, thus endorsing the structural and psychic solipsism of Hamlet's own 'the rest is silence' (5.2.337).

How might the play be different, though, if we thought about it in terms of the time when it was written and first seen? There are a number of echoes between the history plays and *Hamlet*: the stress on father/son inheritance, the unquiet presence of the past, the rivalry between legitimate and illegitimate successors, foreign quarrels versus domestic politics. Like the plays based on narratives from medieval English history, *Hamlet* dramatises different models of kingship and succession, and interrogates past, present and potential occupants of the Danish throne. From the opening scenes, in which the Elsinore sentinels threaten a figure bearing 'that fair and warlike form / In which the majesty of buried Denmark / Did sometimes march' (1.1.47–9) – an oblique figure for regicide which anticipates both the Ghost's description of his murder and its representation as 'The Murder of Gonzago' – the play repeatedly rehearses images of political violence. Why, for example, are the people apparently so ready to back Laertes, who seems such a random choice for king; or how is it that the hostile Hamlet-double Fortinbras is able to march unhindered into Denmark and into the throne?

The question that must have been pivotal to succession-junkies at the end of the sixteenth century – why doesn't Hamlet himself inherit on the death of his father? – is one the play can scarcely articulate but one which haunts its presentation of monarchy. Reactivating the play's history play credentials brings this issue to the fore. Instead of Hamlet as everyman – a character with whose inner struggle we commoners are encouraged to identify – we might instead see Prince Hamlet as a frustrated political subject – perhaps his 'antic disposition' (1.5.172) might be structurally analogous to that of another Prince, Hal, dallying in the Eastcheap taverns in *1* and *2 Henry IV* – denied agency in quite specific affairs of state, rather than through more general psychic alienation. The sense of dynastic foreclosure with which the play reverberates is played out in its final scene, in which the Danish succession is ultimately decided by conquest, and Fortinbras's thin-lipped eulogy on the dead prince takes on the exultant quality of a sneer: 'he was likely, had he been put on, / To have proved most royal' (5.2.376–7). In dramatising the terminus of a bloodline, *Hamlet*'s ending may be the most apocalyptic of Shakespeare's visions of the political consequences of the extinction of the Tudors on the death of Elizabeth – and what is valuable about this sort of interpretation is the political corrective it gives to readings of the play focused minutely on the psychodrama inside Hamlet's own mind.

Jacobean patronage: *King Lear* and *Macbeth*

A number of studies of Shakespeare's plays have seen the break between the reigns of Elizabeth and James as a crucial division. While a number of Shakespeare's plays are known to have been performed at Elizabeth's court (including *Love's Labour's Lost* and *The Merry Wives of Windsor*), the Queen's direct involvement in the theatre was rather less than that of her successor. When James VI of Scotland came to the English throne in 1603, one of his first actions was to take on the patronage of Shakespeare's company, and the Lord Chamberlain's Men became the King's Men. What effect did this have on their chief playwright? Well, it is clear that Shakespeare's Jacobean tragedies all speak to this particular political climate – but in some complicated ways.

Let's start with *King Lear*. If we look again at Shakespeare's sources for *King Lear* we can find a number of registers operating within the play: the folkloric Cinderella antecedents, the comic historical chronicle play called *King Leir*, domestic melodrama via contemporary gossip about a nobleman called Brian Annesley, whose youngest daughter protects him from her sisters who want to have him certified insane so they can annex his property. An important contemporary source, however, is a more immediate political one. One dominant strand of James VI and I's agenda on acceding to the English throne was a policy of uniting England and Scotland. Arguing that his two kingdoms, adjacent and ruled by the same monarch, should be united into one, James proposed it not as a radical innovation (never a good thing) but as a return to how things used to be in the ancient island kingdom of Britain, which was once unified until Brute divided it between his three sons.

The political buzzwords of 1605, then, were 'unification of the kingdoms' – just in the way that phrases from modern news media and advertising such as 'weapons of mass destruction' or 'I did not have sexual relations with that woman Miss Lewinsky' or 'Coke: it's the real thing' come to be widely understood, echoed, circulated and parodied (these examples will come – perhaps as you read it they already have – to date this book as surely as the recognisability of the 'unification of the kingdoms' has, in this respect, dated *King Lear*). This gives a climate in which Gloucester's ominous phrase 'the division of the kingdom' (1.1.3–4) – almost the first words of the play – must have struck a particular contemporary note. Gloucester tells us that the king is proposing to act contrary to the received political wisdom of the time. We could argue that, seen in this context, the play was more a political tragedy than a personal one – and that the division of the kingdoms, powerfully symbolised by the actual sketching out of new boundaries on a map, just as James promulgated his plans for unity by commissioning maps of ancient Britain – is not just an arbitrary signifier of family disunity but a powerful political metaphor related to James' plans for the union of England and Scotland. The relationships within the play are thus politicised: Lear's identity as king becomes more prominent than his familial role; the daughters, including Cordelia whose return from France with an army is differently treated in q and f (see chapter 3, 'Texts', for more on this), become political rivals rather than merely unfilial serpents' teeth; Lear's recognition of the sufferings of his people 'O I have ta'en / Too little care of this' (3.4.32–3) gains in weight if the play is seen to participate in a discourse about good government. If the play doesn't quite come out saying unity is strength, it does suggest that disunity is weakness and that the consequences of Lear's abdication and the breaking up of the kingdom are disastrous.

Perhaps, then, *King Lear* might be seen to begin from an immediate political impulse. But as with the Elizabethan history plays, there is something in excess of propaganda here in *King Lear* – that quality of doing more than is required which the nineteenth-century critic William Hazlitt usefully called Shakespeare's habitual 'supererogation'. So *Lear* is not just a parable about the folly of breaking up a kingdom, nor a creative depiction of Brute's division of ancient Britain, but its immediate political echoes give a useful counter to over-generalised accounts of timeless 'tragedy'.

There are other ways to see Shakespeare's company playing to their new patron's tastes. *Macbeth* famously speaks to the king's well-publicised interest in witchcraft – he had published in Scotland a book called *Daemonologie*, which London publishers scrambled to reprint on his accession to the English throne – although Shakespeare had already written about witchcraft in the character of Margery Jordan in *2 Henry VI*. In deriving his material from Holinshed's *History of Scotland*, however, Shakespeare represents that Scottish ancestry which James claimed to trace back to the descendants of Banquo. When the witches' final apparition reveals to Macbeth a line of kings with the last one holding up a mirror, it may be that at the first performance James himself would have been reflected in the mirror, thus extending the lineage into the current generation.

And, of course, it is only in Jacobean performances of the play that one of the witches' other prophecies finally comes true – the prediction that Banquo 'shalt get kings, though thou be none' (1.3.65), and in fulfilment of which Fleance must escape his murderers in 3.3. The Stuart genealogy had as its mythical claim to royal status the marriage of Fleance's son to a princess, and thus what remains in the text as a loose end – *how* will Banquo's descendants become kings – is settled in a historically specific performance context. It is probable that the idea of equivocation in the play – most explicitly in the Porter's speeches in 2.3 – links to contemporary allegations, following the Gunpowder Plot in 1605 and the trial of Henry Garnet, a leading Jesuit, that Jesuits countenanced lying in the name of religion. But lest this all seem too sycophantic, there are counter-arguments too: *Macbeth* does not unambiguously flatter James. Scotland, after all, is in a pretty lawless and bloody state until help arrives – and that help comes from England. Writing for the popular theatre, Shakespeare is more likely to be influenced by public demand than by royal command.

Historical specificity: gender roles

So far I've discussed history as if it concerns things that were relevant then but obscured now: the Elizabethan succession, James' theatrical patronage. On the one hand, it doesn't take much of a leap of imagination to see that a play about kings and political life might be interpreted topically; on the other, kingship and rule, even if updated to modern democratic contexts, still look like quaintly historical categories. In the rest of the chapter I want to use history to think about historical continuity and disruption – to examine aspects of the plays we may think do not need to be made historical, and to see what difference it makes when we do. Take, for example, apparently 'universal' markers: cultural institutions such as marriage, gender roles, the idea of race. These may seem to us so familiar as to require no elucidation, but when we consider them historically they emerge as local and specific – then, as now.

Let's begin with that crucial element of Shakespearean comedy: marriage. Modern marriage, in most Western contexts, denotes a freely-chosen partnership of compatible, monogamous, heterosexual individuals who have got to know each other through courtship, who talk of their relationship in terms of romantic love and mutual companionship, and who live together. (Of course, *actual* modern marriages are far more various than this general outline suggests, but we might still recognise this as a normative statement.) Shakespeare's comedies are full of people heading towards marriage. But the two uses of the term 'marriage' here may be the equivalent of 'false friends' in the learning of a new language: those words that look as if you know what they mean because they are similar to a word in your own language, but turn out to mean something different after all. Can we, or how can we, access early modern marriage practices through the plays? How far might we assume that the courtships of, for example, Beatrice and Benedick in *Much Ado About Nothing* or Perdita and Florizel in *The Winter's Tale* follow contemporary expectations and mirror early modern experience? And how is this different from our own assumptions about marriage?

Again, caution against over-literal interpretation is required: the fictional world of the plays doesn't give us a transparent window into the world of their first audiences. But, with the help of some historical material suggested in the 'where next?' section, we could still see some early modern anxieties being played out. The urgency with which Beatrice and Benedick's friends bring about their unwilling union, and the way in which the play constructs their marriage as the happy ending to which it is structurally bound, may tell us something about the contemporary importance of marriage and the impossibility of the single life both partners initially espouse. In fact Shakespeare's plays have very little room for young people – particularly women – to reject marriage: like Beatrice, Katherina in *The Taming of the Shrew*, Olivia in *Twelfth Night*, and Isabella in *Measure for Measure*, all declare themselves opposed to husbands and none is left unmarried at the end of her play (unless Isabella rejects the Duke's proposal – see chapter 2, 'Performance', for more discussion of the staging possibilities of the conclusion).

The importance of family, particularly paternal, consent in marriage is also played out in the comedies. Like Egeus in *A Midsummer Night's Dream* and Portia's dead father in *The Merchant of Venice*, Polixenes wants to control his son's marriage choices: his fury on seeing that Florizel has apparently thrown his royal self away on a shepherdess is a frightening echo of Leontes' earlier passionate jealousy. Although contemporary marriages among the upper classes were often contracted between families rather than individuals, the acceptance of the children involved was widely seen as a precondition of a sound marriage. There was, however, a general assumption that parents would be consulted about their children's plans: court records attest to the legal sanction parents could exact when they were excluded from marriage negotiations.

Shakespeare's plays often tread a careful line between sympathy for children making their own marriage choices and the rights of parents to be involved. Sometimes the strategy is to structure the plays so that the young people are effectively orphaned and therefore cannot gain parental consent when they make their choices, such as, for example, Ferdinand in *The Tempest*, or Rosalind in *As You Like It*; sometimes the technique is derived from older comic forms, such as Roman New Comedy, which depend for their generic resolution on the circumvention of the blocking parent figure, as in *A Midsummer Night's Dream* and, in a different key, *Othello*. For the most part, however, as with *The Winter's Tale*, the children's own choice is ratified as eminently suitable: left to their own devices, they choose partners of an appropriate social status who might well have been chosen for them by their parents. Thus Perdita is not a shepherdess, and Florizel has bestowed his affections wisely; Phoebe's mistaking of 'Ganymede' as a potential partner in *As You Like It* is a social transgression more on grounds of class than of gender. By contrast, Malvolio, we remember, is humiliated at the end of *Twelfth Night* because of his presumption of marrying above his station. While on the one hand Shakespeare's plays seem to challenge parental authority and champion individual choice and romantic love, they do this by representing the end result as entirely socially consonant.

Much interest in recent criticism has been focused on the impact of male actors in female roles in the Shakespearean theatre, particularly in those plays where cross-gendered disguise is a part of the plot. So when Rosalind appears in Arden she is a male actor playing a female character (Rosalind) playing a man (Ganymede). As with readings of the English history plays, critical debate has tended to focus on whether these layered gender representations are orthodox or radical – whether they reinscribe gender orthodoxy or subject it to a destabilising critique. By passing as men, female characters in the plays may seem to challenge the legibility of binary sexual difference, and draw a disconcerting attention to the performance by male actors of their own 'femaleness'. Within the plots, however, women do not tend to use this to gain forms of power typically associated with masculinity. No one in Shakespeare's plays dresses as a man in order to be a pirate or a doctor or to challenge the assumptions which set out certain public possibilities for men and largely domestic or private ones for women, and it may be unreasonable, in historical terms, to expect that they might. Even Portia only wows the Venetian court as the formidably knowledgeable and eloquent lawyer Balthasar in order to preserve her husband's best friend. Instead, women dress as men to further romance plots and to gain access to their loved ones – girls' stuff. As with Rosalind and Viola, Julia's disguise as Sebastian in *Two Gentlemen of Verona* is rewarded by marriage: she persuades her former love Proteus away from his infatuation with Silvia and marries him, just as Viola is the only one of the married foursome at the end of *Twelfth Night* to get the partner she has wanted from the outset, and Rosalind's relationship with Orlando looks positively mature when compared with the abrupt courtship of Celia and Oliver, the lackadaisical union of Phoebe and Silvius and the wry pairing of Touchstone and Audrey. We might deduce from this that female–male cross-dressing does not pose a social threat: it is rewarded rather than punished, but equally we might argue that in playing with gender hierarchies, it expands possibilities that are not fully closed down at the end of the play (see chapter 3, 'Texts', for a related discussion of the ending of *As You Like It*). Looked at on their own terms, then, the plays are not stable as either orthodox or radical: they participate in ideologies of gender rather than represent them as fixed.

It's interesting to look at this pattern of cross-dressed women alongside another possible cultural 'false friend' – the issue of sexuality. It is a truism of historical criticism that sexual identities, and in particular the labels 'homosexual' or 'gay', are not legible in the early modern period in the way they might have become in the later twentieth century. It's equally true, however, that highly charged same-sex relationships or encounters *were* thinkable and possible during the Renaissance: while the period predates the terms 'homosexual' and 'homosexuality', it does not predate those emotional and sexual bonds we might now group under those labels. And male–male friendships enjoyed a high status in Renaissance society: Montaigne's essay 'Of Friendship' talks of this bond in terms we might now allocate to marriage: 'one soul in two bodies'. Shakespeare's plays often give us versions of intense male – and, less often, female – relationships, and in the comedies we see that these relationships are potentially at odds with the formal drive to marriage. Portia's joking about the rings at the end of *The Merchant of Venice* has a serious point: having heard her new husband state that he would 'sacrifice' 'my wife and all the world' (4.1.280) to gain Antonio's life, she needs to reinforce marital commitment over the men's deep friendship. So too Beatrice's 'Kill Claudio' (4.1.279) in *Much Ado About Nothing*: if Benedick loves her, he must show it by severing himself finally from his best friend. Perhaps the cross-dressed heroines of *Twelfth Night* or *As You Like It* offer a symbolic way in which the conflict between male–male friendships and heterosexual marriage can be reconciled: Orsino and Orlando gain wives who can simultaneously pass as the male companions so valorised by Montaigne.

Here, thinking historically works to contextualise strong same-sex bonds in the plays within a discourse of friendship. The loss through this procedure is that it may seem to closet any suggestion of homosexuality in a historical blur. But other historically supported, less conservative, readings, are possible. Let's take, for example, the relationship between Antonio and Sebastian in *Twelfth Night*. Antonio has rescued Sebastian from drowning, and is so devoted to him that he endures the danger of returning to Illyria for his friend's sake and gives him free access to his purse during their stay. In a couple of lines of soliloquy after their first scene, Antonio speaks of his affections: 'come what may, I do adore thee so / That danger shall seem sport, and I will go' (2.1.35–6). The word 'adore' is a strong one: where it's used elsewhere by Shakespeare it tends to refer either to the love of mortals for gods, or for an exalted form of romantic courtship. It's a word in emotional excess of the ostensible situation, just as the character of Antonio himself seems in excess of the plot, an unnecessary addition. Perhaps we could use this to activate a different current of meaning in this play so preoccupied with homoerotic relationships which are substituted by marriage: the relationship between Viola and Olivia, between Cesario and Orsino, and here, between Antonio and Sebastian. Like his namesake in *The Merchant of Venice*, there is no place for Antonio in the marital conclusion of *Twelfth Night*, but, again, like his namesake, he represents a form of self-sacrificial, possibly erotic, love which is subtly at odds with the self-interest of many of the other characters.

Race and *Othello*

Attempting to resituate Shakespeare as a dramatist of his own period can look like an evasion of our contemporary critical concerns, but as the discussion of gender roles above suggests, often it is intimately connected to them. Reading gender roles or questions of sexuality in Shakespeare's comedies is both historically situated and engaged with the interest of much recent criticism. In fact, working with Shakespeare in his historical period is itself a challenge to earlier forms of criticism which were concerned to free him from historical specificity to do cultural duty as the transcendental bard. One final sustained example, however, may help to clarify some of the weaknesses as well as the strengths of a historical approach.

By considering the issue of race in *Othello*, we already approach a topic of considerable cultural importance now, as well as then, but one which is discontinuous. That is to say, the meanings attached to blackness now may not be the same as those attached to blackness then. And, what's more, *Othello* constructs, or at least is contemporaneous with the construction of, the very racial categories we might read back into it: we can't fully escape the play's own ideological frame to analyse it. Reading historical context is as much about situating ourselves and our critical perceptions as it is about dustily restoring the literary text to its own cultural moment. How, therefore, can we – *can we?* – historicise Shakespeare's extraordinary decision to make a black character the hero of his tragedy, given the overwhelming prevalent association of blackness with devilry and wickedness – a characterisation Shakespeare seems happy to deploy for Aaron in *Titus Andronicus*. The question of the meaning and significance of race in *Othello* has been answered in two distinct ways – and these can give us a useful way of thinking about the strengths and the limitations of historical analysis.

The first answer includes two interchangeable possibilities: that the play is essentially liberal, or that it is essentially racist. Either we argue that *Othello* anticipates the twenty-first century's concern for tolerance and individualism by presenting us a black character as a hero, or that the play endorses the fears that an apparently assimilated black man will 'revert' to barbaric violence under strain. Either reading can be sustained with reference to the text of the play on the page, and thus, although they come to apparently opposite conclusions, their method – which presupposes that the 'meaning' of the play is always contained within it – is identical.

The second answer might recapitulate similar conclusions, but proceeds from a crucially different argument: that the play needs to be understood *historically*. It is a product of, and participates in, a particular discourse around blackness available to a London writer and his audiences at the beginning of the seventeenth century. So the play cannot do other than operate within its own historical assumptions. This second reading locates its meaning not in the text itself but in the text in its context. Something outside the play – here a pre-existing discourse of assumed attitudes or prejudices – fixes the play for us. It is a reading which turns away from the text towards an idea of historical context. Or, rather as was argued in chapter 2 on performance, reading historically, like reading theatrically, defers interpretative authority out of the autonomous printed text and into the dense and historically specific web of culture of which it is a part.

To take this historical reading of *Othello* we need, therefore, some documentation. We can't generate from our reading of *Othello* assumptions about how early modern audiences would have perceived the play, and then use these assumptions to validate our own interpretations; rather, we need to access some of the material which might have shaped those contemporary views. The following three extracts present some related historical material which it is useful to bring into juxtaposition with Shakespeare's play. Below I begin to sketch out some of the points of interest from them.

(1) *An open letter to the Lord Mayor and Aldermen of London, from Queen Elizabeth* (1596)

> Her Majesty understandeth that there are of late divers blackmoors brought into this realm, of which kind of people there are already here too many, considering how God hath blessed this land with great increase of people of our own nation as any country of the world, whereof many for want of service and means to set them on work fall to

idleness and great extremity. Her Majesty's pleasure therefore is that those kind of people should be sent forth of this land, and for that purpose there is direction given to this bearer Edward Banes to take of those blackmoors that in this last voyage under Sir Thomas Baskervile were brought into this realm the number of ten, to be transported by him out of the realm

Elizabeth's communication with the civic authorities in London speaks of 'too many' moors working as servants – a relative number given some context by the mention of 'ten' to be transported by Banes. It sets up an opposition between this 'those kind of people' and 'people of our own nation'; it constructs 'blackmoors' as an economic threat; it proposes repatriation as a solution. The individuals concerned here do not seem to register as people: they are cargo, 'brought into this realm' and now to be 'transported' away.

(2)   A section from Leo Africanus' book *The History and Description of Africa*. Trans. John Pory, 1600
      What vices the foresaid Africans are subject unto

Let us consider, whether the vices of the Africans do surpass their virtues and good parts. Those which we named the inhabitants of the cities of Barbary are very proud and high-minded, and wonderfully addicted unto wrath; insomuch that (according to the proverb) they will deeply engrave in marble any injury be it never so small, and will in no wise blot it out of their remembrance. So rustical they are and void of good manners, that scarcely can any stranger obtain their familiarity and friendship. Their wits are but mean, and they are so credulous, that they will believe matters impossible, which are told to them. So ignorant are they of natural philosophy, that they imagine all the effects and operations of nature to be extraordinary and divine. They observe no certain order of living nor of laws. Abounding exceedingly with choler, they speak always with an angry and loud voice. Neither shall you walk in the day-time in any of their streets, but you shall see commonly two or three or them together by the ears. By nature they are a vile and base people, being no better accounted of by their governors then if they were dogs. They have neither judges nor lawyers, by whose wisdom and counsel they ought to be directed. Their minds are perpetually possessed with vexation and with strife, so that they will seldom or never show themselves tractable to any man; the cause whereof is supposed to be; for that they are so greedily addicted unto their filthy lucre, that they never could attain unto any kind of civility or good behaviour. All the Numidians, being most ignorant of natural, domestical, and commonwealth-manners, are principally addicted unto treason, treachery, murder, theft, and robbery. . . . Likewise the inhabitants of

Libya live a brutish kind of life; who neglecting all kinds of good arts and sciences, doe wholly apply their minds unto theft and violence. Never as yet had they any religion, any laws, or any good form of living; but always had, and ever will have a most miserable and distressed life. There cannot any treachery or villainy be invented so damnable, which for lucre's sake they dare not attempt. They spend all their days either in most lewd practices, or in hunting, or else in warfare: neither wear they any shoes nor garments. The Negroes likewise lead a beastly kind of life, being utterly destitute of the use of reason, of dexterity of wit, and of all arts. Yea they so behave themselves, as if they had continually lived in a forest among wild beasts. They have great swarms of harlots among them; whereupon a man may easily conjecture their manner of living.

Here Leo Africanus, himself a Muslim who converted to Christianity, attributes a number of negative essential qualities to Africans. The charge of 'wrath' and the remembering of injuries might be thought relevant to the depiction of Othello. There is a strong indication of sexual predation in the last sentence. Perhaps the image of the naked or barefoot African would have shaped expectations about the visual presentation of a Moorish character on the stage.

(3)   Speeches by Moorish characters in drama before *Othello*

> Now I have set these Portugals aworke
> To hew a way for me unto the crown,
> Or with your weapons here to dig your graves.
> You dastards of the night and Erybus,
> Fiends, Fairies, hags that fight in beds of steel,
> Range through this army with your iron whips,
> Drive forward to this deed this Christian crew,
> And let me triumph in the tragedy
> Though it be sealed and honoured with my blood,
> Both of the Portugal and barbarous Moor.
> Ride Nemesis, ride in thy fiery cart,
> And sprinkle gore amongst these men of war,
> That either party eager of revenge,
> May honour thee with sacrifice of death,
> And having bathed thy chariot wheels in blood,
> Descend and take to thy tormenting hell,
> The mangled body of that traitor king,
> That scorns the power and force of Portugal,
> Dammed let him be, dammed and condemned to bear
> All torments, tortures, plagues and pains of hell.
>
> George Peele, *The Battle of Alcazar* (1594)

I'll follow you, now purple villainy;
Sit like robe imperial on my back,
That under thee I closelier may contrive
My vengeance; foul deeds hid do sweetly thrive:
Mischief erect thy throne and sit in state
Here, here upon this head; let fools fear fate.
Thus I defy my stars, I care not I
How low I tumble down, so I mount high.
Old time I'll wait bare-headed at their heels,
And be a foot-boy to thy winged hours;
They shall not tell one minute out in sands,
But I'll set down the number, I'll still wake,
And waste these balls of sight by tossing them,
In busy observations upon thee.
Sweet opportunity I'll bind myself
To thee in base apprentice-hood so long,
Till on thy naked scalp grow hair as thick
As mine: and all hands shall lay hold on thee,
If thou wilt lend me but thy rusty scythe,
To cut down all that stand within my wrongs,
And my revenge. [...]
Oh for more work, more souls to post to hell;
That I might pile up Charon's boat so full,
Until it topple o're, Oh 'twould be sport
To see them sprawl through the black slimy lake.

Thomas Dekker (?) *Lust's Dominion, or the*
Lascivious Queen (1599)

In plays before *Othello* in which black characters appear – we might include in this Aaron, or the scene in which Portia dismisses the Prince of Morocco, her unsuitable suitor – they are marked by a bombastic lust for violence and revenge, and a self-conscious amorality. These characters glory in their own malevolence, unchecked by any ethical scruples.

So, we might say that this material functions rather like the sources discussed in the last chapter (the issue of the 'strong poet' is relevant here too: can Shakespeare reshape expectations or do they have an intrinsic inelasticity?) Just as what is ultimately so fatally predetermined about *Romeo and Juliet* might be interpreted as the inescapable fact that the story already exists and the lovers have therefore already died, maybe here the weight of expectation about the outcome of a racially 'mixed' marriage defies the play's attempt to recast the relationship between Othello and Desdemona. However much Shakespeare's depiction of Othello begins by departing from the stereotype established by his cultural predecessors, in the end it all comes to the same thing.

But perhaps this is to underestimate the performed play's ability to undercut its own categories even as it tries to establish them. Any account of Shakespeare's representation of women has, at some point, to take on board the undeniable fact that there were no women on the Renaissance stage: all female roles were taken by men. There has been a strong critical movement which has used this fact to recuperate the representation of women on the stage as representations rather than essences – as ways of performing an idea of 'woman' rather than as authentic 'women' – and this has opened up a space between real women and represented ones. Perhaps we could argue something analogous for *Othello*: by putting alongside the historical documentation offered above some of the evidence about how black characters would have been represented on early modern stages. Since there were no black actors, blackness was indicated by dye or paint and there are records of coarse-haired or woolly wigs among theatrical props. Thus, in reminding us through performance that Othello is always a white man in disguise the play gives us a space to question racial stereotypes even as it endorses them. Blackness is not seen as intrinsic, unchangeable; rather it is extrinsic, a matter of props, of representational theatrical strategies, the black makeup that can always be wiped away to reveal the whiteness underneath.

It is clear from beginning to assess the context of race in *Othello* that historical readings do not settle or close down interpretations, rather they provoke them. We can't defer to some sort of authoritative answer from history about what the plays meant to their first audiences, and in any case audiences then were probably no more homogeneous than we are now: instead, we can see that thickening the historical moment from which they emerge can recalibrate them in some unexpected ways. As with all the other approaches to Shakespeare, thinking historically exposes us to counter-opinions, different possibilities, and the interpretative fluidity this study has been concerned to show. Neither we nor the plays can or should transcend history: in historicising the context of Shakespeare's plays we also historicise our own readings. For us, as for the Elizabethans, history is about our here-and-now as much as it is the distant past.

History: where next?

- I've suggested that the references to Ireland in *Henry V* can be used to read the play as a feel-good fantasy of victory in which the historical French stand in for the contemporary Irish. Two articles exploring this idea in more detail are Joel Altman, 'Vile Participation': The Amplification of Violence in the Theatre of *Henry V*' in *Shakespeare Quarterly* 42 (1991) and Michael Neill, 'Broken English and Broken Irish: Nation, Language, and the Optic of Power in Shakespeare's Histories', *Shakespeare Quarterly* 45 (1994). If the argument is true, why do we get that deflating, anticlimactic Epilogue, in which all that's been fought for is lost in a few lines? Is it significant that the Epilogue, like all the other Chorus speeches, is not included in the 1600 Quarto text but only in the 1623 Folio? Could other contemporary plays be read as oblique feel-good productions? What about *Much Ado About Nothing* (1599) – in which the juxtaposition of war and wooing is differently structured from *Henry V* – or *As You Like It* (1599) – which also has some unexpected references to Ireland, including Rosalind's dismissive "tis like the howling of Irish wolves against the moon' (5.2.92–3)? A great book on all this is James Shapiro's *1599: A Year in the Life of William Shakespeare* (London, 2005).

- On different ideological readings of the history plays, see my *Blackwell Guides to Criticism: Shakespeare's Histories* (Blackwell, 2004). The argument might be polarised (and oversimplified) between, say, E. M. W. Tillyard and Graham Holderness. Tillyard: Shakespeare 'expressed a universally held and still comprehensible scheme of history: a scheme fundamentally religious, by which events evolve under a law of justice and under the ruling of God's Providence, and of which Elizabeth's England was the acknowledged outcome' (*Shakespeare's History Plays*, 1944); Holderness: 'It is via the strategic interrelating of different discourses that the plays speak of their own time, the later sixteenth century. They do not address the present directly, by universalist historical generalization or contemporary political allegory [. . .] competing social forces produced the competing ideologies of Renaissance historiography; the plays reflect on those ideologies, and thereby indirectly on the social forces themselves' (*Shakespeare Recycled: The Making of Historical Drama*, 1992). We might compare this with a pair of contemporary views: Thomas Heywood's *An Apology for Actors* (1612) suggests that 'domestic histories' create patriotic fervour: 'what English blood, seeing the person of any bold Englishman presented, and doth not hug his fame and honey at his valour, pursuing him in his enterprise with his best wishes . . . what English prince, should he behold the true portraiture of that famous King Edward the Third, foraging France, taking so great a king captive in his own country, quartering the English lions with the French flower-deluce [*fleur de lys*], and would not be suddenly inflamed with so royal a spectacle, being made apt and fit for the like achievement?' (reprinted in Brian Vickers, ed., *English Renaissance Literary Criticism*, Oxford University Press, 1999).

On the other hand, Sir Henry Wootton's letter to his nephew in which he describes the production of *Henry VIII* seems to suggest that the staging of authority cheapens it: 'The King's players had a new play called *All Is True*, representing some principal pieces of the reign of Henry VIII, which was set forth with many extraordinary circumstances of pomp and majesty, even to the matting of the stage; the Knights of the Order with their Georges and garters, the Guards with their embroidered coats, and the like: sufficient in truth within a while to make greatness very familiar, if not ridiculous' (quoted in E. K. Chambers, *The Elizabethan Stage* (Oxford University Press, 1923), 2, 419).

- In thinking about *Hamlet* as a history play, I've drawn on the ideas in Steven Mullaney's essay 'Mourning and Misogyny: *Hamlet* and the Final Progress of Elizabeth I' in *Shakespeare Quarterly* 45 (1994) and reprinted in Kate Chedgzoy, *Shakespeare, Feminism and Gender* (Palgrave, 2001), and on Margreta de Grazia's *Hamlet without 'Hamlet'* (Cambridge University Press, 2006). It is interesting to compare the roles of Fortinbras in the films by Almereyda and Branagh, as well as – if you can get hold of it – in the bleakly political film by Grigori Kozintsev (1964), in which the accession of Fortinbras is announced rather as the accession of Claudius with which the film begins, suggesting a grinding political circularity about the historical process which is indebted to Polish theatre director Jan Kott's view of the English histories in his influential *Shakespeare our Contemporary* (1964).

- On the relation between history and literature, the chapters 'The Text and the World' and 'History' in Andrew Bennett and Nicholas Royle's excellent *Introduction to Literature, Criticism and Theory* 3rd edn, Pearson, 2004) are recommended, as is Stephen Greenblatt's essay 'Culture' in Frank Lentricchia and Thomas McLaughlin's *Critical Terms for Literary Study* (2nd edn, Chicago, 1995). More specifically on Shakespeare – although Greenblatt discusses *The Tempest* – try David Scott Kastan's *Shakespeare after Theory* (Routledge, 1999).

- To find out more about the social and cultural history of Elizabethan and Jacobean England, the following introductory essays are recommended as overviews with useful suggestions for further reading: Martin Ingram, 'Love, Sex and Marriage', in *Shakespeare: An Oxford Guide*, eds. Stanley Wells and Lena Cowen Orlin (Oxford University Press, 2003); Susan Dwyer Amussen, 'The Family and the Household', in *A Companion to Shakespeare* ed. David Scott Kastan (Oxford University Press, 1999).

- Other plays to look at in the context of a movement from same-sex to opposite-sex relationships might include *Two Noble Kinsmen* and *Two Gentlemen of Verona*, or, in reverse from marriage to same-sex relationships, at

Aufidius' welcome to the exiled Coriolanus in *Coriolanus*. On the historical construction of sexuality, see Valerie Traub, *The Renaissance of Lesbianism in Early Modern England* (Cambridge University Press, 2002), Stephen Orgel, *Impersonations: the Performance of Gender in Shakespeare's England* (Cambridge University Press, 1996), and Mario diGangi, *The Homoerotics of Early Modern Drama* (Cambridge University Press, 1997). Montaigne's essays, in a translation by John Florio from 1603 that we know Shakespeare used for *The Tempest*, are available via the Renascence Editions website http://darkwing.uoregon.edu/~rbear/ren.htm; the same site has Francis Bacon's *Essays* which are also pithy, engaging observations on a range of topics from friendship to travel to gardens.

- On *Othello* in historical context, Virginia Mason Vaughan's *Othello: A Contextual History* (Cambridge University Press, 1994), is highly recommended. Routledge's series of 'Literary Sourcebooks' gathers together material on historical context: Andrew Hadfield's volume on *Othello*, which includes the materials quoted here, was published in 2003, and there are other Shakespeare volumes on *King Lear* (ed. Grace Ioppolo, 2002), *The Merchant of Venice* (ed. S. P. Cerasano, 2004), *Macbeth* (ed. Alexander Leggatt, 2005) and *Hamlet* (ed. Sean McEvoy, 2005). For a collection of contemporary extracts on different aspects of early modern life and thought, Kate Aughterson's comprehensive *The English Renaissance: An Anthology of Sources and Documents* (Routledge, 1998) is invaluable. Dympna Callaghan's essay 'Othello was a White Man' discusses the implications of performed blackness to the play (in her *Shakespeare Without Women: Representing Gender and Race on the Renaissance Stage*, Routledge, 1999); Virginia Mason Vaughan's *Performing Blackness on Renaissance Stages 1500–1800* (Cambridge University Press, 2005) is interesting on the evidence for the ways in which blackness was represented. Both *The Battle of Alcazar* and *Lust's Dominion* are available online from Renascence Editions (http://darkwing.uoregon.edu/~rbear/ren.htm).

在莎士比亚戏剧的研究中，大家更关注的似乎是剧中一些"永恒"的东西，即没有很强的时间概念的主题。但是，我们同时也应注意到他的剧中那些有着明显的时间性的内容，那些明显是为了他的同代人而创作的东西。考虑到文艺复兴时期英国戏剧创作的特点——每个剧目只演出很少的几场，而且都集中在几周之内——可以断定莎士比亚的剧在当初创作时面向的是他的同代人，目的是为他们提供一种享受。考虑到莎剧的素材往往取自经典作品或通俗故事，那么又能在多大程度上讲莎剧反映了剧作家生活的那个时代的政治气候、他的同代人的思想状况、现实生活呢？

Bibliography

Adamson, Sylvia et al. (eds.), *Reading Shakespeare's Dramatic Language: A Guide* (London: Thomson, 2001)

Adelman, Janet, *Suffocating Mothers: Fantasies of Maternal Origin in Shakespeare's Plays, 'Hamlet' to 'The Tempest'* (London: Routledge, 1992)

Alexander, Gavin (ed.), *Sidney's 'The Defence of Poesy' and Selected Renaissance Literary Criticism*, edited by Gavin Alexander (London: Penguin, 2004)

Altman, Joel D., "'Vile Participation": The Amplification of Violence in the Theatre of *Henry V*', *Shakespeare Quarterly* 42 (1991)

Amussen, Susan Dwyer, 'The Family and the Household', in David Scott Kastan (ed.), *A Companion to Shakespeare* (Oxford: Blackwell, 1999)

Aughterson, Kate (ed.), *The English Renaissance: An Anthology of Sources and Documents* (London: Routledge, 1998)

Barton, John, *Playing Shakespeare* (London: Methuen, 1984)

Bate, Jonathan, *The Genius of Shakespeare* (London: Picador, 1997)

Bate, W. Jackson, *The Burden of the Past and the English Poet* (London: Chatto and Windus, 1971)

Belsey, Catherine, *The Subject of Tragedy: Identity and Difference in Renaissance Drama* (London: Routledge, 1991)

Bennett, Andrew, *The Author* (London: Routledge, 2005)

Bennett, Andrew and Nicholas Royle, *Introduction to Literature, Criticism and Theory* (3rd edn, Harlow: Pearson Longman, 2004)

Berry, Cicely, *The Actor and his Text* (London: Virgin, 1993)

Bloom, Harold, *Shakespeare: The Invention of the Human* (London: Fourth Estate, 1999)

    The Anxiety of Influence (2nd edn, Oxford: Oxford University Press, 1997)

Bradley, A. C., *Shakespearean Tragedy* (London: Macmillan, 1904)

Bullough, Geoffrey, *Narrative and Dramatic Sources of Shakespeare* (London: Routledge and Kegan Paul, 1957–75)

Burke, Seán (ed.), *Authorship, from Plato to the Postmodern: A Reader* (Edinburgh: Edinburgh University Press, 2000)

Burt, Richard, and Lynda E. Boose (eds.), *Shakespeare the Movie II: Popularising the Plays on Film, TV, Video, and DVD* (London: Routledge, 2003)

Callaghan, Dympna, *Shakespeare Without Women: Representing Gender and Race on the Renaissance Stage* (London: Routledge, 1999)

Callow, Simon, *Henry IV Part 1 and Part II: Actors on Shakespeare* (London: Faber, 2002)

Cartmell, Deborah, *Interpreting Shakespeare on Screen* (Basingstoke: Macmillan, 2000)

Cerasano, S. P. (ed.), *The Merchant of Venice: A Sourcebook* (London: Routledge, 2004)

Cerasano, S. P. and Marion Wynne-Davies (eds.), *Gloriana's Face: Women, Public and Private, in the English Renaissance* (London: Harvester Wheatsheaf, 1992)

Chambers, E. K., *The Elizabethan Stage* (Oxford: Clarendon Press, 1923)

Clare, Janet, *'Art made Tongue-Tied by Authority': Elizabethan and Jacobean Dramatic Censorship* (2nd edn, Manchester: Manchester University Press, 1999)

Cloud, Random, '"The Very Names of the Persons": Editing and the Invention of Dramatick Character', in David Scott Kastan and Peter Stallybrass (eds), *Staging the Renaissance: Reinterpretations of Elizabethan and Jacobean Drama* (London: Routledge, 1991)

    'The Marriage of Good and Bad Quartos', in *Shakespeare Quarterly* 33 (1982)

Cordner, Michael, 'Actors, Editors, and the Annotation of Shakespearean Playscripts', *Shakespeare Survey 55* (2002)

Cox, John (ed.), *Shakespeare in Production: Much Ado About Nothing* (Cambridge: Cambridge University Press, 1997)

Crystal, David, *The Cambridge Encyclopedia of the English Language* (Cambridge: Cambridge University Press, 1999)

de Grazia, Margreta, 'The Scandal of Shakespeare's Sonnets', *Shakespeare Studies* 46 (1993), reprinted in *Shakespeare and Sexuality*, ed. Catherine Alexander (Cambridge: Cambridge University Press, 2001)

    Hamlet without 'Hamlet' (forthcoming, Cambridge: Cambridge University Press, 2007)

de Grazia, Margreta and Stanley Wells (eds.), *The Cambridge Companion to Shakespeare* (Cambridge: Cambridge University Press, 2001)

de Grazia, Margreta, and Peter Stallybrass, 'The Materiality of the Shakespearean Text', in *Shakespeare Quarterly* 44 (1993)

diGangi, Mario, *The Homoerotics of Early Modern Drama* (Cambridge: Cambridge University Press, 1997)

Duncan-Jones, Katherine, *Ungentle Shakespeare: Scenes from his Life* (London: Arden Shakespeare, 2001)

Dutton, Richard, *Mastering the Revels: The Regulation and Censorship of English Renaissance Drama* (Basingstoke: Macmillan, 1991)

Dymkowski, Christine (ed.), *Shakespeare in Production: The Tempest* (Cambridge: Cambridge University Press, 2000)

Edelman, Charles (ed.), *Shakespeare in Production: The Merchant of Venice* (Cambridge: Cambridge University Press, 2002)

Fielding, Emma, *Twelfth Night: Actors on Shakespeare* (London: Faber, 2002)

Fitter, Chris, 'Historicising Shakespeare's *Richard II*: Current Events, Dating, and the Sabotage of Essex', *Early Modern Literary Studies* 11.2 (September, 2005) at http://purl.oclc.org/emls/11-2/fittric2.htm

Frances, Shirley (ed.), *Shakespeare in Production: Troilus and Cressida* (Cambridge: Cambridge University Press, 2005)

Goldberg, Jonathan, *Sodometries: Renaissance Texts, Modern Sexualities* (Stanford Calif.: Stanford University Press, 1992)

Greenblatt, Stephen, *Will in the World: How Shakespeare Became Shakespeare* (London: Jonathan Cape, 2004)

Griffiths, Trevor, *Shakespeare in Production: A Midsummer Night's Dream* (Cambridge: Cambridge University Press, 1996)

Hadfield, Andrew (ed.), *Othello: A Sourcebook* (London: Routledge, 2003)

Hankey, Julie (ed.), *Shakespeare in Production: Othello* (2nd edn, Cambridge: Cambridge University Press, 2005)

Hapgood, Robert (ed.), *Shakespeare in Production: Hamlet* (Cambridge: Cambridge University Press, 1999)

Holderness, Graham, *Shakespeare Recycled: The Making of Historical Drama*, (London: Harvester Wheatsheaf, 1992)

Holmes, Jonathan, *Merely Players? Actors' Accounts of Performing Shakespeare* (London: Routledge, 2004)

Honan, Park, *Shakespeare: A Life* (Oxford: Oxford University Press, 2000)

Howard, Jean, 'Crossdressing, the Theatre and Gender Struggle in Early Modern England', *Shakespeare Quarterly* 39 (1988)

Ingram, Martin, 'Love, Sex and Marriage', in *Shakespeare: An Oxford Guide*, eds. Stanley Wells and Lena Cowen Orlin (Oxford: Oxford University Press, 2003)

Ioppolo, Grace (ed.), *King Lear: A Sourcebook* (London: Routledge, 2002)

Jackson, Russell (ed.), *The Cambridge Companion to Shakespeare on Film* (Cambridge: Cambridge University Press, 2000)

Jones, James Earl, *Othello: Actors on Shakespeare* (London: Faber, 2003)

Jorgens, Jack, *Shakespeare on Film* (Bloomington and London: Indiana University Press, 1977)

Kastan, David Scott, *Shakespeare after Theory* (London: Routledge, 1999)

Kastan, David Scott (ed.), *A Companion to Shakespeare* (Oxford: Blackwell, 1999)

Kermode, Frank, *Shakespeare's Language* (London: Penguin, 2001)

Kiernan, Pauline, *Staging Shakespeare at the New Globe* (Basingstoke: Macmillan, 1999)

Knights, L. C., *Explorations: Essays in Criticism* (London: Chatto and Windus, 1946)

Kott, Jan, *Shakespeare our Contemporary* (New York: Doubleday, 1964)

Kozintsev, Grigori, *King Lear: The Space of Tragedy* (London: Heinemann, 1977)

Leggatt, Alexander (ed.), *Macbeth: A Sourcebook* (London: Routledge, 2005)

Lentricchia, Frank and Thomas McLaughlin, *Critical Terms for Literary Study* (2nd edn, Chicago: University of Chicago Press, 1995)

Loehlin, James (ed.), *Shakespeare in Production: Romeo and Juliet* (Cambridge: Cambridge University Press, 2002)

Madelaine, Richard (ed.), *Shakespeare in Production: Antony and Cleopatra* (Cambridge: Cambridge University Press, 1998)

Maguire, Laurie E., 'Feminist Editing and the Body of the Text', in Dympna Callaghan (ed.), *A Feminist Companion to Shakespeare* (Oxford: Blackwell, 2000)

Marcus, Leah, *Unediting the Renaissance: Shakespeare, Marlowe, Milton* (London: Routledge, 1996)

Marshall, Cynthia (ed.), *Shakespeare in Production: As You Like It* (Cambridge: Cambridge University Press, 2004)

Maus, Katherine, *Inwardness and Theater in the English Renaissance* (Chicago and London: University of Chicago Press, 1995)

McEvoy, Sean (ed.), *Hamlet: A Sourcebook* (London: Routledge, 2005)

Mullaney, Steven, 'Mourning and Misogyny: *Hamlet* and the Final Progress of Elizabeth I', *Shakespeare Quarterly* 45 (1994) and reprinted in Kate Chedgzoy, *Shakespeare, Feminism and Gender* (Basingstoke: Palgrave, 2001)

Neill, Michael, 'Broken English and Broken Irish: Nation, Language, and the Optic of Power in Shakespeare's Histories', *Shakespeare Quarterly* 45 (1994)

Issues of Death: Mortality and Identity in English Renaissance Tragedy (Oxford: Oxford University Press, 1997)

Orgel, Stephen, *Impersonations: the Performance of Gender in Shakespeare's England* (Cambridge: Cambridge University Press, 1996)

Palfrey, Simon, *Doing Shakespeare* (London: Arden Shakespeare, 2005)

Pequigney, Joseph, *Such is My Love: A Study of Shakespeare's Sonnets* (Chicago and London: University of Chicago Press, 1985)

Redgrave, Vanessa, *Antony and Cleopatra: Actors on Shakespeare* (London: Faber, 2002)

Reeves, Saskia, *Much Ado About Nothing: Actors on Shakespeare* (London: Faber, 2003)

Rice, Philip and Patricia Waugh (eds.), *Modern Literary Theory* (London: Edward Arnold, 4th edn, 2001)

Rodenburg, Patsy, *Speaking Shakespeare* (London: Methuen, 2005)

Rose, Mary Beth, 'Where are the Mothers in Shakespeare: Options for Gender Representation in the English Renaissance', *Shakespeare Quarterly* 42 (1991)

Schafer, Elizabeth (ed.), *Shakespeare in Production: The Taming of the Shrew* (Cambridge: Cambridge University Press, 2002)

Shapiro, James, *1599: A Year in the Life of William Shakespeare* (London: Faber, 2005)

Sinfield, Alan, *Faultlines: Cultural Materialism and the Politics of Dissident Reading* (Oxford: Clarendon Press, 1992)

Smiley, Jane, *A Thousand Acres* (London: Flamingo, 1992)

Smith, Emma (ed.), *Blackwell Guides to Criticism: Shakespeare's Tragedies* (Oxford: Blackwell, 2004)

    Blackwell Guides to Criticism: Shakespeare's Histories (Oxford: Blackwell, 2004)

    Shakespeare in Production: King Henry V (Cambridge: Cambridge University Press, 2002)

Snyder, Susan, 'The Genres of Shakespeare's Plays', in Margreta de Grazia and Stanley Wells (eds.), *The Cambridge Companion to Shakespeare* (Cambridge: Cambridge University Press, 2001)

Spurgeon, Caroline, *Shakespeare's Imagery and What it Tells Us* (Cambridge: Cambridge University Press, 1935)

Stern, Tiffany, *Making Shakespeare: From Stage to Page* (London: Routledge, 2004)

Tillyard, E. M. W., *Shakespeare's History Plays* (London: Chatto and Windus, 1944)

Traub, Valerie, *The Renaissance of Lesbianism in Early Modern England* (Cambridge: Cambridge University Press, 2002)

Urkowitz, Steven, 'Good News about 'Bad' Quartos', in Maurice Charney (ed.), *'Bad' Shakespeare: Revaluations of the Shakespeare Canon* (Rutherford, NJ: Fairleigh Dickinson University Press, 1988)

Vaughan, Virginia Mason, *Othello: A Contextual History* (Cambridge: Cambridge University Press, 1994)

    Performing Blackness on Renaissance Stages 1500–1800 (Cambridge: Cambridge University Press, 2005)

Vickers, Brian, ed., *English Renaissance Literary Criticism* (Oxford: Oxford University Press, 1999)

Walter, Harriet, *Macbeth: Actors on Shakespeare* (London: Faber, 2002)

Warner, Marina, *From the Beast to the Blonde: On Fairy Tales and their Tellers* (London: Chatto and Windus, 1994)

Warren, Michael, and Gary Taylor, *The Division of the Kingdoms: Shakespeare's Two Versions of 'King Lear'* (Oxford: Oxford University Press, 1983)

Wells, Stanley and Lena Cowen Orlin, *Shakespeare: An Oxford Guide* (Oxford: Oxford University Press, 2003)

Wilders, John (ed.), *Shakespeare in Production: Macbeth* (Cambridge: Cambridge University Press, 2004)

Worden, Blair, 'Which Play was Performed at the Globe Theatre on 7 February 1601?' *London Review of Books* (10 July 2003)

Index